SMALL AND MEDIUM TOWNS AND THEIR ROLE IN REGIONAL DEVELOPMENT

Small and Medium Towns and Their Role In Regional Development

A.C. MINOCHA

H.S. YADAV

GIAN PUBLISHING HOUSE
NEW DELHI - 110002

GIAN PUBLISHING HOUSE
4348, Madan Mohan Street
4-C Ansari Road, Darya Ganj,
New Delhi-110002

ISBN 81—212—0264—7

This publication is financially supported by the ICSSR. The responsibility for the facts stated, opinions expressed, or conclusions reached, is entirely that of the authors and that the ICSSR accepts no responsibility for them.

PRINTED IN INDIA

Published by Mrs. Gayatri Garg for Gian Publishing House, New Delhi and Printed at Godwall Printers, Delhi.

PREFACE

The process of urbanisation though slow in some parts, is more or less on the same pattern—haphazard, unplanned, exploitative and dysfunctional. The spatial organisation is attuned to the requirements of growth plus strategy, with towns degenerating into centres of exploitation of rural hinterland and focal points of suction mechanism. Our urban centres, by and large, have not transmitted growth impulses to their respective regional economies. The massive public investment in a few pockets of heavy and basic industries which are "export-based", have further helped in the concentration of population and activities in a few urban centres which are generally rootless and incapable of acting as agents of growth and change. While the production process continues to be strongly rooted in rural economy, the hierarchical organisation of space is increasingly becoming top heavy in favour of large cities. This model of urban growth has resulted in unplanned urbanization, by and large, to the disadvantage of small and medium towns.

Madhya Pradesh is a State of very small towns with more than 75% of all towns belonging to this category, with population of less than 20,000 each. In 1981, nearly 47% of urban population was found to be living in Class I cities, numbering 14, 18% in intermediate towns, mumbering 21, and 35.16% in small towns numbering 261, out of total of 303 towns. The state does not have a single metropolitan town.

No comprehensive study of the process of urbanisation in Mdhya Pradesh has been made so far. It is to fill up this gap that the present study was undertaken. The focus of the study is on small and medium towns. The study is mainly analytical. It is concerned with the analysis of the growth or decline of small towns against the background of urbanisation and econmic development in the state. The causes of urbanisation and interaction between urbanisation and socio-economic aspects of towns have been studied, to formulate a sound base for fruitful planning policies.

The spatial aspect of urbanisation in M.P., has been studied in details against the background of distribution of activities. The study shows that the eastern region of the state which is a mineral and forest belt, has recorded the highest rate of growth of urban population during 1971-81, though the region has lowest level of urbanisation, only 14.2% as aginst 20.3% of the State. The share of this region in total urban population of the state has gone up from 18.8% in 1971 to 20.4% in 1981, whereas that of western region which is more urbanised region, has gone down from 30.5% to 28%, in the same period. This indicates that relativcly less urbanised regions of the State are showing faster rate of urbanisation than the relatively more urbanised regions and there is a consequent narrowing down of inter-regional disparities in urbanisation. Our analysis shows that agricultural development gives rise to the emergence of small towns, whereas industrialisation tends to strengthen agglomeration tendencies and gives rise to greater concentration of population at few centres. The regional variations in the levels of different size-class of towns in the overall urban hierarchy and their differential growth rates, have been explained, among other factors, in terms of difference in regional pattern of growth.

The study discusses, in particular, the growth and pattern of urbanisation in Malwa region of Madhya Pradesh which includes 13 districts, mainly of western and to a small extent of inland western regions of Madhya Pradesh. This region is agriculturally more developed and has four Class I towns. Chapters III and IV deal with the process and pattern of urbanisation in Malwa region against the background of socio-economic facets of the region. Nearly 32% of total urban population of M.P. lives in Malwa region, though this percentage is gradually declining. The region has nearly 28% of all the towns in the State. A probe is made into the causes of growth/decline of the towns of this region.

In this study, five small and medium towns have been selected from Malwa region for detailed investigation. Chapter V presents the economic base of these five towns, in terms of location, occupational structure, land use pattern and the cropping pattern of their hinter lands. The economic base comprises the structure of rural economy of these towns which largely determines the flow of marketed surplus and the extent of interaction with the urban economy. We have made an analysis and the changes therein. We have also shown crop combinations obtainable in the five tehsils of those small towns and the changes taking place therein to measure the extent of commercialization of agriculture.

The focus of Chapter V is on rural-urban interaction on the basis of empirical facts that we collected during the course of survey. The theoretical, empirical and administrative boundaries of the hinterland of five towns, have been delineated with the help of cartographic technique.

Urbanisation in the State has not assumed any serious proportions, despite absence of any well-defined urbanisation policy. Town plans for some towns have been designed but seldom the actual growth has taken place according to these plans. There is no regional planning in the State. It is high time that the state formulates an urbanisation policy, not as an isolated measure, but as an integral part of the overall plan of the State. Small towns can play their role effectively provided they are developed in respect of infra-structure and functions and facilities and have sufficient communication linkages with their respective hinterlands. The last chapter draws attention to some of the important conclusions and urban development policy issues, and also presents the outlines of urbanization policy in the State.

The study was sponsored and financed by the Indian Council of Social Science Research, New Delhi. We would like to express our gratitude to the Council, for the financial assistance and timely release of instalments of grant.

We gratefully acknowledge the contribution of the staff working in the project M.S. Phogat. Shri P.K. Varma deserves appreciation and thanks for typing and stencilling the Report.

We record our thanks to the faculty members of the Depatment with whom we had useful discussions on many aspects of the problem.

We hope that this study, despite limitations, which we are well aware, will create interest in the approaches that we have adopted.

Department of Regional Planning and Economic Growth, Bhopal University, Bhopal (M.P.)

A.C. Minocha
H.S. Yadav

CONTENTS

LIST OF MAPS

CHAPTER 1

THE ROLE OF SMALL AND MEDIUM TOWNS IN REGIONAL AND NATIONAL DEVELOPMENT

This chapter examines the actual and potential role of small and medium towns in regional and national development.

Before assigning them any place in the regional and national economy, it would be essential to make an attempt to define the terms.

The term "urban" has been differently defined in different countries, and even in the same country in different censuses. The primary consideration for deciding the status of any settlement as rural or urban, has been the administrative set-up and size in terms of population and not necessarily its social and economic characteristics.

In the Indian censuses, the definition of a town remained more or less unchanged for the period 1901-1951, and that it was only in 1961 that some modifications were introduced to make the definition more satisfying from the statistical point of view. But an interesting feature of the Indian census has been the latitude given to the Census Superintendents in respect of classification of places as rural and urban. In 1901, a town included :

(i) every municipality of whatever size,

(ii) all civil lines not included within municipal limits,

(iii) every other continuous collection of houses particularly inhabited by not less than 5000 persons which the provincial superintendent may decide to treat as town for census purposes.

The definition suffered not only from lack of scientific and relatistic criteria but also from lack of uniform application throughout the country. It gave a lot of discretion to the census authorities to determine whether a place was a town or not. Not all municipalities, civil lines and cantonments have a population of more than 5000 each. Many of the places designated as towns were not more than overgrown villages.

The definitions of town adopted in 1961 census and also used in subsequent censuses, with minor changes, is as follows :

(i) The place should be a municipal corporation, a municipal committee, a town area committee or a notified area committee or cantonment board.

or

(ii) a population of 5000 and above,

(iii) a density of not less than 1000 per square mile,

(iv) Three-fourths of its population is engaged in non-agricultural occupations and the place has a few pronounced urban characteristics.

Again, a lot of discretion has been given to the census authorities because urban characteristics and amenities have not been defined. Moreover, the State Government has the power to declare any area as urban by creating a municipal committee, notified area committee or a town area committee, even at places with less than 5000 population. It can enlarge the area of an urban local body. The growth of urban population in India is due to inclusion of new towns on their being declared as municipal towns, extension of area of existing towns, natural rate of growth of population and migration.

Absence of any precise and scientific basis for designating places as urban has given lot of latitude to the census authorities and this fact has vitiated temporal and spatial comparisons of urban growth in the country.

In the Indian censuses, there are six size-classes of towns, based on population. These are :

Class	I	100000 and above
Class	II	50,000 to 99,9,99
Class	III	20,000 to 49,9,99
Class	IV	10,000 to 19,9,99
Class	V	5,000 to 9,999
Class	VI	less than 5000

This again is not a scientific classsfication as it does not take into account characteristics other than population. The basis of classification is arbitrary. At the same time, there appears to be no other alternative but to accept the classification for analytical purposes as there are no other sources from where to get data in respect of other characteristics. Apart from population, other criteria that could be used to define the demographic definition of a town may be population density, the proportion of working force engaged in non-agricultural activities, physical characteristics, the mix and diversity of economic activities, the relationship of towns with other towns of different sizes.

Since the concept of town has varied from country to country, international comparisons, on the basis of national data are very shaky.

Now the question that needs to be examined is : What is a small and medium town ?

The concept of small and medium town is relative and the range of towns belonging to this category of towns in the hierarchy, will vary among countries depending upon the pattern of urban settlements, their level of economic development and the structure of their economies. There is no general agreement on how small and medium towns should be defined. Some analysts have insisted that small towns must perform "central place functions" and, therefore, serve people living in rural areas and other towns. They have to serve as channels through which economic and social interactions occur. Osborn in his comparative analysis of middle level towns in Malaysia and Indonesia used the term cannoting "functional intermediacy in the flows of power, innovations, people and resources among places." Some cities with population of above 100000 may not perform these functions if they do not have urban employment and economic characteristics and don't serve population living outside of their own boundaries, they cannot be regarded as intermediate towns in the functional sense.[1] The determination of functional intermediacy requires detailed analysis of individual cities. We do not have such type of information about cities at the aggregative level in the census data. Information in respect of flows of people and commodities is still more scanty. Thus our analysis falls back on population size as an initial criterion for indentifying the small and middle level towns. Relative population size is both convenient and initially useful criterion for identifying small and medium towns, because a good deal of empircial evidence, both in developed and developing countries shows positive correlation between city size and functional complexity.[2]

Lubell[3] has categorised urban places in developing countries into three levels :

(i) Metropolis, a large city usually the national capital of a small country or a major regional capital in a large country, like Calcutta, Bombay, Madras.

(ii) Secondary centres—small cities ranging in population from 1,00,000 to 2.5 million or more.

(iil) The rural-urban interface-small cities or rural growth centres ranging according to country, downward in population from 1,00,000 or more.

The above classification excludes the middle sized and small towns and fails to distinguish between cities which are industrial and those which perform agricultural and rural service functions.

The range of population size of small and intermediate towns varies from country to country. A recent U.N. Report designated small and medium towns in the range of 20,090 to 100,000 and reported that these towns constituted 22% of the urban population of less developed countries in 1950, 16.7% in 1970, and is predicted to have declined absolutely in 1970-80.

In highly developed and urbanised countries, the largest city may have more than 10 million people and middle level towns may be in the range of 2 to 3 million population. In countrics with primate city settlement system because of very concept of primacy, the primate city, by definition, has substantially large proportion of population than the next 2 or 3 large cities. For example, in Egypt, the Cario metropolitan area has grown to nearly 6.5 million people by 1975, almost 3 times the size of the next largest city. Alexandria, which was nearly 10 times the averge size of all other cities with more than one lakh population. In Mexico, there is distinct size difference between Maxico city with 12 million population in 1975 and the second largest metropolitan city with 2 million people. Jakarta is at least 3 times larger than the size of Bandung and Surabaya which are three times larger than the average intermediate city. Even in countries like India, where there is low level of primacy or with dual primacy, a distinct population size gap appears between the largest cities and secondary metropolitan cities and middle level towns. In India, for instance, Bombay and Calcutta are estimated to have nearly 10 million population each, in 1981, the next largest metropolitan cities Delhi, Madras, Ahmedabad, Bangalore, Hyderabad, Kanpur and Pune, have 1 to 5 million population each. Thus whether the country has high or low level of primacy, there is strong population size difference among classes of cities and there are substantial gaps between metropolitan cities and other middle level towns. In more developed and urbanised countries, the intermediate level cities are generally those which have population in the range of 100000 to 20.5 lakhs. In Latin American countries, many countries of Africa and some countries of Middle East and Asia, largest cities are quite small and there are few urban centres of above one lakh population. In such countries, the intermediate towns may be in the range of 40,000 to 1,50,000 population.

In China, cities with population of 5 lakh and above are designated as large cities, with population in the range of 20,0000 and 5 lakhs as intermediate towns. The small towns are of 3 categories, countries, and mining towns, satellite towns in the peripheries of large cities and rural market centres.

In Philippines, intermediate cities are considered in the range of 60,000 to 99,9,99, small cities in the range of 40,000–59,9,99 and large cities, with population of one lakh and above In Korea, small and intermediate towns are in the population range of 20,000 to 1 lakh.

Andrade[5] has designated urban centres with population in the range of 20,000 to one lakh in Latin American countries as intermediate cities but such a classification may be criticised on the ground that (i) cities with over one lakh population sometimes exhibit such characteristics on account of which they can be classified as intermediate. (ii) Population cannot be good indicator of its size class as it does not reveal the functions. (iii) Because of vast under-utilised human resource in the form of underemployment in developing countries, it is doubtful whether population criterion can be adequately used to calculate the size of productive base and market potentiality. Andrade, therefore, makes a plea for conducting surveys to arrive at a defiinition of small and intermediate cities.

In India, the census has classified urban settlements into 6 classes on the basis of population. The line of demarcation between villages and small towns in the lowest range is very thin. There are urban settlements below 5000 population (class VI) if there is a municipality or a town area committee or notified area cammittee or a cantonment Board. A number of small towns has rural characteristics and less than 5000 population, with more than 50% of workers engaged in agricultural and allied activities, but have been designated as town by constituting urban local bodies, sometimes on the grounds of political expediency.

In Madhya Pradesh which is a state predominantly of small towns, there is not a single metropolitan city. The primacy index is very low (0.43). There are only 14 Class I towns according to 1981 census. The highest population among Class I cities is that of Indore (8,27,071), followed by Jabalpur (7,57,726) and Bhopal (6,72,329) and the lowest is that in Rewa (1,00,519). This class of towns includes some urban settlements which still have rural characteristics and perform functions and facilities for the rural hinterlands. Some of them are market towns for their respective hinterlands. There appears to be not much difference between the economic base of Rewa which is a class I city and of Satna or Rajnandgaon which are class II towns, whereas the difference in population between them is of a few hundreds or a thousand.

In the present study, we have taken towns in Madhya Pradesh as small which have population of less than 50,000 and medium or intermediate towns as such which have a population of 50,000 or more but less than one lakh. In terms of size-class of towns, we have included class II towns in the category of medium towns and Class III, IV, V and VI towns in the category of small towns. We are quite conscious of the fact that this classification is arbitrary and unscientific. Since the average size of town in Madhya Pradesh is small, it would be appropriate to take towns with less than 50,000 as small towns. We have taken towns with less than 20,000 population as very small towns. In fact, such settlements are overgrown villages. This classification of towns into large, medium and small, may not be valid in the context of a country or a state which is highly urbanised.

What should be the role of small and medium towns in regional development ? Lot of theoretical literature is available on the subject. At best, we can review such literature and offer our comments or judgement regarding the desirability or otherwise of the role of such towns in the hierarchy of settlements.

The propensity to concentrate human settlements and allied activities and functions at spatially strategic points in space is as old as human civilization. With the passage of time, this phenomenon evolved from amorphous and homogeneous to the distinctly heterogeneous settlements. The impetus behind such progression in urbanisation is industrialisation and trade and commerce. The process of urbanization implies both the multiplication of points of concentration and increase in the size of individual clusters. It relates to the movement of people out of agricultural communities into non-agricultural communities.

Urbanisation is a specific process of re-organisation of space which is operationalised through spatial redistribution of population among a hierarchical system of settlements of various sizes and having mixes of urban/rural attributes along a continuum in response to vertical shifts within the workforce.[6]

Urbanisation is seen as the product of increasing economic specialisation and advanced technology. Brian Berry supports the view that urban growth is simply a concentration of differentiated but functionally integrated specialisation in rational localities. The geographers' approach emphasises the part played by physical environment, and studies urban centres with reference to their regional setting. Dickson's city region highlights the relevance of this geographical concept and explains in an economic sense that the city reflects the region and the city depends upon its region for its needs, stemming from agricultural production, and in its turn, the region is dependent on the city for all those functions which hinge on exchange, manufacture and services. There is mutual interdependence between the town and the countryside in economic as well as social and political consideration. Rural-urban interaction arises and strengthens on account of intimate relations between urban areas and the surrounding countryside. Therefore, the study of towns cannot be taken up in isolation from the rural hinterlands.

Industrialisation has introduced the process of polarisation in rural-urban communities and to the expansion of urban areas into the countryside on an unprecedented scale. The development of all forms of modern means of communication and transport brings the rural areas more closely into the urban orbit. As a consequence, spatially the once clear-cut division between rural and urban areas is now blurred and there is vast zone of transition known as "rurban".

Rural urban interaction takes place in a two-way process. The city or town extends its sphere of influence on the countryside and the countryside reacts to this urban influence through responses in spatial socio-economic and demographic changes. The rural areas supply their agricultural products to the town market and purchase their inputs and other articles from these markets. The surplus rural population migrates to town in search of employment and this migration is caused, both by 'pull' and 'push' factors.

The boundaries of towns and cities are extended by the State Governments and the fringe areas are gradually merged into growing urban complex, which for some time, retain their rural character. It is this area where urbanisation impringes on rurality and where rural-urban continuum is most effectively observed.

According to EAJ Johnson, in a primarily agricultural community, trade in agricultural products is the most important channel for accomplishing rural-urban interaction.

In India, there is a sharp polarisation between urban and rural areas. It is rural-urban dichotomy that prevails in the Indian context. The towns are not playing their role expected of them in their respective regional economies. There is absence of spatial and functional integration. The relationship is exploitative and dysfunctional. The urban/rural areas are differentiated by the number and quality of functions. The per capita income in rural areas is much below the urban. The rural areas are denied most of the modern facilities that are made available to the urbanities. The levels of health, literacy and housing are much lower in rural areas compared to urban areas. The rural educated people do not like to settle in rural areas but tend to migrate to cities to take up non-agricultural occupations. At present there are poor linkages between different levels of the hierarchy of settlements. Such types of links can be forged and strengthened in a framework of multi-level planning in which spatial and sectoral plans are integrated. At present there is no scientific basis being followed in the location of functions and facilities in different settlements in the hierarchy.

The minimum number of people required to support a facility would include not only the size of population of the place where the facility is located but also the number of people living in the surrounding areas, who are willing to travel a given distance. Reciprocal relationships between the centre and its catchment area and among centres constitute the logic of the Central Place theory. While the validity of the theorem of central place is questioned, the logic of the theory holds good. A centre can be central to its catchment area and yet function as satellite to a metropolitan city. With changing, levels of development, and also owing to policy interventions, the hierarchy gets disturbed. The travel-behaviour patterns of both consumers and producers also undergo changes in favour of larger settlements where superior and varied services are available owing to larger thresholds.[7] In states like Madhya Pradesh where density of population is low, national norms for the location of functions and facilities will have to be lowered. In the hierarchy of settlements, small towns will be assigned an important role, particularly in agricultural economy. The economic base of the town lies in rural hinterland. If agriculture grows at a faster rate and rural incomes increase, more marketable surplus will flow to the town markets and more inputs and other commodities will be purchased from the market, the size of the town will tend to grow.

The less developed countries are showing a policy preference for small and intermediate towns and decentralised pattern of spatial development. A substantial number of less developed countries find the existing spatial distribution of population as unacceptable because of concentration of population in few metropolitan centres, and deceleration of migration towards few metropolitan centres has been offered as a possible solution to the problem of unsatisfactory spatial distribution of population. The free play of market forces is encouraging further concentration of population in large cities.

Three types of arguments are generally adduced[8] to support the bias in favour of small and medium towns.

(i) *The argument of efficiency*

Beyond a certain size of population, the economies of scale are exhausted and diseconomies may become more pronounced. The per capita unit cost of providing infrastructure and basic urban resources rises disproportionately beyond a particular size. Which city size is conducive to efficiency ? No conclusive evidence is available. But too small a town may not permit the economical operation of a number of functions.

(ii) *The equity consideration*

A more equitable distribution of population over space is more conducive to the objective of national development. The argument is based on the ground that undue concentration of population in a few large cities creates 'dualism' and a state of 'dependency' and hampers national integration.

(iii) *The failure of trickle-down mechanism*

Growth once concentrated in a few large cities has a tendency to perpetuate itself rather than to trickle down to small urban centres. The experience of more developed countries in respect of trickle-down process is not relevant for the EDC's because of difference in the institutional framework of the two set of countries.

A Seminar[9] on Urban Development Strategies at the Centre of Regional Development held at Nagoya, Japan in, Oct.-Nov. 1974 emphasised that in the case of developing countries, (i) there is a case for the development of small and medium towns from the point of view of maximising employment generation as the "employment multiplier" is found to be the highest in medium size cities according to some studies. (ii) There is a case for development of small towns from the point of view of giving effect to an amenity-based strategy of decentralising social services in rural areas. This is an organic-relationship approach.

The following specific roles can be assigned to small and medium towns : countering primacy, facilitating multiple growth via decentralisation, offering rural areas accessibility to higher urban services, providing linkages to rural and urban areas and promoting spatial integration via more dispersed population.

In China, it is shown by Yu Deyin and Sun Zongfen[10] and Tridib Banerjee that small towns are beneficial to rational distribution of productive forces and the control of size of large cities, (ii) favourable to accumulation of large incidence of labour surplus through transfer of population from agricultural to non-agricultural activities, (iii) conducive to economic cooperation between town and country-side as well as between workers and peasants and (iv) leads to a progressive rise in the level of health, education and culture in rural areas. Benerjee[11] observes in his study that the Chinese strategy to develop the lower order cities was "an evolutionary process of experimenting with different policies and evaluating their results—a commitment to industrial development without sacrificing agricultural productivity, larger investment in transportation energy and infrastructure, decentralisation of industries from coastal provinces . . . a strong emphasis on rural industrialisation, agricultural modernisation and integration of small and large industries and a strong population policy."

Niles Hansen[12] in his paper "diffused urbanisation from below involving the development of small and intermediate towns as feasible recipe for the developing countries so that expanding urban system is organically linked to the target population (the poor) throughout the development process."

But there is no guarantee that the problem of poverty would be tackled simply by decentralising production. The beneficiaries of decentralisation may be the richer sections of the community in an institutional framework, characterised by skewed distribution of incomes and wealth.

In China the model of growth is different from that of India. Rural industrialisation, collectivisation and mechanisation at the farm level and rejuvenation of small and medium cities through the infusion of light industry, are some of the highlights of the Chinese model. The communes in rural areas have their own workshops for grain milling, oil pressing and other kinds of food processing. A number of small iron and steel plants, chemical fertilizer plants and other chemical plants are owned and operated by the communes. The strengthening of collective economy gives impetus to the development of small cities, whereas in the market economy of India, the affluent sections of the rural community are the major beneficiaries of rural development programmes. The development of towns will benefit those who can avail of facilities available there. The Rural poor will be squeezed out of the rural economy to swell the ranks of unemployed in small towns or big cities. The Green Revolution had led to this type of development. In the rural areas, land reforms have not been effectively implemented and the rural economy continues to be semi-feudal, though in certain parts of the country, capitalist farming has also emerged. In such a model of growth, only those who own assets and have marketable surplus, will gain from higher procurement prices and developmental schemes.

The development of small towns can help distribution of products of enterprises in large and intermediate cities and set up integrated Industrial-commercial enterprise. In small towns, the processing industries serve agricultural production and the handicrafts which use local materials and fuel. The small towns can perform this role in prosperity of a type different from the present which is confined to a few pockets and few individuals.

Different small and intermediate towns with a different history of development as well as economic and social conditions will play different roles. Some of them will function as administrative headquarters, others will be industrial and commercial centres. Some may be centres of tourist interest, others may be market towns. These towns can help in the economic development of the region and the spatial distribution of industries. Some of them can support agriculture. Some of these may be in the nature of satellite towns in the periphery of large cities which can play an active role in the control of further sprawl in the urban areas and also can promote economic development of surrounding rural areas and improve physical and cultural life of the peasants. Some small towns are rural market towns whose main economic activities are the collection and distribution of grains, non-staple products, and indigenous products as well as exchange of handicraft products. A number of rural enterprises can be set up in small towns which can bring about the following changes : (i) changes in economic structure of towns, from towns dominated by agriculture to those dominated by industry combined with agriculture, (ii) will increase industrial accumulation and support agriculture, (iii) will increase links with higher level settlements, (iv) promote construction works in rural areas and market towns, and (v) absorb surplus population of rural areas.

Small and medium or medium towns are expected to play an increasingly important role in achieving national development goal of social, regional and personal equity. But such an approach may not be feasible without some powerful and centrally controlled policies about the mobility of people and location of economic activities. These towns can play an effective role only when there is comprehensive approach to rural development and to whole economy. They will play the role of stimulating modern development in the following abbreviated manner :-

(i) as centres where the provision of urban services, facilities and articles are provided for rural settlements ;

(ii) as a concomitant and complementary development to rural development ;

(iii) as an "interface" between urban development and rural development especially in terms of information flows ;

(iv) as an attempt to create a locally-oriented intermediate regional marketing system, forming a coherent nodal system of points in the national transportation and marketing net-work ;

(v) to stem the incessant flow of rural migrants by creating "urban jobs" in rural areas ;

(vi) to create viable income generating opportunities attractive to rural folk so as to reduce the number of migrants ;

(vii) to create diversified income base for the local authorities whose conventional sources of income are inadequate.

The above can be visualised in an integrated system of rural urban settlements where there is regional planning and not in the present one where planning is mostly sectoral. We have not yet delineated viable rural urban communities for the purpose of planning. The planning process is being diluted and the instruments of state policy are becoming ineffective in regulating economic activities, with the result that the end product is quite different from what wc visualise in the plans. The towns and cities are developing on different lines from what have been envisaged in the town and city plans. The local bodies and other urban authorities which are supposed to prepare plans and programmes of development, have failed to perform their functions. Mostly they take an isolated view of urban problems. Towns' plans at present are, by and large, physical plans for land-use patterns rather than regional plans for the development of the entire regional economy in which a town or city is expected to play an effective role.

Generally, we adopt population growth as the only criterion to measure the growth or decay of towns and cities. This approach is unwarranted in the context of regional planning. Towns should be evaluated in terms of their key functions, such as re-inforcing rural-urban linkages, stimulating the productivity of agriculture on both demand and supply sides, efficiency in public service provision and raising the income and welfare levels of both their residents and of hinterland population. The aim of small city development strategy should be to maximise some equity-oriented social welfare function.

In spite of emphasis on the development of small and medium towns in our five year plans, these towns have not performed the roles expected of them. They have played so far a relatively weaker role in absorbing population and creating more spatial distribution of population and activities. The rural-urban dichotomy continues. This may be attributed to the following factors :

(1) The institutional framework is exploitative.

(2) Absence of comprehensive planning in the country.

(3) Absence of national urbanisation policy in the country.

(4) No delineation of regions on the basis of functional linkages and, therefore, no scientific location of functions and facilities.

(5) Agricultural prosperity is confined to a few areas and to large cultivators.

(6) No regionalisation of the country for the purpose of planning.
(7) Inadequate infrastructure in most of the towns.

The need to tackle the problem of industrial dispersal has been recognised in all the plan documents since the beginning of planning in India. But the policy instruments designed exclusively for the purpose, were not instituted till the 70s. A variety of instruments have been devised to translate the approach of industrial dispersal into action. The more important of these are : central Government subsidy on investment in backward areas, the scheme of concessional finance, fiscal incentives, the location of public sector enterprises, licensing policy, the location of industrial estates and a number of promotinal activities of the state Governments. But most of these measures have not succeeded in creating viable growth centres where forces of agglomeration have attracted industries. Even small and medium industrial units tend to be concentrated in metropolitan centres. Such small towns have attracted some industrial units which are within the proximity of large cities. But in majority of cases, the type of units that have come up do not have much linkages with the regional economy, with the result that these towns exist in isolation from their regions of location. Smallness is sufficient to make a unit eligible for assistance from the Government and financial institutions. No attention is paid to the line of manufacture, the location, the ownership and the linkages of such units.

The intimate link between industrialisation and urbanisation has not been adequately reflected in policy design. Planning for industrialisation and urbanisation have to go together. In fact, a programme to disperse industries to new centres, the programme to develop medium sized towns and the objective of controlling metropolitan congestion, are complementary to each other.

Even small scale industrial units are concentrated in large cities and developed states. In 1972, the industrially developed states accounted for nearly 60% of units and 63% of employment, in 1976, the share of these states increased to 64%. Even within developed states, there is concentration of units in few areas. For example, in Gujarat, 26% of units in the state are concentrated in Ahmedabad district, in Maharashtra 31% in Bombay (Greater) district and 23% in Thane district, in Tamil Nadu, 28% in Madras district, in West Bengal 42% in Calcutta district, in Karanataka, 34% in Bangalore district and in UP 28% in Varanasi district.

The impact of location of an industrial unit on the overall development of the area depends upon the extent to which the benefits of industrial employment accrue to local people and the stimulus to further development provided by the influx of industry is availed of in the local areas. The local impact can be considered to be negligible if new industry is brought staffed by labour from outside and with all multiplier effects and other spin-offs being realised outside the area. At present there is no selectivity in approach to enable decentralisation in really backward areas. There is a scramble among states to get as many large projects from the centre as possible.

The result is "enclave" type of development with "export" industries having poor linkages with the state economy. This is the type of industrial development which Madhya Pradesh is witnessing.

Towns can grow not only through industrial development but also through agricultural growth in the area. Most of the towns are in the nature of market towns which have their economic base in rural economy.

The evidence of different states in India whether small and medium towns are actually able to perform their role, is scanty. It is the purpose of the present study to make a detailed investigation into the role which these towns have been performing in the State. The economic functions performed by small and medium towns have to be determined from case histories of individual urban centres. A few broader generalisations about the social and economic characteristics of small and intermediate towns which need testing, are outlined below :

1. Small and intermediate towns exhibit characteristics both of rural and urban areas and generally perform functions found in both rural and urban settlements. They blend both

urban and rural characteristics. They exhibit urban characteristics in their economics which are dominated by commercial and service activities and may have a large manufacturing sector composed of small-sized firms. The middle level towns may have a large proportion of working force in agro-processing, marketing and sometimes manufacturing activities. In some small towns, agricultural activities still predominate. Some of these are overgrown villages but where municipal bodies have been created by the State Government. It is only with industrialisation that some economic characteristics of middle level towns become increasingly urban and different from those of smaller towns. Middle level cities have higher rates of inmigration. Fertility rates among women begin to decline. Yet when all these changes occur, middle level towns remain a blend of urban and rural life styles. Hazelhurst observed of intermediate cities in India that "their multiformity is typically reflected in patchwork of small-scale industrial and commercial enterprises for they incorporate economic functions of both market towns and small-scale manufacturing centres."[13] The blending of city and country is vividly described by Hazelhurst who observes :[14]

"To the occasional visitor, middle range cities contain a bewildering variety of economic activity. Often the first glimmering of the city's economic life is encountered at the railroad station or bus stand, typically congested with tea stalls, sweet shops and rickshaw drivers. Turning to the streets of the bazaar, one finds some areas heavily populated with hawkers, who might be selling fruit and vegetables or odds and ends of cloth... Behind the hawkers are the shops of residents businessmen, one finds, for example bicycle shops and bicycle machanics, small scale metal workers who manufacture trucks and agricultural implements, the shops of medical practitioners and dispensers of medicine, cloth shops and shops labelled simply "general merchandise", gold merchants and grain merchants... Both traditional consumer goods and luxury goods of more recent origin, can be found in the bazaar of the middle range city."

The mingling of rural and urban characteristics persist even in some of the class I cities with a population of over one lakh. Periodic markets still play an important part in the economy of Bhopal, Gwalior, Bhilai and other cities of Madhya Pradesh. These periodic markets play more important role in small and middle level towns which serve as important consumer and marketing centres for their own population and for their hinterlands. Srivastava[15] notes the mix of urban and rural activities found in the periodic markets, which are particularly large in the "Ranehi metropolitan area." They draw buyer from both urban and rural areas and sellers from far-flung villages and towns. He describes the bi-weekly markets of Ranchi as being "as large as to resemble a small fair". These markets attract and bring together in economic and social exchange, both urban merchants and rural farmers.[16]

> "From the countryside, the tribal population brings vegetables, rice and other grains, parched grains, crude sweetmeat, made mostly with gur, seasonal fruits . . . goats, crude agricultural implements, country-woven cloth and sundry other articles. The rural sellers buy some of these articles or the manufactured and the more sophisticated articles from the towns"

The above description of periodic markets by Srivastava, equally applies to small and intermediate and even large towns of M.P.

Many intermediate towns are caught in the middle of development problems. (i) They are growing in population and expanding in physical size and their economies are becoming more diversified but they often lack resources to cope with these changes and the capacity for influencing the direction of change. (ii) The economies of middle level towns tend to be dominted by commercial and service activities, with manufacturing employment concentrated primarily in small-scale industrial sector. These towns tend to differ in their economic composition and mix of activities depending upon size, location and patterns of post investment. Studies done of some Asian countries suggest that the following occupational structures are characteristics of cities in different size classifications :[17]

(a) Cities with population smaller than 100,000 have high proportion of employment in agriculture and related marketing and commercial activities, in small-scale cottage and artisan manufacturing, and lower order services that have relatively low growth rate in total urban emp loyment.

(b) Cities with a population of 100,000 and 250,000 have generally high rates of employment in small-scale manufacturing and in consumer-oriented commercial and service activities and have relatively high rate of total urban employment.

(c) Cities with population of 250,000 to half a million are characterised by an increasing rate of growth in the producer-oriented commercial sector. They tend to have substantial manufacturing and tertiary activities, with increasing rates of growth in the producer-oriented commercial and service sectors and

(d) Cities of I million or more have relatively high proportion of employment in manufacturing, but their occupational structure is dominated by producer-oriented commercial and service sectors.

Cities smaller than 1,00,000 may not have sufficient threshold population to support large scale commercial and manufacturing activities that are dependent on local markets, they do offer sufficiently large markets to sustain lower order, small scale consumer and service functions, agricultural marketing and service activities. Lo and Salih suggest that in Asia manufacturing efficiency increases with city size up to about I million and then begins to decline, while producer-oriented tertiary activities continue to increase in efficiency with population size after cities pass the 1 million mark.

It is interesting to note that the percentage of workers in manufacturing rises with city size, while with employment in household industry, it shows a negative correlation. The changes in urban economic structure occur with continuing urbanisation, rapid industrialisation, and deliberate attempts made by the Government to decentralise urban economic activities from primate city. The economic base of middle level towns is dominated by the informal tertiary sector which is composed of very small commercial activities in which participants barely manage to eke out a living. But this informal sector is seen as a major channel of upward mobility for most of the poorer residents of small and middle level towns because of its low level of skill and educational requirements and the low cost of operation.

(3) Middle-size cities tend to have a disproportionately small share of manufacturing activities and employment compared to their share of population than the largest cities and contribute less to national output. This may be due to historical factor, when under the colonial Governments, most of the investment was made in larger cities.

(4) Intermediate cities tend to have a greater diversity and better quality of social services and facilities than smaller towns and rural areas, but they have proportionately smaller share and poorer quality of services and facilities than the largest cities.

The large gap between the national or state capital and intermediate towns in economic activities, job opportunities and the quantity and quality of social services and facilities, creates a vicious cycle that perpetuates the weak economic position of middle level cities. Poor conditions in these towns make the large cities more attractive to the professionals, skilled workers and entrepreneurs who might generate economic growth and promote better living conditions in intermediate towns. USAID analysts in[18] Colombia observed the adverse effects of the inferior quality of services, infrastructure and facilities in middle-sized cities of that country on improving their economies :

> "Why should doctors, or any professional want to reside in an intermediate city when there are, for example, far superior educational, housing, sanitary, recreational and cultural facilities in the major cities ? And without these professionals how can intermediate cities develop ? This is not to suggest that all intermediate cities should have public facilities that rival those of largest cities. However, the evidence available suggests that intermediate cities are

so far worse off at this point in time and that their future development is threatend."

The Demographic characteristics of small and intermediate towns

(1) Middle sized cities in developing countries have been growing rapidly both in number and population since 1951. United National demographic data indicate that the number of intermediate cities more than doubled between 1950 and 1980 from 301 to 644.

(2) Relatively, however, intermediate cities have been growing slower than cities in the larger and smaller size categories. Only in those countries of Asia where the largest cities have already reached enormous sizes, have the population of middle level cities grown faster than the largest metroplis.

(3) Intermediate and small towns have played relatively weak role, absorbing population increases in most developing countries or in creating a more balanced spatial distribution of population. Even though small and intermediate towns have increased in number and population, their percentage share in total urban population has not increased greatly, and sometimes declined. Kingsley Davis points out that there was a 15% shift in population from rural to urban areas in Latin America between 1950 and 1970, yet cities in the 100,000 and 500,000 range increased their share of population by less than 1 per cent during the same period. The majority of the migrants went to the largest cities in South America. In Asia, migration from rural areas and small towns has played a major role in the expansion of primate cities and in the growth of the largest metropolitan areas. The World Bank estimates that during the 1950s half of growth of Bombay's growth could be attributed to migration. Over 80% of all rural migrants in Indonesia went to Jakarta during the 1960s. The relatively weak role that middle level cities play in absorbing population growth in India is reflected in the fact that cities of over 1,00,000 accounted for less than 10% of India's total population in 1971. Less than 3% of Indians lived in cities of 50,000 and 100,000. More than 80% of the Indian population was scattered in a half million villages containing

less than 10,000 each, and more than half of settlements has less than 500 people.[19]

Middle level towns seem to play the weakest role in the urban system of nations in Africa and Middle East.

A rapid growth of urban population in regions without a corresponding change in the structure of the economy leads, generally to weakening of the agrarian base. This generates the "colonial pattern of the development of under-development" wherein expansion of urban centres is contingent upon the exploitation of the hinterland, which becomes increasingly pauperised through the powerful affluent enclaves and indigent hinterland and the gap between the two widens with time. It follows, therefore, that in evaluating the urban process, their impact on rural base of the region which supports the urban infrastructure, must be taken into account. Under conditions of healthy urbanisation, it is not the urban centre but the system of centres which grows and develops. Under conditions of 'urban accretion', on the other hand, the spatial structure of nodal settlements gets disrupted, thereby smaller towns start decaying or experience low rate of growth under the shadow of higher order of towns. In the face of a weak base of lower order towns, the phenomenal growth of large towns reflects a state of disequilibrium in the structure which tends to be detrimental to the economic development of the region.[20]

REFERENCES

1. Dennis A Bondinelli—A comparative Analysis of demographic, social and economic characteristics of intermediate cities in developing countries—in "Small cities in national development"—edited by Om Prakash Mathur—p. 254.
2. Brian J.L. Berry and Frank E Horton ; eds. Geographic Perspectives on Urban System—Prentice Hall 1979.
3. Harold Lubell—Urban development policies and programmes (working paper) Agency for International Development 1979, p. 34.
4. U.N.—Patterns of Rural and Urban growth-Population Studies 1968, New York, 1980.
5. Thompson Almeida Andrade—Decentralisation from large to small and intermediate cities—a critical view—in Small cities and National Development, edited by O.P. Mathur p 240.

6. Urbanisation in a fragmented world : Some aspects of international inequities—Moonis Raza, Atiya Habeeb, Y P. Aggarwal—Urban India, January, 1984—Vol. 4 No. I—p. 5.
7. V.L.S. Prakasa Rao—Urbanization in India a special dimensions, 1983—pp. 153-167.
8. Small cities in National Development. Edited by Om Prakash Mathur, p. 7.
9. Report of the Seminar on "Urban Development strategies in the context of Regional Development" held at Nagoya, Japan—UN Centre for Regional Developmemt.
10. Yu and Sun Zongfen—"The strategic objective of urban development in China" in Small cities and National Development, Edited by O.P. Mathur UN Centre for Regional Development Nagoya, Japan-1982.
11. Tridib Banerjee, Sirgrid Schenk and William Wiekhan—"The bottom-up approach to the development of lower order cities : Learning from China—in "Small cities and national development" Edited by O.P. Mathur.
12. Niles Hansen—"The role of small and intermediate cities in National Development process and strategies—"Small cities and National Development—Edited by Om Prakash Mathur, Nagoya, Japan—1982.
13. Lighton W. Hazelhurst "The middle range city in India"—Asian survey No. 7. 1968, p. 540.
14. *Ibid.*
15. E. Ahmed and B. Srivastava—"Growth, Morphology, and Ethnic Character of Ranchi-Dhurwa urban complex." in S.M. Alam and VV Pokshinshevsky eds., Urbanisation in Developing countries (Hyderbad, Osmania University Press) 1976, p. 513-42.
16. *Ibid.*
17. Fu-Chou LO and Kamal Salih—"Growth poles and regional policy in open dualistic economies : Western theory and Asian Reality" in LO and Salih-eds. Growth strategy and alternative approaches, 1978.
18. USAID—Urban-Regional sector analysis, page 46.
19. Govt. of India—Department of Statistics-Statistical Abstract of India 1974 (new Series 20) Ministry of Planning.
20. Amitabh Kundu—Measurement of Urban Process. A study in Regionalism, Popular Prakashan—Bombay-pp. 34-35.

CHAPTER 2

THE PROCESS AND PATTERN OF URBANISATION

This chapter makes an attempt at presenting the process and pattern of urbanisation in Madhya Pradesh against the background of economic development in the State. The growth of towns is not a function of size only but also of their location and, therefore, any isolated consideration of towns and cities, without reference to their location and functions, would not be adequate.

The use of population data as a measure of growth has been questioned by Harry Richardson and others. Richardson has pointed out that if population grows in a small city on account of rural surplus and/or excessively high fertility rates, then it would be a symptom of failure of policies rather than of success. Richardson has argued that "population growth is a very poor measure of urban growth used only because the data for variables other than population are sparse.[1] In these respects, rapid population growth might be more of an index of failure than of success. If towns perform their functions successfully in relation to their rural population, namely, generation of employment opportunities in the off-season, reinforcing rural-urban linkages, stimulating the productivity of agriculture, efficiency in public service provision, raising the level of incomes, both of their own residents and of hinterland population, their success may not be reflected in population growth but in circular migration, much of which will not be reflected in official population statistics but which is an important index that measures the intensity of rural-urban linkages.

Thompson Andrade[2] has also argued that the population dimension can hardly express the size of productive base in countries where there is high degree of sub-utilisation of labour and, therefore, it is not a valid indicator for measuring growth or growth potential of small cities. Using population growth as an indicator of "urban success" would mask real failure in the form of poor performance of their functions. Treating stagnant or declining population share as a symptom of urban size-class weakness, is very dangerous. One of the most obvious reason is that a number of rapidly growing towns in the upper range of a class tend to be promoted out of it to the extent that the contribution of a particular size-class to urban growth is continually eroded by "size-class jumping" and the erosion is not compensated by new entrants.

Although it is apparent that population growth indicators have their limitations, it is difficult to substitute other criteria without a massive detailed research. Because of non-availability of adequate data at the macro level, we are constrained to use. by and large, population and related measures to indicate the "growth" or "decay" of different size class of towns. The primary source of information, the national censuses, are always somewhat out of date, and relatively little social and economic information beyond population characteristics, are generally available. In many cases, data are not disaggregated by citiess but are reported by states or districts. Problems of comparison are computed by another fact that city boundaries change from one census to another.

In a subsequent chapter relating to detailed studies of individual towns, we will be more concerned with other indicators of economic and social change along with population growth, to asses the role of small and medium towns in Madhya Pradesh. Wherever permitted by data availibity, we have deployed temporal-spatial framework of analysis, in this chapter.

The Model of Urbanisation

The present state of Madhya Pradesh was constituted on first November, 1956, after the integration of a number of erstwhile princely states and parts of former British India. Its agricultural economy was feudal in character, a large part of land was under the control of non-cultivating landlords, some of whom had purchased land or won rights on it as a result of peasant indebtedness. Even today, the State is characterised by semi-feudal relations of production, though capitalist form of production has emerged in certain parts, particularly where modern inputs have been provided by the Government. Through subsidies, infra structural development, like irrigation, power and banking. Government programmes and their funds have played an essential role in helping this new class to increase its production base. On the political side, the new institutions of Panchayati Raj, cooperative credit, education and village development, have helped this new class maintain its hegemony in a new way over the increasingly proletarised rural majority. A new class of vested interests has emerged among the tribals and scheduled castes who constitute nearly one-third of total population of theState. The exploitation of tribals has been intensified in areas where new industrial units have come into being. The tribal economy has not yet been drawn into the vertex of money-commodity relationship. But the village traders and the wholesalers are thoroughly integrated into the overall industrial and commercial structure. One of the reasons as to why capitalistic farming has not yet developed as quickly as in Punjab and Haryana, is lack of infrastructure and irrigation facilities. A feudal or semi-feudal economy which holds back the forces of production, does not give rise to rapid urbanisation, although a few market centres and seats of administration may emerge on the scene. It is under capitalist farming where more surplus is generated, released and marketed that towns may grow as market centres or where the capitalists may combine agro-industries or other urban occupations, along with agriculture.

The process or urbanization in Madhya Pradesh (M.P.) though slow in many parts of the State, is more or less on the pattern of the whole country-haphazard, unplanned, exploitative and dysfunctional. The spatial organization is attuned to the requirement of growth plus strategy and high rate of capital foamation, with towns degenerating into centres of exploitation of rural hinterland and focal points of suction mechanism. Our urban centres, by and large, have not generated growth impulses to their respective regional economies. The massive public sector investments in a few pockets in heavy and basic industries have further helped in the concentration of population and activities in a few urban centres which are generally rootless, incapable of acting as agents of growth and change, without much trickle-down effects. With the emergence of new class of contractors, traders and Government functionaries in the new and existing industrial and commercial centres, the towns are squeezing out maximum surplus from their respective hinterlands. The market towns tilt the terms of trade in favour of big cultivators and their trading partners. The exploitative mechanism exists right from the top of the hierarchy to the lower order settlements, with chain of intermediaries at different levels. The hinterland of new industrial centres is so poor and backward that it is not capable of taking advantage of the process of 'growth' initiated at these new centres.

While the production process in the country continues to be strongly rooted in rural economy, the hierarchical organization of space which is unplanned, is increasingly becoming top heavy in favour of big cities and consequently dysfunctional. The State did not witness anything like the 'Green Revolution' except in a few pockets where there was assured water supply and this has led to accretion of population in a few market towns and also to the emergence of a few new towns. So far, the pursuit of indentifying backward regions has been so single minded that the need to understand the nature and causes of backwardness has almost been completely neglected. The urge to measure backwardness has drowned the need to analyse. Our whole approach to regional disparities has been ambivalent.

Urbanisation in India has taken place without any national urbanisation policy. A few scholars, have viewed this phenomenon as "over-urbanisation,"[3] a situation in which urban population is not accompanied by a corresponding growth of workforce in non-agricultural sector. Mcgee[4] has termed this as "pseudo-urbanisation", to describe the phenomenal growth of cities, in the face of mounting unemployment, lopsided occupational structure, inequalities in the distribution of income and other assets, overcrowding in slums, mushrooming of squatter settlements and inadequate sanitary and transport facilities. One urban economist recommends the use of the term "subsistence urbanization", implying a situation in which an average urban dweller is denied all amenities except the bare necessities of life and sometimes even these are denied. Kundu and Raza[5] have used the term "urban accretion" which may be defined as "distorted growth of urban centres in relation to their own economic base on the one hand, and to the regional economy on the other."

Whatever name we may suggest, the process of urbanization in India, by and large, is taking place in an unplanned manner in response to market forces. With the further dilution of planning in the country and amendment of industrial policy in favour of large business houses and multinationals, the industrial development would further encourage agglomeration in a few pockets of the country, with the object of exploiting the rural hinterland. The new industrial centres that are emerging are mostly in the proximity of existing big centres, without many forward and backward linkages. The four states of Maharashtra, Gujarat, Tamil Nadu and West Bengal, taken together, accounted for nearly 58% of the total value added by manufacture in the country in 1975-76. Even in so called industrialised states, there are few pockets of Industrial development. In fact, Maharashtra minus Bombay-Thane-Pune belt, is as backward as any other backward state of India.

Although we have been talking about regional planning in a multi-level planning framework since the beginning of the fourth plan, no concrete steps have been taken in this direction with the result that there is no rational distribution of population between different sizes of settlements and no scientific location of functions and facilities. There has been very little sectoral and functional integration in our planning process. In more recent years, whatever little of the edifice of planning was left, has been diluted and we have been increasingly abdicating the field in favour of private sector, with public sector playing the role of providing necessary infrastructure to the private sector.

Madhya Pradesh is no exception to the model of urbanisation that has emerged on the Indian scene. Being relatively more underdeveloped, it manifests more heavily entrenched feudal interests, with slow rate of growth of capitalist mode of production. The resource potential of the State which is very rich is being exploited mostly by the outsiders in collaboration with the local capitalists.[6] The towns and cities are helping the Kulaks and the petty bourgeoise class in the process of exploitation of resource-potential of the State, and the Government is creating the necessary infrastructure for such an exploitation.

Growth of Population in Madhya Pradesh

Let us present a profile of population growth in Madhya Pradesh since 1901, against the background of which we will discuss the process and pattern of urbanization. Table 2.1 presents this profile.

The population of Madhya Pradesh increased by little more than 3 times over the period of last 80 years (1901-81), whereas in the country as a whole, the increase has been little less than 3 times. There has been rapid increase in population in the State since 1961, particularly after the creation of new state of Madhya Pradesh in 1956. The pattern of decadal growth rate has been more or less the same as recorded in the whole country. The rate of growth of population in M.P. has been higher than that of India since 1961. The density of population in the state is little less than one-half of the Indian level. The level of urbanisation in the state has been lower than the Indian average all through the censuses, but since 1951 the level has been rising rapidly in the State, with the result that the gap between the state level and the national level of urbanisation is gradually reduced. The sex ratio has tended to fall in the state from 990 in 1901 to 941 in 1981 but has been all through higher than the Indian average

TABLE 2.1

Year	MADHYA PRADESH Population (lakh)	Decadal growth rate (%)	Density of population (%)	Level of urbanisation (%)	Sex ratio	INDIA Population (lakh)	Decadal growth rate (%)	Density of population	Level of urbanisation (%)	Sex ratio
1	2	3	4	5	6	7	8	9	10	11
1901	169	—	38	8.38	990	2384	—	77	11.0	972
1911	194	15.3	44	6.68	986	2521	5.7	82	10.4	964
1921	192	—1.4	43	7.51	974	2513	—0.3	881	11.3	955
1931	214	11.4	48	8.30	973	2790	11.0	90	12.2	950
1941	240	12.3	54	9.81	970	3107	14.2	103	14.1	945
1951	261	8.7	59	12.02	961	3611	13.3	117	17.6	946
1961	324	24.2	73	14.29	953	4392	21.6	142	18.3	941
1971	417	28.7	94	16.29	941	5482	24.8	177	20.2	930
1981	512	25.2	118	20.31	941	6838	24.8	221	23.7	935

Growth of Urbanization in Madhya Pradesh

Table 2.2 Shows that the level of urbanisation in Madhya Pradesh has been much lower than the level in India, though the difference between the two figures is gradually narrowing down, more particularly in 1981. The co-efficient of variation in the level of urbanisation in M.P. between 1901 and 1981, has been 33.52% as against 28.90% in India, indicating larger variations in M.P. than in the country as a whole.

M.P. is one of the less urbanised states of India, with only 20.31% of its population as urban, compared to 23.7% of India, 35.03% in Maharashtra, 32.98% in Tamil Nadu, 31.08% in Gujarat, 28.9% in Karnataka and 27.7% in Punjab, as revealed by 1981 census. The rate of growth of percentage of urban population to total population in the State has been faster, than that of the country as a whole. The State is fortunate in one respect that urbanisation has not yet assumed any serious dimensions, despite absence of any urbanisation policy. The State does not have a single metropolitan city and the rate of growth of class I towns has slackened in 1971-81, compared to 1961-71.

The number of towns in the State has gone up from 113 in 1901 to 303 in 1981. This increase in number has been more rapid, particularly between 1971-81. This is due to the emergence of new towns in the State. The emergence of new towns largely depends upon the administrative decision of the State Government which can declare any area as municipality. The comparison in number of towns since 1901 has been vitiated on account of frequent changes made in the concept of town in different censuses.

Urbanisation in the State was slow till 1951. This was quite consistent with the overall pattern of slow economic development with low rate of population growth during this period. The real spurt in urban growth was witnessed since 1951. During 1951-81, the urban population increased by more than 3 times, rural population less than doubled and total population doubled.

Table 2.2 also shows that growth of population in M.P., has been faster since 1961 and also the decadal growth rate of urban population has accelerated since then. This may

TABLE 2.2

Levels of Urbanization and Decadal Growth Rates : M.P. and India

Year	Level of Urbanization		Totals Number of towns		Decadal Growth rate Madhya Pradesh			Decadal Growth rate India			URGD	
	M.P.	India	M.P.	India	Total	Urban	Rural population	Total	Urban	Rural population	M.P.	India
1	2	3	4	5	6	7	8	9	10	11	12	13
1901	8.65	11.0	113	1834	—	—	—	—	—	—	—	—
1911	6.68	10.4	110	1776	+15.3	—10.91	+17.78	5.7	+ 0	+ 6.1	—28.69	— 6.1
1921	7.51	11.3	115	1920	— 1.38	+10.87	— 2.26	—0.3	+ 7.9	— 1.8	+13.13	+ 9.7
1931	8.30	12.2	136	2049	+11.39	+23.03	+10.45	11.0	+11.7	+ 9.1	+12 58	+ 8.3
1941	9 81	14.1	162	2210	+12.34	+32.78	+10.49	14.2	+28.2	+11.1	+22.29	+17.1
1951	12.02	17.6	194	2844	+ 8.67	+33.16	+ 6.01	13.3	+35.2	+ 8.2	+27.15	+27.0
1961	14.29	18.3	208	2330	—24.17	+47.70	+29.95	21.6	+23.4	+18.8	+26.75	+ 4.6
1971	16.29	20.2	232	2531	+28.67	+46.63	+20.68	24.8	+23.6	+19.7	+20.95	+12.3
1981	20 31	23.7	303	3245	+25.17	+56.07	+19.16	24.8	+38.6	+17.5	+36.91	+21.1
C.V.	33.52	28.90	—	—	40.93	68.65	59.88	—	—	—	—	—

Source : Census of India, 1971—M.P. Series 10—11 Part II (A)
Census of India, 1981—Series II M.P. Paper I of 1981
Census of India, 1981—Provisional papers Total Series I Paper II of 1981

TABLE 2.3

The size-class Distribution of Towns in Madhya Pradesh and Decennial growth rate by size-classes

Census	Number of towns in size class							Decadal growth rate of population (Percentage)					
Year	I	II	III	IV	V	VI	Total	I	II	III	IV	V	VI
1	2	3	4	5	6	7	8	9	10	11	12	13	14
1901	1	3	11	20	52	26	113	—	—	—	—	—	—
1911	1	3	8	20	56	22	110	—27.39	—26.53	—25.71	+3.32	+12.8	—14.98
1921	3	—	10	23	50	29	115	225.67	—	35.18	10.11	— 9.44	33.9
1931	3	2	11	30	53	37	136	20.15	—	7.59	27.87	4.2	20.26
1941	3	5	16	31	69	38	162	43.33	192.07	19.35	4.64	27.6	— 0.86
1951	5	5	22	35	73	55	194	84.51	5.15	41.44	15.63	7.17	6.20
1961	8	5	30	56	93	16	208	73.52	7.03	55.96	61.41	30.12	—55.81
1971	11	11	41	72	90	7	232	69.12	83.05	41.04	30.4	1.88	—56.97
1981	14	28	41	113	104	3	303	62.23	173.85	—3.60	64.30	18.66	54.75

Census year	All Classes	Proportion of population in each class to total urban population					
		I	II	III	IV	V	VI
15	16	17	18	19	20	21	22
1901	—	9.5	18.0	23.1	18.0	24.3	7.1
1911	−10.91	7.8	15.0	19.8	21.8	29.0	6.6
1921	+10.87	22.6	—	22.9	21.3	24.3	8.9
1931	+23.03	22.2	6.6	20.3	22.3	20.6	7.8
1941	+32.78	24.0	14.3	18.4	17.5	19.9	5.9
1951	+33.16	33.2	11.3	19.4	15.3	16.1	4.7
1961	+47.70	39.1	8.2	20.6	16.2	14.5	1.4
1971	+46.83	43.05	10.26	19.81	14.37	10.09	0.42
1981	+56.07	46.84	18.00	12.24	15.13	7.67	0.12

be partly due to the fact that with the creation of new State of M.P. in 1956, a number of large industrial projects has come up and commercial and industrial activities have expanded at certain places. Some of the district towns have gained population because of expansion of administrative services and tertiary activities. The table also shows that with the exception of 1911 when the decadal growth rate of rural population in M.P. was higher than that of urban growth rate, in all other census years, the growth rate of urban population has been much faster than that of rural population. In 1981, the decadal growth rate of urban population has been more than two times the growth of total population and nearly three times the growth rate of rural population. With the exception of 1911 and 1951, in all other census years, the decadal rate of growth of urban population in M.P., has been higher than that of the country as a whole. The Co-efficient of variation of urban population between 1901 and 1981, has been higher (68.65) compared to C V of rural growth rate (59.88) and total population decadal growth rate (40.93), indicating greater variations in urban decadal growth rates compared to rural and total.

Because of large variations in the rates of growth of both rural and urban population, URGD (Urban-Rural Growth Differential) measure shows large variations between decades. According to this measure, URGD in M.P. was the highest in 1971-81 decade, whereas it was the highest in India in 1941-51 decade. The 1981 census has revealed the highest rate of growth of urban population and a decline in the rate of growth of rural population from 20.68% in 1971 to 19.16% in 1981. This may be indicative of increase in migration from rural to urban areas. During 1971-81, decennial growth rate has fallen by 6.52% in respect of rural population and has increased by 9.94% in respect of urban population. The URGD has been higher in M.P. than the all-India corresponding figures since 1921, indicating higher pace of urbanisation in the State compared to the country as a whole. Fluctuations in levels of urbanisation and decennial rates of growth have also been caused by frequent changes made in the concept of "urban" in Indian censuses.[7] It is only since 1961, that the definition of urban has been systematised and made uniform across the states. The classification of towns has an element of arbitrariness and has been subject to administrative and political pressures. This problem was practically severe in the classification of towns in the lower scale since at this level, the distribution between village and town would necessarily involve judgement and discretion, even in applying the more rigorous tests of urbanisation.

Another feature regarding urbanisation in Madhya Pradesh is relatively less stable structure of settlements compared to India. While total urban population has increased by more than seven times between 1901 and 1981, the number of urban settlements has increased by little less than 3 times. Whereas in the country as a whole, total urban population has increased by six times, the number of settlements increased by only 80%. In India, therefore, most of the urban growth was because of enlargement of existing towns at every level and not merely because of addition of new towns. In Madhya Pradesh, on the other hand, growth of new urban centres has been higher than the country as a whole and rapid growth rate of urban population has been more due to inclusion of new towns than due to enlargement of areas of existing towns.

Size-Class Distribution of Towns

Table 2.3 presents the size-class distribution of towns and decennial growth rates since 1901.

The table shows that the number of towns in M.P. has increased from 113 in 1901 to 303 in 1981, the largest increase having taken place during 1971-81. The number of towns in the population range of 10,000 to 20,000 (class IV) has gone up considerably in the last three censuses, from 35 in 1951 to 56 in 1961, 72 in 1971 and 113 in 1981. Class II towns have shown an appreciable increase in numbers from 11 in 1971 to 28 in 1981. There has been a marked decline in the number of class VI towns from 55 in 1951 to 16 in 1961, 7 in 1971 and only 3 in 1981. More than 75% of all towns in the State belong to classes IV, V and VI in the population range of less than 20,000. Vast majority of towns in the State are, therefore, very small towns.

The distribution of total urban population among different

size-class of towns and their proportion of total population, may show another interesting dimension of the process of urbanisation in Madhya Pradesh. The predominance of Class I towns in urban population is evident from the fact that percentage of urban population living in these towns has gone up from 39.1% in 1961 to 46.84% in 1981. In the country as a whole, a much higher percentage of urban population (56.21% in 1971 and 60.37% in 1981) was living in Class I cities. The decennial growth rate of this class of towns has shown a decline from 84.51% in 1951 to 69.12% in 1971 and 62.23% in 1981, though the number of towns in this class has gone up from 5 in 1951 to 8 in 1961, 11 in 1971 and 14 in 1981. The concentration of nearly 47% of urban population of the State in only 14 cities, as compared to 53% of population in the remaining 299 urban settlements, reveals imbalance in the pattern of urbanisation in M.P., even when only 20% of total population of the State is urban.

The table also shows percentage changes in the number of towns and percentage changes in growth of population in different size-class of towns in the State. The rate of growth of population of all class of towns has been the fastest between 1971-81 (56.07%) compared to 46.63% during 1961-71 and 47.70% during 1951-61. This higher growth rate of urban population during 1971-81 is due to faster population growth of class II towns (173.85%), followed by Class IV towns (64.3%) and Class I towns (62.23%). Other classes of towns either had negative rates of population growth or growth rates lower than the growth rate of total urban population. In 1961-71 also, the fastest rate of growth was manifested by Class II towns, followed by Class I towns. But during 1951-61, the highest percentage growth of population was recorded in respect of Class I towns, followed by Class IV towns (61.41%) and Class III towns (55.96%). The fastest rate of growth (173.85%) during 1971-81 was registered by Class II towns and this may be largely due to increase in the number of such towns from 11 in 1971 to 28 in 1981 (154% increase). The rapid growth of Class II towns may be attributed to factors like (i) increase in the number of towns and (ii) a number of towns in lower class have jumped over the fence or what Richardson calls 'size class jumping' on account of which the contribution of this size-class is continually eroded. This erosion is not compensated by new entrants and (iii) higher natural growth and in-migration due to expansion of commercial and industrial activities. The number of Class III towns remains the same between 1961-71 and 1971-81, but their share in total urban population has gone down from 20.6% in 1961 to 19.81% in 1971 and further to 12.24% in 1981 and their decennial growth rate of population has been negative during 1971-81 (—3.60%). This may be due to upward mobility of such towns of this class as were on the verge of becoming Class II and their replacement by such towns of lower class whose population was just equal to the lower range of higher class of towns. Of the 14 towns of this class, 16 towns had declining growth rate during 1971-81 to such an extent that they had offset the higher growth rate of remaining 24 towns which had an increasing growth rate. The table shows that urban growth during 1971-81 is virtually confined to two size class of towns, Class II and Class IV which have manifested higher rates of growth of population compared to previous decades. Interestingly, Class IV towns (population range 10,000 to 20,000) have registered a higher decadal rate of growth compared to Class I towns, but their share in total urban population has increased only marginally from 14.37% between 1961-71 to 15.13% between 1971-81.

The table also shows that decadal rates of growth of population of Class I, Class II, Class III, Class V towns have been generally higher than the decadal growth of respective number of towns. In the case of Class VI towns, there has been negative growth both in respect of decadal growth of population as well as number of towns. Higher decadal growth rate of population compared to decadal growth rate of number of towns, may be interpreted as increase in population in a particular class of towns more due to increase in existing population of towns rather than to increase in number of towns.

Since no town devolves out of Class I, while many may graduate into it, the illusion is created that cities are growing at a faster rate. To compare growth rate of size-class of towns across the decades, we are in fact comparing non-comparable entities. For instance, the growth rate of Class I cities is compared in respect of 11 towns in 1971 and 14 in 1981. Therefore, to obtain a realistic picture of the growth rates of urban population by size-class, the population at the two census points must be for only those towns that belonged to that category in the base year.[8] This analysis has been made in a subsequent section.

Small and Intermediate Towns

It would be interesting to look at the problem from another angle : disaggregation of total urban population into percentage shares of towns in different ranges of population, small towns, intermediate towns and large towns.

In the present study, we have re-classified six size-class of towns into following categories :

1. Small towns up to population of 49,9,99 (Class III, IV V & VI)
2. Medium or intermediate towns in the population range of 50,000 to below one lakh. (Class II towns)
3. Large towns (Class I towns) with a population of one lakh and above.

The Table 2.4 presents the distribution of urban population of Madhya Pradesh according to above classification.

This table shows that M.P. is predominantly a state of small towns with less than 50,000 population each. The comparability of data through different censuses has been vitiated by frequent changes in the concept of town in the censuses. The number of small towns increased from 109 in 1901 to 261 in 1981 but the percentage share of this category of towns in total urban population has plummetted from 72.5% in 1901 to 35.16% in 1981. The number of very small towns with population of less than 20,000 each, has gone up from 98 in 1901 to 220 in 1981 but the percentage share in total urban population has appreciably declined from 49.4% in 1901 to 22.9% in 1981. This decline may be partly due to

TABLE 2.4

Census Year	Very small towns (less than 20,000)		Small towns (up to 49,9,999)		Intermediate (50,000 to 99,99,9,99)		Larger towns	
	Number of towns	Percentage of urban population	Number	Percentage of urban population	Number of Towns	Percentage of urban population	Number	Percentage of urban population
1901	98	49.4	109	72.5	3	18.0	1	9.5
1911	98	57.4	106	77.2	3	15.0	1	7.8
1921	102	54.4	112	77.4	—	—	3	22.6
1931	120	50.7	131	71.2	3	6.6	3	22.6
1941	138	43.3	154	61.5	5	14.3	3	24.0
1951	162	36.1	184	55.5	5	11.3	5	33.2
1961	165	32.1	195	52.5	5	8.2	8	39.1
1971	169	24.6	210	44.7	11	10.26	11	45.0
1981	220	22.9	261	35.16	28	18.0	14	46.8

definitional changes and partly due to graduation of towns of this category to next higher category. The number of medium size towns has increased from 3 to 28 but there are wide fluctuations in the percentage share of this category of towns in the total urban population. Since 1961, there has been consistent increase in the share of these towns in total urban population of the State, from 8.2% in 1961 to 10.26% in 1971 and 18.0% in 1981. Only towns with population of one lakh and above have shown increase in percentage share to the extent that in 1981 nearly 47% of total urban population was living in this category of towns. Thus with the exception of large towns and to some extent of intermediate towns, the percentage shares of small and very small towns in total urban population of the State, have gone down. Obviously, there is imbalance in the distribution of urban population among different categories of towns in the State.

The phenomenon of relatively slow growth of small towns in the urban hierarchy has been variously interpreted. Some feel that their slow growth is only transitional and as "trickle-down" forces are strengthened, small and medium towns will find thair place in the urban hierarchy. To some, the erroneous development strategies which have been highly capital intensive and agglomerative, pursued by the Government in the sixties and seventies, are responsible for the emergence of lop-sided and concentrated problem of urbanisation. It is generally observed that "policy makers in India aimed at industrialisation without urbanisation and achieved urbanisation without industrialisation."

Urbanization in Madhya Pradesh and India

It would be interesting to compare the growth rates of urban population and distribution of urban population by size-class of towns in M.P. with India. Table 2.5 presents this comparative picture.

The decadal rate of growth of population of Class I towns has declined in M.P. from 69.12% in 1971 to 62.23% in 1981, whereas in India, this percentage has gone up from 52.67%. to 56.83%. In M.P. Class II towns have manifested the highest rate of growth of population from 83.05% in 1971 to 173.85%, whereas in India, this class of towns has shown increase in growth rate from 40.94% to 51.22%. In M.P. Class III towns have shown negative growth rate in 1980 (—3.60%) compared to a very high rate of growth of 41.04% in 1971, whereas in India this class of towns have shown a marginal decline in growth rate from 29.27% to 28.41%. Class IV towns in M.P. have shown faster growth rate compared to their counterparts in India, where this class of towns have registered a declining growth rate from 18.85% to 15.44%. Class V towns have shown higher rate of growth in the country as a whole, compared to M.P. Class VI towns in M.P. have shown negative growth rate, whereas in India this class of towns has manifested a very high growth rate. Thus there have been differential growth rates in different size class of towns, in M.P. and India.

The table also presents the distribution of urban population among different size-class of towns in Madhya Pradesh and India. The percentage share of class I towns in total urban population of M.P. has increased only marginally from 45.05% to 46.84% whereas in India, this percentage has increased at a higher rate from 56.21% in 1971 to 60.37% in 1981. In respect of Class II towns which have shown the highest rate of growth of population in the State, the percentage share has increased appreciably from 10.26% in 1971 to 18.0% in 1981. But in India, the share of this class of towns has increased only marginally from 11.24% to 11.65%. The percentage shares of Class III towns have gone down both in M.P. and India The percentage share of class IV towns has increased in M.P. but declined in the country as a whole. The shares of Class V and VI towns declined in MP but increased marginally in the country as a whole.

Table 2.5 shows that in Madhya Pradesh, the share of small towns in the population range of below 50,000 namely Class III, IV, V and VI towns, has declined from 44.69% in 1971 to 35.16% in 1981, whereas in the country as a whole, this percentage has declined from 28.55 to 27.98. Although a much higher percentage of urban population is living in small towns in M.P. compared to India, the decline in the share of this class of towns is much faster in Madhya Pradesh

TABLE 2.5

Distribution of urban population and growth rates by size-class of towns in 1971 and 1981 : M.P. and India

Size range and class of towns		Number of towns				Percentage of total urban population				Growth rate (decadal) of population (percentage)			
		1971		1981		1971		1981		1971		1981	
		M.P.	India	M,P.	India	M.P.	India	M.P.	India	M.P.	India	M.P.	India
1	2	3	4	5	6	7	8	9	10	11	12	13	14
I	100,000 & above	11	45	14	216	40.05	26.21	46.84	60.37	69.12	52.67	62.23	56.83
II	50,000—99,999	11	178	28	270	10.26	11.24	18.0	11.65	83.03	40.94	173.85	51.22
III	20,000—49,999	41	570	41	739	19.81	16.32	12.24	14.35	41.04	29.27	—3.60	28.41
IV	10,000—19,999	72	847	113	1048	14.37	11.20	15.13	9.52	30.14	18.85	64 30	24.03
V	5000— 9,999	90	641	104	742	10.08	0.57	7.67	3.61	1.88	—10.38	18.6	15.44
VI	below 5000	7	150	3	230	0.42	0.46	0.12	0.50	—56.97	19.70	—54.75	60.74
	Total	232	2431	303	3245	100	100	100	100	46.63	37.91	56.07	46.02

than in the country as a whole, whereas gainers in M.P. are medium towns in the range of 50,000 to 99,999 whose share in total urban population has gone up from 10.26% in 1971 to 18.0%in 1981, in India, the gainers are mostly Class I towns. The 1981 census has shown a very fast rate of growth of population of Class II towns and deceleration in the rate of growth of Class I towns in Madhya Pradesh. The pattern of urbanisation and distribution of urban population among classes of towns is somewhat different in Madhya Pradesh from that of India. This difference is more marked in 1981 census compared to the earlier censuses.

Let us now present a comparative picture of Madhya Pradesh and other states of India, as revealed by 1981 census.

Regional Variations in Pattern of Urbanisation in India

West Bengal and Maharashtra have the highest concentration of urban population (over 70%) in Class I towns. This is followed by Tamil Nadu, Karnataka, Gujarat and Haryana. Punjab provides an example of urbanisation that has taken place primarily as a result of rapid agricultural development combined with agro-based industries. Only 46.4% of total urban population is living in class I cities. There are 37 Class II and III towns, accounting for 34.5% of urban population. Madhya Pradesh has nearly the same percentage of urban population as that of Punjab living in Class I towns but it is spread over 14 towns as against 7 in Punjab, indicating smaller size of Class I cities compared to Punjab. In Madhya Pradesh, a larger proportion of urban population was residing in very small towns of less than 20,000 population, the highest among the major states in India (23.92%), followed by Orissa (23.78%) and UP (22.26%). All the three states are industrially under-developed. Barring Maharashtra and West Bengal, a sizeable proportion of urban population lives in class II and III towns in different states of India. The states where more than one-third of the urban population resides in these towns are Kerala (41.38%), Andhra Pradesh (37.12%), Punjab (34.6%) and Bihar (33.64%). In M.P. nearly 30% of urban population is living in these two classes of towns. The regional variations in the levels of towns of different size-classes in the overall urban hierarchy, and their differential growth rates can, to a large extent, be explained in terms of differences in the regional pattern of economic growth in general and industrial development in particular.

Urban Growth Rates in Different States

The following table presents urban growth rates in major states of India during 1971-81.

TABLE 2.6

State	Percentage Growth rate	URGD 1961-71	URGD 1971-81
Orissa	68.29	3.05	3.82
UP	61.22	0.99	3.01
Haryana	59.16	0.30	2.74
Delhi	57.73	—	—
Rajasthan	57.15	0.96	2.14
M.P.	56.07	1.53	2.74
Bihar	54.40	1.93	2.55
Karnataka	50.39	1.10	2.39
Andhra Pradesh	48.26	1.25	1.37
Punjab	43.66	0.38	2.10
Gujarat	40.82	1.21	1.48
Maharashtra	39.82	1.40	1.76
Kerala	37.63	0.85	1.78
West Bengal	31.78	0.16	0.92
Tamil Nadu	27.78	1.74	1.27
India	46.20	1.26	2.07

The table shows that interestingly the states which have shown the highest growth rates are the ones which have an urban-rural composition which is less than the national average of 23.7%. These include Orissa, U.P., Haryana, Rajasthan, Madhya Pradesh, Bihar and Andhra Pradesh. The first six States have been considered to be non-urban and rural-oriented. Orissa, Rajasthan, M.P., Bihar and UP are also considered backward states. At the same time, the more advanced and more urbanised States such as Gujarat, Maharashtra, Punjab, Tamil Nadu and West Bengal, have recorded urban growth rates which are less than the national average of 46.20%. One clearly noticeable pattern is that there is a slight tapering off urban growth in the more highly urbanised states and a sharp increase in the backward states. The U.R.G.D. was found to be the highest (3.82) in Orissa followed by UP (3.01), M.P. (2.74) and the lowest in West Bengal (0.92), followed by T.N. (1.27).

The wide variety of urban patterns that are discernible in India, is a very interesting phenomenon. Punjab, Haryana and western UP, have a large number of small towns and all of them show healthy growth characteristics. This is due to the strength of the agrarian economies and there seems to be reason to believe that the close links exist between agricultural surplus and marketing and service function centres in mandi towns. The principal variation within the region that can be observed, however, is the strength of Class I towns in Haryana (probably as a result of the growth of towns around Delhi), of Class III and IV towns in Punjab and Class III, IV, and V towns in UP.

South-central and south-eastern UP and northern Bihar have very similar urban growth characteristics. The urban settlements are not closely clustered as in the agriculturally prosperous regions, but are growing very fast (more than 50% in a decade). This areas has similar topographical and demographic characteristics, very large holdings in the hands of landlords and very small average size of holdings, most of the peasantry living on the verge of subsistence, urban population not exceeding 10% of total population in the regions. Such an economy does not lend itself to strong marketing functions.

South Bihar, parts of south-eastern Bengal, eastern Orissa and south-eastern Madhya Pradesh seem to have some similarity in respect of urban growth. The area is minerally rich, urban-populated on account of hills and forests and is the region where large scale industries such as mining, metallurgical industries and power are located. The urban settlements are scattered, but those which show remarkably high growth characthristics. Dhanbad, Bokaro, Ranchi, Jameshedpur in Bihar, Rourkela, Sambalpur, Koraput in Orissa, Bilaspur, Korba, Raipur, Durg, Bhilai, in M.P., are more or less similar in terms of their employment and growth profiles. The spread effects of these cities within the regions are limited, but viewed autonomously, each of them is a powerful urban centre. For instance, Korba in Bilaspur district of M.P. has recorded a decadal growth rate of 155.58%. The town is near to Raigarh district from which it seems to attract a substantial amount of labour, the rural growth rate of Raigarh district was 9.8% during 1971-81 and of Bilaspur 16.84%. The urban growth for Raigarh district was 54.47% and for Raigarh town 59.62%. There has been substantial migration from rural areas to new urban centres. In such regions there would naturally be an enormous gulf between the rural and urban areas with no continuum between the two economies, a situation quite contrary to Punjab and western U.P. which exhibit strong rural-urban continuum.[9]

Madhya Pradesh and Rajasthan have shown high rates of urban growth, 56.1% and 57.2% respectively during the decade 1971-81. Both states are backward, sparsely populated and have a large land area. In terms of development potential M.P. is by far the richer, with its ample water resources, varied soil types and plenty of mineral and forests. Rajasthan is handicapped by climate and geography, the whole of western Rajasthan is desert.

Growth of Towns in M.P.

The Class I towns have registered a decline in the decadal growth rate of population from 69.12% in 1971 to 62.23% although the number of towns in this class has gone up from 11 to 14. This may be partly due to the fact that in 1981, out of 14 towns 7 had increasing growth rate compared to 6 out of 11 in 1971 and consequently there has been increase in the number of towns with declin ing growth rate. Another factor may be that in 1971, out of 11 towns of this Class, 4 had registered decadal Growth rate higher than the state average, whereas in 1981, the number of such towns was only 3 out of total of 14. Decline in growth rate may also be attributed to lower rate of natural growth, lesser migration due to lack of expansion of commercial and industrial activities. This deceleration in the decadal growth rate of Class I towns in 1981 is a peculiar phenomenon to be observed in Madhya Pradesh, perhaps not to be found in most of the other states and needs to be thoroughly probed when more data in respect of migration and occupational classification of workers become available. The contention of Director of Census Operations, M.P., that there seems to be the end of the "Urbanisation Cycle" in Class I cities of M.P., seems to be unwarranted.

Of the 14 Class I cities in the state, only three, viz. Bhopal Durg-Bhilainagar and Raipur have shown faster rate of growth than the State average rate of urban growth, Bhopal being the capital seat of Madhya Pradesh and location of BHEL, Durg-Bhilai and Raipur because of location of steel plant and number of other industrial units. Other important towns of M.P. belonging to this class like Indore, Gwalior, Jabalpur, Ujjain, Sagar, Bilaspur, Ratlam and Khandwa, have grown at rates lower than the urban growth rate in the State.

The Class II towns have shown the fastest rate of growth in 1981 (173.85%) compared to 83.05% in 1971. This may be partly due to increase in the number of towns from 11 to 28 and partly due to increase in number of such towns which have recorded decadal growth rate of population higher than the urban growth rate in the State, from 3 to 6. Most of these 6 towns are industrial or coal-mining centres.

Class III towns whose number has remained constant in the census years 1971 and 1981, have shown a negative rate of growth(—3.6%) in 1981, partly due to decline in the number of such towns from 14 to 2, showing decadal growth rate higher than the state average and partly due to increase in the number of such towns from 5 to 16 which have recorded declining population growth. A number of fast growing towns of this class have graduated to the next higher class.

Next to Class II towns, the Class IV towns have shown the highest rate of growth in 1981 (64.3%) even higher than Class I towns. This may be due to increase in the number of towns from 72 in 1971 to 113 in 1981. Of the 113 towns of this class, more than half belong to the category of towns which had increasing decadal growth of population.

Class V towns have shown a slower rate of growth in 1981 but higher g'owth rate when compared to that registered in 1971. The number of towns belonging to this class has gone up from 90 to 104. But the number of towns with increasing decadal growth rate has gone down from 23 to 15 and with declining growth rate has increased from 5 to 23.

Class VI towns have shown the highest negative decadal growth rate in 1981 (—54.75%) as well as in 1971 (—56.97%). The explanation for this may be decline in the number of towns from 7 to 3. In fact, this is the only class of towns whose number has gone down.

Towns which have shown faster rate of growth compared to growth rate of urban population in the State are not mostly district headquarters. Of the 24 towns belonging to this category, only 8 are district headquarters, the rest are either new industrial centres or project towns or coal mining centres. Very few towns have grown because of agricultural growth. Among 3 Class I towns showing faster rate of growth, Bhopal, is the capital seat of the State, Durg-Bhilai and Raipur have grown faster because of industrial development. All the Class II towns belonging to this category are newly emerging industrial centres or coal-mining centres, such as Korba, Dewas, Rajhara, Parasia. Two Class III towns which belong to this category, are agricultural marketing centres. Of the 12 Class IV towns, only two are industrial centres, 2 are project towns and the rest are agricultural market centres. This analysis shows that most of the fast growing towns in the State are either industrial centres or coal-mining centres.

Let us know look at the decadal growth rates of class I cities individually to see as to which of them have registered higher rates of growth and which have decelerated in the last 30 years. The following Table 2.7 presents data relating to the growth rates of Class I towns in the state.

The Table 2.7 shows that in 1951-61 only five of the 14 Class I cities had manifested growth rate of population higher than the urban growth in the State. The number of such towns in 1971-81 was reduced to three. In 1951-61, the highest rate of growth was recorded by Durg-Bhilai (557.96%), followed by Bilaspur (121.71%) and Bhopal (117.87%). This may be attributed to location of steel plant at Bhilai, capital head-quarters of M.P. at Bhopal and expansion of commercial and industrial activities at Bilaspur. In 1961-71, the highest rate of growth of population was again witnessed by Durg-Bhilai (83.99 %), followed by Bhopal (72.62 %). In 1971-81, also the highest rate of growth was witnessed by Durg-Bhilai (99.96 %), followed by Bhopal (74.69 %). Out of 14 Class I towns, the population growth rates declined during 1971-81 in 7 towns compared to 1961-71 decade.

TABLE 2.7

Showing growth of Class I Towns in Madhya Pradesh

Name of the city	Population growth rate (decadal)		
	1951-61	1961-71	1971-81
1	2	3	4
1. Indore	27.05	42.03	47.44
2. Bhopal	117.87	72.62	74.94
3. Jabalpur	42.81	45.73	41.67
4. Gwalior	24.43	35.12	37.83
5. Durg-Bhilai	557.96	83.99	99.96
6. Raipur	55.66	47.35	64.56
7. Ujjain	11.05	44.66	35.15
8. Sagar	30.73	47.87	33.99
9. Bilaspur	121.71	50.79	42.94
10. Ratlam	37.96	36.33	31.23
11. Burhanpur	17.16	28.32	33.99
12. Murwara	78.47	43.10	44.56
13. Khandwa	22.27	34.48	34.03
14. Rewa	45.38	60.65	45.30
15. M.P. urban population	47.70	46.63	56.07
16. All Class I towns	73.52	69.12	62.23
17. CV of Class I towns	159.18	30.54	39.27

The co-efficient of variation of population growth rate of these 14 Class I towns was the highest in 1951-61 (159.18 %).

This was due to the fact that growth of population was the fastest in Durg-Bhilai, Bhopal and Bilaspur which slackened in subsequent decades. In the next two decades, the CV came down to 30.54 and 39.27 respectively.

There appears to be no firm relationship between the number of cities, their growth rate and the number of small and intermediate towns and their growth rate of population. As the table shows, Bilaspur district has the largest number of small and intermediate towns (10) but the annual growth rate of population of Bilaspur city, the growth rate of urban population in the district and also annual growth rate of population of small and intermediate towns, do not appear to be very high. Durg district has the highest annual rate of population growth during 1971-81 and also the highest rate of growth of urban population in the district among such districts which have Class I cities. The annual growth rate of population of small and intermediate towns is also the highest in Durg District.

It cannot be established whether small and intermediate towns have higher or lower annual growth rates of population in such districts where big cities are located. It is generally observed that in districts where big cities are located, small and intermediate towns may not grow at a fast rate or decline because of the attraction of migrants to bigger cities. Another view may be that small towns flourish within the proximity of large cities either as satellite towns or as ring towns. No such evidence was available in this regard in the State. One fact is discernible that Durg district which had witnessed the highest growth rate of city population, had also the highest URGD and had also recorded the highest rate of growth of population of small and intermediate towns. On the other hand, Ratlam district which had recorded the lowest rate of growth of population of Ratlam city, had also shown the lowest URGD in the district and the lowest rate of population growth of small and intermediate towns in such districts which had the location of Class I cities. But such relationships in respect of other districts, could not be observed.

The Primacy Ratio

In several countries, including India, the largest city claims an unduly large proportion of the urban population. The urban pattern is characterised by a good deal of primacy even in countries with low level of urbanisation. The statistical measure of primacy is called index of primacy which is defined as the ratio of population of the largest city to the combined population of second third and fourth largest cities. This measure involves the rank-size rule whose applicability is questionable, even though the concept serves the purpose of illustration.

TABLE 2.8

	Index of primacy	
	1971	1981
1. India	0.56	0.46
2. Madhya Pradesh	0.42	0.43
3, Eastern region of M.P.	0.60	0.80
4. Inland Eastern Region	2.70	2.9
5. Inland Western Region	1.4	1.8
6. Western region	1.3	1.4
7. Northern region	2.8	2.8

The illustration is quite revealing. In the country as a whole, we notice a reduction in the degree of primacy in 1981 compared to 1971. In Madhya Pradesh, there appears to be stability in primacy. The low or high primacy measured in numerial terms is not perhaps the best indicator of the dysfunctional role of the urban pattern. For different regions of M.P. the highest primacy index was found in respect of inland eastern region (2.9), followed by northern region (2.8) and the lowest in respect of eastern region (0.80). In inland eastern region, there is a big gap between the population of Jabalpur city and other towns ranked in order of population. Similarly, in the northern region, the primacy index is high because of location of Gwalior, the largest city followed by other towns which are of considerable smaller size. In the eastern region, the index happens to of low order, because there is not very large gap between the population of Durg-Bhilai, the largest town and other towns. In the inland western region, there is a big gap between the population of Bhopal city and towns occupying next three ranks. Although, the primacy index for the state as a whole is not very high, there are regional variations, indicating the gap between the population of the largest city and the town occupying the next three ranks.

Sex Composition

There has been a continuous decline in sex ratio in the State since 1901. In 1981, the sex ratio of 1971 (941) has been maintained. Sex ratio is generally lower in urban areas than in rural areas. The following table presents females per 1000 males in Madhya Pradesh.

TABLE 2.9

Sex Ratio

Census year	Total population	Urban population
1901	990	937
1911	986	913
1921	974	878
1931	973	872
1941	970	882
1951	967	907
1961	953	856
1971	941	968
1981	941	883

Whereas sex ratio of population as a whole was continuously declining since 1901 till 1971, that in urban areas of the State was showing a different behaviour. It declined from 937 in 1901 to 872 in 1931 but in the two decades 1931-51, increased to 882 in 1941 and 907 in 1951. In the decade 1951-61, the ratio again assumed the declining trend when it was 856 in 1961, the lowest ratio recorded in the century since 1901. Since then again it has assumed the upward trend.

Big urban centres and industrial and mining towns are generally characterised by low sex ratio. Similarly project towns also exhibit low sex ratio. But when these big towns cross the initial stage of development, the sex ratio tends to stabilise and improve. For instance, in Bhilai Nagar, the sex ratio was only 486 in 1961, when the town was in its initial stage of development, consequent upon the location of steel plant. By 1971 it was a settled township. The sex ratio in 1971 improved to 795 and further to 853 in 1981.

The spatial pattern of sex composition is characterised by marked variations. It is not confined to rural-urban areas but is a characteristic feature of inter-town analysis. The size of town has an important bearing on sex composition as is evident from the following table ;

TABLE 2.10

Size-Class	Sex ratio in 1981
I	877
II	873
III	891
IV	899
V	899
VI	856
All classes of towns	883
Total population	941

The above statement shows that class I, II and VI exhibit sex ratios lower than the state urban average, whereas class III, IV and V show sex ratios above the state urban average. "Actually speaking the take-off stage of urbanisation is size Class IV. The sex ratio of 899 of size Class V is maintained in size Class IV but as we move upward in the size class, the sex ratio of size class declines to 891 in size class III and further to 873 in size class II. But as we move further to size Class I, the urbanisation prossce gets stabilised and there is slight improvement in sex ratio from 973 in class II to 877 in class I."[10]

As a matter of fact, sex ratio in Class VI should not have been so low as this class of towns is just an extension of rural areas. In M.P. in 1981, there are only 3 towns in this size-class and these are Khajuraho, Panara and Naya Baradwar. Khajuraho is the internationally famous archaeological centre of great tourist interest and is in the same situation today as a project town exhibiting a sex ratio of 797. Panara is a coal-mining town and in coal mines, it is generally the males who are employed as labourers. The third town of this size-class Naya Baradwar has a sex ratio of 892 which is higher than the state average for the urban areas. It is low sex ratio of the first two towns that has brought down the sex ratio of class VI towns in the State.

Density of Population

It is generally said that big towns are more densely populated than smaller towns. Though dwelling density declines towards city fringes, the average density for the city as a whole is likely to be high. There is likely to be less of the agglomerative effect in smaller towns and, therefore, lower densities would occur. There may be deviations in respect of smaller towns which are industrial centres. It is generally found that population per sq. km. is less for each successively smaller size class. In the absence of data relating to density of population in respect of different classes of towns in 1981 census, the analysis of density according to size-class of towns could not be done. Instead, district-wise density data are given and on that basis analysis has been made. The following table presents the number of districts classified according to density range per sq. km.

TABLE 2.11

Density range per sq. km.	Number of districts in M.P.	
	1971	1981
below 50	1	1
50-100	25	11
100-150	12	24
150-200	5	3
200-300	2	4
above 300	—	2
total	45	45

There has been upward mobility of districts from low density range of 50-100 to high density range of 100-150. The number of districts in the density range of 100-150 has gone up from 12 to 24 and the number in the range of 50-100 has come down from 25 to 11. There were 3 districts in the range of 150-200 density in 1981 but in 1971 the number was 5. The 2 districts might have migrated to the higher range of 200-300 in 1981. In the range of 300 and above, there was not a single district in 1971 but in 1981, two districts were found in this range of density.

The state as a whole had density of 118 persons per sq. km. in 1981 as against 94 in 1971. By and large, districts having highly urbanised areas like cities have recorded higher density of population. Indore (361) and Bastar (47) continue to be the districts having the highest and the lowest density of population respectively. There are 22 districts with density higher than the state average.

The following table indicates density of population in class I cities of M.P. in 1981.

TABLE 2.12

City	Area in Km.	Density of population
Gwalior	291.85	1918
Sagar	50.06	4143
Rewa	52.57	1912
Ratlam	39.19	3993
Ujjain	74.84	3766
Indore	113.52	7286
Khandwa	22.57	5071
Burhanpur	12.67	11,140
Bhopal	284.9	2360
Jabalpur	220.8	3432
Murwara	88.57	1412
Bilaspur	51.57	3611
Durg	135.0	3815
Raipur	55.03	6160
M.P.		118

The highest density of population is recorded in Burhanpur (11,140) which is a congested city with lowest area among Class I cities (12.67 km.). The lowest density among Class I cities is to be found in Murwara where area in the municipal limits is large in relation to population. In smaller towns, there is less agglomerative effect and hence low densities. It is generally found that population per sq. km. is less for each successively smaller size class of towns. But in the absence of data, the relationship between density and size-class of towns could not be established.

Literacy Rate

The percentage of literates to total population in the State has gone up from 22.14% in 1971 to 27.82% in 1981, an increase of 25.65% in literacy rate during the decade of1971-81.

The following table presents literacy rates in the State since 1961, along with all India rates for the purpose of comparison.

TABLE 2.13

Literacy rate for total population and for males and females in India and M.P.

Year	Persons		Males		Females	
	India	M.P.	India	M.P.	India	M.P.
1961	24 02	17.13	34.44	27.03	12.95	6.73
1971	29.45	22.14	39.45	32.70	18.69	10.92
1981	36.17	27.82	46.74	39.38	24.88	15.53

The state is quite below the All-India average and the gap is larger in respect of female literacy.

Another table below presents the percentage increase of literacy rates between two censuses to show the pace of development in this field.

TABLE 2.14

Percentage increase in Literacy rate 1961-81

Period	INDIA			MADHYA PRADESH		
	Persons	Males	Females	Persons	Males	females
1961-71	22.61	14.55	44.32	29.25	20.98	62.26
1971-81	22.82	18.48	23.12	25.65	20.43	42.22

The table shows that the rate of increase in literacy rate in the State was higher (29.25%) in 1961-71 decade but slowed down in 1971-81 decade (25.65%). In the first decade, the rate of increase was higher because of high increase in female literacy rate (62.26%) compared to 20.98% in male literacy rate. In the second period, the rate has declined mainly due to decline in the female literacy rate from 62.26% to 42.22%. The population of the state is still predominantly literate, the number of illiterates is little less than 2 and half time of literates.

There are considerable variations in the literacy rate between sexes, between districts and between towns of different size class. The rural literacy rate is 21.15% as against 53.98% in urban areas and 27.82% in the whole state. Male literacy rate has gone up from 17.13% in 1961 to 22.14% in 1971 and 27.82% in 1981, while female literacy rate has increased from 6.73% in 1961 to 10.92% in 1971 and 15.54% in 1981. The pace of increase in the literacy rate among females has been much higher than what was among males.

In 1971 there were 18 districts which had recorded literacy rates higher than the state average of 22.14, in 1981, the number of such districts increased to 19, the state average being 27.82. If we take literacy rate of urban population in different districts we find that out of 45 districts, 20 districts have recorded urban literacy rates higher than the literacy rate of urban Madhya Pradesh (53.98%).

Urbanization and Occupational Pattern

Generally urbanisation is associated with industrialisation. But in M.P. it is not so much industrialisation as development of commercial and trading activities and services which have led to urbanisation. There appears to be no major shift in the percentage distribution of workers between different occupations in the State, as the Table 2.15 shows.

The provisional totals of 1981 census have not yet given the breakdowns of 'other workers'. The percentage of workforce engaged in agriculture has declined from 79.42 in 1971 to 76.27 in 1981 and this decline is mainly caused by decline in percentage of agricultural labourers in the State from 26.56%

to 24.17% in 1981. The percentage of workers in household industries has increased only marginally from 3.64% to 3.80%, despite emphasis on rural industrialisation in the five year plans. This improvement is mainly caused by Sagar & Demoh where bidimaking is the main cottage industry. The category "other workers" includes those who are engaged in all activities other than agriculture and household industries. The percentage of "other workers" has gone up from 16.94% to 19.93% and this increase mainly at the cost of agricultural labourers. The rural economy of the State continues to be characterised by lack of diversification.

TABLE 2.15

	Percentage of workforce			
	1971		1981	
	Total	Urban	Total	Urban
1. Cultivation	52.86	6.6	52.10	7.4
2. Agricultural labourers	26.57	5.7	24.17	6.3
3. H.H. Industry	3.64	7.1	3.80	7.1
4. Other Workers	16.94	80.6	19.93	79·2
Total	100	100	100	100

In the urban economy of the State, a peculiar phenomenon is discernible. The percentage of cultivators and agricultural labourers has increased from 6.7% in 1971 to 7.6% in 1981 and from 5.7% to 6.3% respectively. The percentage of working force in urban areas in household industries has remained constant at 7.1%. The percentage of "other workers" in urban working force has declined from 80.6% in 1971 to 79.2% in 1981. Although "other workers" predominate in the urban work force, the percentage has shown a decline in 1981 compared to 1971. This analysis shows that the percentage of urban working force in rural-based activities, has increased and that of urban based activities like manufacturing and tertiary activities has declined, but the changes, are of such marginal nature as not to warrant any significant change in the occupational structure of the State's urban economy. Many of the urban centres in the State are nothing but overgrown villages.

Out of 54 districts in the State, only in 15 districts, the percentage of workers in household industries (HH) has registered an increase in 1981 over 1971. In 12 out of these 15 districts, this increase has taken place at the cost of cultivators and agricultural labourers and in one district at the cost of cultivators. In all the 30 districts which have witnessed a decline in the percentage of workers in HH industry, the decline has been caused by increase in "other workers" and in 12 districts due to increase in percentage share of cultivators, agricultural labourers and other workers, in 5 due to increase in "other workers" and agricultural labourers and in two districts on account of increase in the share of cultivators. The highest percentage increase in the proportion of household workers has taken place in Damoh district (+9.78%), followed by Sagar (+8.98%), Gwalior (+2.58%) and Bhopal (+2.264%). The increase in other districts is nominal, being less than 1% in 10 years.

Not only the proportion of work force engaged in "other occupations" is low (19.93%), it is highly concentrated in few districts as the following table reveals :

TABLE 2.16

Districts	Percentage of urban population in 1981	Decennial growth rate (1971-1981) of urban population	Percentage of "other workers" to total workers in the district	
			1971	1981
1. Gwalior	55.20	38.45	47.75	49.01
2. Sagar	27.88	41.67	21.42	22.91
3. Ratlam	30.81	33.19	24.76	26.19
4. Ujjain	37.47	36.43	30.48	32.07
5. Indore	65.92	44.16	60.58	61.27
6. Khandwa	26.77	49.70	20.98	23.63
7. Bhopal	76.27	73.99	63.85	66.97
8. Hoshangabad	25.05	43.24	26.88	29.21
9. Jabalpur	45.15	45.25	34.66	39.40
10. Chhindwara	21.18	57.86	18.38	20.34
11. Durg	31.80	100.59	20.46	27.65
State average	20.31	56.07	16.94	19.93

The above 11 districts of the State have registered a higher proportion of urban to total population in 1981 as comapared to the state percentage (20.31%). These 11 districts account for higher percentage of "other workers" than the state average. Nearly 44% of total "other workers" in the State are concentrated in those 11 districts which have relatively higher level of urbanisation than the state as a whole. If we take "other workers" in the urban areas, then 73% of such workers in urban M.P. are concentrated in these 11 districts. If we take 14 Class I cities of the State, then we find that about 51% of total "other workers" in urban areas are to be found in these cities. The highest percentage of "other workers" to total workers is to be found in Bhopal district (66.97%), followed by Indore (61.27%), Gwalior (39.01%), Jabalpur (39.40%), and Ujjain (32.07). In fact, these are the highly urbanised districts of the state.

The above analysis brings us to the following broad conclusions :

(i) The economies of very small towns in the State are dominated by agriculture. Towns with population smaller than 20,000 have high proportion of employment in agriculture and related marketing and commercial activities, in small cottage and artisan manufacturing and lower order services that have relatively a low growth rate in total urban employment.

(ii) The economies of middle level towns tend to be dominated by commercial and service activities, accounting for more than 62% of total workers in Class II towns. The percentage of workers in this sector tends to decline with decline in population size of towns but even then the percentage of workers in this sector seems to be quite high in the range of 35% in Class VI towns and 62% in Class II towns.

(iii) Cities, in general, have a smaller proportion of household sector but in Madhya Pradesh, this percentage appears to be high in urban areas compared to the percentage in the whole State. Even in Class I cities, quite, a large proportion of workers were found in the

HH industries. The growth of Class I and II towns bear some relationship with the growth of organised manufacturing sector in the State but in small towns or other lower order urban settlements, there appears to be no relationship between the two.

(iv) The correlation between the levels of urbanisation and the share of secondary sector in the State Domestic product is highly significant being 0.723, between 1960-61 and 1980-81. Urbanisation, however, is related negatively with the share of primary sector in the SDP. It is more because of construction and electricity than manufacturing (registered) that the percentage of secondary sector in the SDP has increased. In 1980-81, the contribution of manufactured (registered) to the SDP was only 5.8%, the rest was contributed by manufacturing (unregistered), construction and electricity, age and water supply.

(v) Urbanisation in Madhya Pradesh is more due to expansion of tertiary sector and construction and electricity and less due to the process of industrialisation which is taking place at a slow pace.

(vi) There is strong correlation between the level of urbanisation and percentage of workers in activities other than agriculture household industries.

(vii) The composition of occupations varies distinctively between size of towns, indicating that they perform different functions in the regional economy. It is interesting to note that the percentage of workers in manufacturing rises with city size, while with employment in HH industry, it shows a negative correlation.

(viii) In India, the male participation rate in work force in bigger towns is higher than in small towns. But in M.P., Class VI towns have shown the highest male participation rate. This may be due to the fact that a number of very small towns belonging to this class are project towns and mining towns where male participation rates are comparatively higher.

Regional Dimensions of Urban Growth

Table 2.17 indicates the regional pattern of urbanisation in the State. Madhya Pradesh being the largest State of India in terms of area, manifests wide variations among different sub-regions. It is, therefore, necessary to disaggregate the trends in urbanisation at the sub-regional level to capture the spatial aspect of urbanisation in the State. It may be noted that variations in urbanisation between regions are large and of such a nature that are not readily explicable. The regional disaggregation is useful to focus on the regions of highest and the lowest urban growth. The National Sample Survey Organisation has identified economic sub-regions within the State on the basis of uniform agro-climatic factors. Table 3.7 shows that the eastern region has the lowest level of urbanisation (14.2%) as against 20.3% of the State in 1981. The share of this region in total urban population of the State has gone up from 18.8% in 1971 to 20.4% in 1981, whereas that of western region which is highly urbanised region of the State, has gone down from 30.5% to 28% in the same period. This indicates that relatively less developed regions of the state have shown faster rate of urbanisation than relatively developed regions. The eastern region accounted for nearly 33% of the total rural population of the State in 1971, but its share came down to 31.3% in 1981.

The eastern region which besides other areas includes Durg-Bhilai-Raipur, Korba, Balaghat, Baster—the mineral and forest belt of the State, recorded the highest annual rate of growth of urban population during 1971-81 (6.7%), accompanied by a very low rate of growth of rural population, 1.47% and of 1.64% of total population. The URGD is the highest (5.2) in this sub-region, followed by Inland Eastern region (4.1). In these two regions, huge investments have been made in coal, cement, forest-based and mineral-based industries. The Eastern and Inland Eastern regions had lower initial level of urbanisation and sparsely located towns with greater potential for the emergence of new towns and accretion of population to existing towns.

The Co-efficient of Variation of urban population among five regions of Madhya Pradesh has declined from 14.53% in 1971

TABLE 2.17

Regional Pattern of Urbanization in M.P.

Region	Decadal Population Growth						URGD		Level of Urbanization		Share of the Region, in States' urban population	
	Total		Rural		Urban							
	71	81	71	81	71	81	71	81	71	81	71	81
(1)	(2)	(3)	(4)	(5)	(6)	(7)	(8)	(9)	(10)	(11)	(12)	(13)
1. Eastern	26.64	16.41	23.90	14.74	57.70	67.34	33.80	52.60	10.11	14.10	18 8	20.4
2. Inland Eastern	29.17	26.07	25.88	19.96	52.52	61.03	26.64	41.07	14.98	19.14	16.2	17.6
3. Inland Western	32.58	27.48	28.36	19.92	52.58	57.72	24.52	37.80	19.88	29.19	20.5	19.8
4. Western	29.63	28.39	28.24	24.42	36.28	42.54	8.04	18.12	22.98	25.51	30.5	28.4
5. Northern	25.77	27.41	28.36	19.92	52.88	57.72	24.52	37.80	16.62	20.87	14.0	13.8
M.P.	28.67	25 17	25.68	19.16	46.63	56.07	20.95	36.91	16.29	20.31	100	100
C.V.	8.38	17.62	6.64	15.15	14.53	14.25			25.90	23.94		

Region	Share of Region in State's Rural population		No. of Towns		No. of Cities		Number of small and intermediate towns		New Towns Added in 81	Population Growth of of cities 71 81	Urban Population Growth rate		Mean Population of town	
	71	81	71	81	71	81	71	81			71 Un-corrected	81 Co-rrected	71	81
	(14)	(15)	(16)	(17)	(18)	(19)	(20)	(21)	(22)	(23)	(24)	(25)	(26)	(27)
1. Eastern	32.4	31.3	47	58	3	3	43	44	9	74.62	54.0	49.2	27,146	38,817
2. Island Eastern	18.1	18.1	29	59	1	3	24	44	23	42.40	48.0	37.5	37,977	35,471
3. Inland Western	16.0	16.1	49	52	2	2	45	52	12	63.02	46.6	40.6	28,325	36,484
4. Western	20.1	20.9	74	90	4	5	66	76	13	40.90	36.4	32.0	28,155	34,136
5. Northern	13.5	13.7	33	48	1	1	31	45	18	37.83	48.2	36.1	28,370	29,378
M.P.	100	100	232	303	11	14	209	261	75	62.23	46.0	3.90	29,244	34,946
C.V.	—	—	—	—	—	—	—	—	—	—	—	—	—	—

Note : Corrected & Un-corrected population growth rates taken from 'The Morphology of urbanization in India—some results from 1981 census—Rakesh Mohan, EPW Sept. 25, 1982.

to 14.25% in 1981 and of rural population has increased from 6.64% to 15.15% and also of total population from 8.38 to 17.62 in the same period. The CV in the level of urbanisation between different regions of the state has shown a decline from 25.90% to 23.94% between 1971 and 1981 indicating narrowing down of regional disparities in the level of urbanisation in the region of the State.

The western region which is relatively more urbanised, has the largest number of towns, followed by inland western region. This region has the largest number of cities, 5 out of 14 in 1981 and 4 out of 11 in 1971. The region has the largest number of small towns 76 out of a total of 261, followed by inland western region. The number of towns has been nearly doubled in the inland eastern region between 1971 and 1981. The smallest increase in the number of small towns has taken place in the eastern region. The cities of the eastern region have shown the highest rate of growth between 1971-81 (74.62%), followed by inland western region (63.02%). The cities in other three regions have recorded rates of growth which are lower than the rate of growth in the whole state (62.23%).

M.K. Jain and Rakesh Mohan (1981)[10] have argued in this context that the computation of the growth of the population in Class I towns on the basis of the population of the towns identified as cities in the respective censuses has raised a false alarm. They have suggested and rightly so, that in computing growth for different categories, the population at the two points of time must be for only those towns that belonged to that category in the base year. Accordingly, they have calculated the corrected and uncorrected growth rates of population.

Richardson[11] has emphatically pointed out that the effects of size-class jumping on the growth rates are not a mere theoretical possibility ; they are very important in practice. An examination of the growth performance of cities that remain within a size class implies a focus on the 'failures' from the population point of view.

The corrected urban population growth rates for different regions shows wide variations from uncorrected rates. Since the number of new towns added is the highest in inland eastern region followed by northern region, there is wide divergence between the uncorrected and corrected rates of growth, in these regions.

There are not much differences in mean population of towns in different regions of the State. The mean population of town is the highest in the eastern region (38.817), followed by the inland western region (36,484) as against the average of 34,946 for the whole state. The mean size of towns in the inland eastern region has declined in 1981 compared with 1971. The increase in the mean size of town has been the highest in respect of inland western region.

Given the demand for labour in urban area, rural-urban migration takes place readily both in prosperous agricultural region such as western and northern regions as well as agri-culturally poor regions such as eastern and inland eastern regions. A part of labour of eastern and inland eastern region migrates to Punjab and Haryana in search of employment. The systematic testing of this hypothesis would have to wait till the availability of data on migration. Rapid urbanisation has taken place in the eastern region because of public invest-ment in industrial projects based on mineral resources. This region is the mineral belt of the State and a number of indus-trial projects, though having poor linkages with the locai economy, have attracted more population to the industrlal centres.

The regional variations in levels of urban development and the differential growth rates, can to a large extent, be explained in terms of difference in regional pattern of economic growth in general and industrial development in particular. These relationships have been empircially tested in a subsequent chapter.

Let us look at the problems of spatial distribution of population from another angle ; the extent to which different regions are served by towns. Table 3.6 presents this data.

In the whole state, one town on an average is serving rural population of 1,37128 besides its own, and an area of 1463 sq. km. which appear to be quite unfavourable in relation to population as well as area. In 1971 town-Rural population ratio in the State was 1 : 154609 which has come down to 137, and 128 in 1981.

There are regional variations in these ratios. In the western region, the town-rural population ratio is the lowest 1 : 99096 and also the town-area ratio 1 : 956 sq. km., indicating more favourable situation in respect of number of towns in relation to rural population and area. These ratios are the highest in the eastern region, one town on an average for 2,20292 people and one town for an area of 2448 sq. km. The western region which is relatively more developed agriculturally, is better served by towns in relation to its population and area, compared to other regions of the State. The Eastern region which includes Bastar district also, the largest in area in the State, has the lowest density of population (105). The western region has the highest density of population (140) as against 118 in the state as a whole.

The other region which has density higher than the state average is the northern region. Next to western region, this region has favourable town-rural population ratio as well as town-area ratio. The northern and the western regions of the state are better served by towns compared to other regions. These two regions have higher density of population, have larger proportion of districts with town-population ratio below the state average and larger proportion of districts with above state average density of population.

The western and northern regions of the state present a different picture than the eastern and inland eastern regions. The first two regions are, by and large, wheat producing and also produce commercial crops like cotton, sugar cane, soyabeen, opium, whereas the eastern region is mono-cropped and is predominantly rice-producing. There is larger proportion of area under forests in the eastern and inland eastern regions and also higher proportion of tribal population. The eastern region is the mineral belt of the state and recently a number of industrial projects have come up but most of these projects have poor linkages with their respective regional economies. Because of recent industrial development in eastern and inland eastern regions, the average size of town is increasing, particularly of Class II towns.

In evaluating the urban processes, their impact on the rural base of the region which supports the urban infrastructure, must be taken into account. In the light of the above, the percentage of urban to total population would not adequately reflect the actuality and would tend to understate the degree of urban accretion in relatively urbanised regions. To remove this defect, we have worked out the percentage of urban to rural (U/R) as an index of urban accretion.

The U/R is the highest (36) in the western region, followed by inland western region and the lowest in eastern region (18%). In Madhya Pradesh, the western part has a well distributed urban settlement system centred around certain large towns, such as Bhopal, Indore, Ratlam, Khandwa, Burhanpur, Itarsi, etc. Northern M.P. with its well developed irrigation system is gradually presenting a picture of fast-developing small towns. Central and south-eastern M.P. also have a number of fast growing towns, based largely on metallurgical and other mineral-based industries. Large towns are growing faster than small ones, and towns in the eastern region where mineral exploitation is being stepped up, are growing much slower than the new ones, such as Shahdol, Sidhi, Korba, Durg-Bhilai, Hoshangabad, Itarsi, Dewas. In Madhya Pradesh, urban growth is following the generation of new economic activity and the location of major industries in backward regions. This is very different picture from that prevailing in north Bihar. The pressures exerted by a growing rural population with no avenues of employment in the rural areas are not major factors for giving an impetus to urban growth in Madhya Pradesh. It is the dynamism of situation where economic activity has resulted in the growth of towns. There are vast geographical variations within the State. One finds a phenomenon similar to Punjab, in Bhind and Morena districts, the Gujarat pattern in western M.P. and the western Orissa pattern in south-eastern M.P. Since the major portion of Narmada river flows through the state, the impact of this rivers' development is likely to be considerable and a time may come when south-western region will grow in continuum with Gujarat.

Distribution of Urban Population in Different Regions by Size-Class

The urban population is unevenly distributed among different size-class of towns in different regions of the state. Nearly 53% of total urban population of inland eastern region is concentrated in Class I towns and this percentage was little more than 50 in the case of western region of the state. These two regions are followed by eastern region, where 47% of urban population is residing in Class I towns. The northern region indicated lesser degree of concentration, where Class I towns accounted for 38% of total urban population in the region. Of the total population of Class I towns in the State, 30.6% is concentrated in western region, followed by eastern region (20.48%) and inland eastern region (19.8%). The lowest percentage recorded by the northern region is (11.2%). This region is agriculturally relatively more developed. It has only one town, viz. Gwalior, but large number of small and medium towns. This region has better distribution of its total urban population among different size class of towns compared to other regions.

If we take Class II towns along with Class I towns, we find that eastern region has more than 70% of its urban population in these classes of towns, whereas in western region, the two classes of towns together account for nearly 64% of its urban population. Eastern region has the highest percentage of its urban population living in Class II towns. The lowest percentage of total urban population of inland eastern region was living in Class II towns.

If we take the percentage shares of Class III, IV, V and VI towns (below 50,000) together, we find that nearly 41% of total population of northern region was residing in this category of towns, followed by inland western region (39.7%) and inland eastern and western regions (35.6%) and the lowest in eastern region (22.6%).

The northern, western and inland western regions of the state are relatively more developed agriculturally compared to eastern and inland eastern regions. These regions have larger proportion of their urban population in small towns. The eastern and inland eastern regions constitute the mineral and forest belt of the state and are comparatively more developed industrially. In these regions, small towns account for lesser percentage of total urban population. This analysis shows that agricultural development gives rise to the emergence of small size towns, whereas industrialisation tends to strengthen agglomeration tendency and gives rise to greater concentration of population at industrial centres.

If we take towns of less than 20,000 population, we find that in the northern region, 28% of its urban population was living in this class of towns and this percentage being the highest among all the regions of the state. Next comes inland eastern region where nearly 26% of urban population was living in these towns.

Of the total urban population of the state, 28% was living in the western region, followed by eastern region (20.4%), and inland western region (19.8%) and the lowest in northern region (13.8%). But level of urbanisation was the highest in inland western region (29.19%) as against 20.3% in the state as a whole, followed by western region (25.5%) and the lowest in the eastern region (19.14%) as revealed by 1981 census. The decadal growth rate of urban population recorded in 1981 was the highest in the eastern region, followed by inland eastern region. This shows that the two less urbanised regions of the state are having faster rate of urban population growth compared to other regions, thereby leading to convergence in inter-regional disparities in the levels of urbanisation in the state.

The regional variation in the levels of different size class of towns in the overall urban hierarchy and their differential growth rates can to a large extent, be explained in terms of difference in the regional pattern of economic growth and also historical factors.

Of the 93 towns which have manifested annual growth rate of above 4% in 1981 following is the regional location :—

TABLE 2.18

Location	No. of towns having above 4% annual growth rate	Total No. of towns	No. of New towns
1. Eastern	32	54	9
2. Inland Eastern	13	59	23
3. Inland Western	17	52	12
4. Western	14	90	13
5. Northern	19	48	18
Total	95	303	75

The Eastern region has the largest number of towns with more than 4% annual growth rate and the inland eastern region the largest number of new towns.

Conclusions

An analysis of urbanisation in M.P. shows that decennial growth rate of Class II and Class IV towns has gone up and that of Class I and other classes has gone down during 1971-81. Only 35 towns out of 303 in 1981 as against 40 out of 232 in 1971, have manifested growth rates higher than the state average. Of the total towns, 106 have shown increasing decadal growth rate, 98 declining and one constant growth rate. There are 76 new towns. We have seen that Class III and VI towns have witnessed negative growth rates and Class I towns have shown declining growth rate during 1971 – 81. Thus we find that most of the small and medium towns in the state are languishing and with the exception of a few Class I and II towns, even larger cities had a declining rate of growth, although the disparities between different classes and between different districts, have narrowed down. This has taken place without any conscious policy of the state in respect of urbanisation.

M.P. continues to be an under-developed state, with vast resource-potential which is being increasingly exploited for the benefit of the few. The pace of industrial and agricultural development has been slow in the 70's compared to 60's. The per capita Net State Domestic Product at constant prices has come down from Rs. 488 in 1970-71 to Rs. 457 in 1978-79, a decline of .086% per annum. The annual rate of growth of NSDP has been only 1.71%. In the 70's the annual average growth rate was 1.29% as compared to 8% in Punjab, 6.6% in Haryana. The productivity per hectare of important crops has gone down.

The state does not have diversified industrial structure[11] as revealed by the dominance of six industries, viz. electrical machinery, generation and distribution of electricity, iron and steel, cement, paper and paper board and textiles, which accounted for 73.9% of total fixed catital, 61% of total employment 65.13% of total output and 75.42% of total value added by manufactures in 1977-78. There are only 13 districts which account for 68% of all industrial units, 98% of fixed capital, 92.10% of value-added by manufacture, 93.75% of total output and 86.39% of total employment in the manufacturing sector of the state in 1977-78.[12] Moreover, in each of these districts, there is the dominance of one or the other industry. The fast-growing industries are 'export-based', in the nature of iron and steel, electrical machinery, cement and a number of luxury goods industries. The lagging industries, are mostly agro and forest-based. The multiplier of heavy and basic industries has not been very high and trickle down effects limited. Export-led growth is bound to lead to concentration of industries and population in a few centres. The industrial structure of the state is lop-sided and unbalanced, as revealed by the dominace of a few industries which constitute the industrial core of the state. There has been little development of consumer industries. The agro-based industries are lagging behind because of lack of adequate demand. Indiscriminate subsidies and assistance are being given by the government and the financial institutions to all sorts of industrial units in backward districts. Mostly industrial units are coming up in such backward districts which are within the proximity of large cities—Dewas near Indore, Mandideep near Bhopal, Bamore near Gwalior. Most of the small units are also concentrated in larger cities. Despite stress laid in our five year plans on the development of rural industries as an essential ingredient of rural development strategy and despite a number of promotional and protective measures, the picture of household industries that we have seen, is really depressing. The policies and programmes for rural industrialisation have included measures without serious efforts to improve technology and productivity of these industries and the institutional framework of the rural economy, with the result that necessary conditions for realising the advantages of protective measures have not been created. No radical measures have been introduced in the rural economy to widen the demand base of these industries. The so-called direct attacks on poverty involve just limited orders of financial transfers without corresponding curbs on accretion to the physical assets or consumption of the better off-sections. It is agricultural prosperity in a different institutional framework that can sustain rural industries, and not the present highly skewed asset and income distribution. In the present exploitative society, household workers like other workers continue to be exploited by a chain of intermediaries. The spatial aspect of industrialisation, that is, location of units in relation to human settlements depending upon local resources and local markets, has not received the attention of the planners. An integrated rural development programme has not only to be sectorally integrated but also spatially integrated, in an altogether different institutional framework which generates incomes and employment for the bottom 30% of population. Most of the towns are market towns and their growth depends upon their economic base. It is agricultural prosperity in a different socio-economic setting that generates surpluses and provides market for industrial goods. Agriculture continues to be traditional, largely depending upon monsoons. Irrigation facilities are hardly available to 12% of net cropped area. The cropping intensity is low. A large number of labour from Chhattisgarh and also from drought-affected areas migrates to other states in search of employment. Feudal or semi fedual conditions prevail in most of the areas of the state. Decline in the percentage share of agricultural workers in the total workers in the state may be partly due to out-migration to other states. The 60's had witnessed comparatively high rates of growth of agriculture and industry. This period had witnessed large immigration into M.P. in new industrial centres. The seventies witnessed sluggishness in growth rate.

The growth of small towns is linked with agricultural economy, the economic base. At the farm level, it means transition from subsistance agriculture to market-oriented agriculture, not only a few big cultivators but also of small and marginal farmers who can be made viable and surplus generating through appropriate technology and diversification of activities. Diversification of activities would create employment opportunities at larger number of centres which would serve as counter-magnets to bigger cities and also can absorb the rural unemployeds.

For an optimal spatial equilibrium, it is necessary that each category of town is supported by a certain number of higher as well as lower order towns. The economic base of the region can be developed and strengthened not mearly by techno-economic approach, of delivery of package of inputs but also through institutional changes of far-reaching importance. Dispersed and localized Industrial activities with number of linkages, yield better average income than large industrial projects unrelated to local economy.

Appendix

Details of Regions of Madhya Pradesh

REGION	Name of districts
1. Eastern Region	Surguja, Raigargh, Bilaspur, Raipur Durg, Balaghat, Baster=7
2. Inland Eastern region	Sidhi, Rewa, Satna, Shahdol, Panna, Jabalpur, Mandla and Seoni=8
3. Inland Western region	Damoh, Sagar, Vidisha, Sehore (which included Bhopal at that time) Raisen, Narsinghpur, Chhindwara, Hoshangabad, Betul=9
4. Western region	Mandsaur, Rajgarh, Shajapur Ujjain, Dhar, Jhabua, Ratlam,

	Indore, Dewas, Khargone, Khandwa=11
5. Northern region	Chhaturpur, Bhind, Tikamgarh, Gwalior, Morena, Shivpuri, Guna, Datia=8
	Total number of districts 43

Districts created after 1971 census are Bhopal (bifurcation of Sehore district and Rajnandgaon bifurcation of Durg district). The number of districts in the state has gone up to 45.

REFERENCES

1. Harry Richardson—"Policies for strengthening small cities in developing countries"—in Small cities and National Development—edited by Om Prakash Mathur—In Centre for Regional Development, Nagoya, Japan, 1982.
2. Andrade—"Decentralisation from large to small and intermediate cities"—in Small cities and National Development" edited by OM Prakash Mathur (1982).
3. Kingsley Davis and Hilda H. Golden—"Urbanisation and the Development of pre-industrial Areas"—Economic Development and cultural change, III No. I (October 1954).
4. Mcgee T.G. (1976) The South-East Asian city. G. Bell, London.
5. Kundu and Raza, M (1975) Urbanisation and Regional Development in India-Allied Publishers-New Delhi-p. 11.
6. There was a net inflow of (—) 1882 crore Rs. in the state in 1978-79. Total outflows amounted to Rs. 3245 crores and inflows Rs. 1363 crores. Madhya Pradesh accounted for 14.28 of total outflows and 6.0% of total inflows of the country. Inter-state flow of goods and Regional Development—R. Mehta Proceeding of a Seminar held at Nainital—April 1982.
7. The term was used rather loosely in princely states. Nearly 40% of the area of present M.P., consists of areas of former princely states.
8. M.K. Jain—Inter-State variations in the trends of urbanization in India, 1951-71 (Bombay-International Institute of population studies 1977).

— Mohan Rakesh-Existing urban Policies and Growth Trends of Urbanization-Urban India (No. I 1981).

— Amitabh Kundu-Theories of City Size Distribution and Indian Urban Structure : A Re-appraisal, Economic and Political Weekly, July 30, 1988.

9. Emerging Regional Patterns—M.N. Buch—Urban India-January 1984 No. 7 page 17-39.

10. Census of India—1981 M.P. page 27.
— Rakesh Mohan—Existing urban Policies and Growth trends of urbanisation 'Planning Commission' (1981) Urban India No. 1.
11. Harry W. Richardson. Policies for strengthening Small town in developing countries, Published in Small cities and National Development, edited by OM Prakesh Mathur—UN Centre for Regional Development, page, 327-328,
— The specialisation co-efficient of M.P. declined from 0.432 in 1960 to 0.39 in 1965 and 0.382, indicating high degree of specialization-Indian Industrialization Regional Structure & Planning Choice—Y.K. Alagh, Man and Development Vol. V No. 1 March 1983.
12. Minocha. A.C.—Changing Industrial Structure of Madhya Pradesh—Margin—NCAER-New Delhi-October, 1981, Vol. 14 No. 1

CHAPTER 3

THE PHYSICAL FRAMEWORK OF MALWA REGION AND ITS SOCIO-ECONOMIC FACETS

The growth of towns in a region cannot be studied in isolation from its economic base and the socio-economic changes taking place in the regional economy. Towns grow or stagnate because of certain factors operating in the hinterland factors operating in the hinterland for which weakening of the linkages of the towns with the surrounding areas.

The modernisation of a regional occupational structure measured frequently in terms of shift of resources from primary to secondary and tertiary sectors, may be reflected in occupational changes having bearing on growth of urbanisation. Similarly movement from subsistence farming into industrial agriculture, exemplifies occuptional modernisation within the primary sector, thereby leading to greater demand for modern inputs and greater linkages with the town economy. The development programmes initiated in the regional economy would further strengthen linkages between rural and urban areas. The rural-urban continuum makes a strong case for integrated development of rural and urban settlements.

This chapter deals with the delimitation of the boundary of the region under study, the socio-economic profile and the physical setting against the background of which the process of urbanisation has to be viewed. The location, the physical features, the demographic characteristics, the infrastructure, all are relevant to the changing structure of regional economy. It is against the background of the Malwa region, that in a subsequent chapter we will discuss the growth/stagnation of five selected towns of the region in relation to their respective hinterlands.

The Malwa region of Madhya Pradesh selected for the study of small and intermediate towns. The region Malwa lies in the north-western part of Madhya Pradesh. Malwa constitutes a separate sub-region with reference to its geography, history, culture, geology and to some extent its economy. The region is homogenous with regard to its physical features, geological formation, cultural traits and economic development. Although the Malwa region seems to be well defined and demarcated region with its distinct geology landscape, yet controversy remains unresolved particularly about its eastern boundaries, regarding the inclusion/exclusion of Raisen, Bhopal, Vidisha, Sagar and Guna districts. Some researchers have included them while others exclude some or all of these districts from the boundary of the Malwa region.

Delimitation of The Region

With a view to delineating the Malwa region, four criteria have been adopted in the present study, geology, language, historical factors, and physiography. The region has distinct geological formation, bounded by clear physiographic boundaries with similar cultural traits throughout. Although historically, the region has remained an important political unit, the extent of political boundaries has varied since Vedic period till independence and even after independence.

The Malwa region is well defined by its geograpical landscape. The region is bounded by Vindhya ranges in the south, and in the north of these ranges, the widespread plateau is known as the Malwa plateau whose height varies between 450 and 600 metres above the mean sea level. Vindhya ranges separate the region from the Narmada-Son river plains in the south with steep scarpment towards the rivers and gentle slope in the north. River Mahi water-divide from the western boundary of the region which covers some parts of

Rajasthan and Gujarat states also. Vindhya scarpland forms the north-eastern boundary along the Bundelkhand plateau which separates the Malwa plateau from Gangetic plains. The Bundelkhand plateau has separate geological features, with peneplain and eroded surface, distinct from Malwa plateau and Vindhya scarpment. Aravalli ranges make the northern boundary of the region. Thus the Malwa region is well bounded geographical region with plateau topography of small hillocks and table lands with deep eroded river channels. The region Malwa has the spread up to Narmada in the south, Bhander ranges and Sagar plateau in the east, covering parts of Sagar district and parts of Guna district in the north-east. In the west, it extends to parts of Rajasthan and Gujarat.

Spate[1] classified the Malwa as a separate sub-region of central Vindhyan country and delimits the region as :

"Malwa forms great triangle, based on Vindhyan hills and bounded on the northwest by the great boundary fault of the Aarvallis, on the east by the sharply-defined scarp overlooking Bundelkhand. Most of it is drained by the Chambal and its right bank tributaries but it includes in the south-east the upper courses of the Ken and Betwa in the south-west a very irregular and dissected Deccan Lava brow overlooking the wild Bagar."

Geographically bounded Malwa region almost covers 15 districts of north western Madhya Pradesh. The districts included are Mandsaur, Ratlam, Ujjain, Dewas, Indore, Jhabua, Rajgarh, Shajapur, Sehore, Bhopal, Raisen, Vidisha and parts of Sagar and Guna.

Geology of The Region

The area with Deccan Trap has deposits in north-west M.P. is known as Malwa plateau, which is homogeneous is terms of geological features. These deposits were of heavy basalt which came out of volcanic cracks at the end of Cretaceous period. The entire south and western parts of M.P. is covered by the Deccan trap deposits. Parts of mainly three divisions of Indore, Bhopal and Jabalpur have been covered by these rocks, the thickness of these rocks (lava) lessens towards north and west and even at the fringes of Malwa plateau, the Vindhyan rocks are seen at the surface.

All the flows of the trap are unifoım in layers having a thickness between 3 to 7.5 metres. There are also deposits of ash and scoriae which give the idea that volcanic activity also took place with explosions. The erruption of main mass of lava was, however, of quite non-explosive type, the fissure erruption. In the areas of Deccan Trap, 5 to 10 flows have been marked. The chemical formation of Basaltic lava is the same throughout the region with slight difference of colour and cluster.

In the east, Sagar-Damoh edge forms the boundary of Deccan trap but it cannot be considered as the last limit as reminiscences are seen up to Chhota Nagpur plateau. In the north and north-east mixed features of Deccan trap and Vindhyan rock are seen. Vindhya rocks are also exposed around Bhopal and Sagar also. The first cycle of erosion in Eaocene period started after the periods of Cretaceous deposition and the eroded surface of Deccan trap is known as the Malwa Plateau.

The geogloical features also provide the regional boundaries of Malwa similar to the physical features of the land except that the Deccan trap deposits are extended beyond the Narmada river valley also. The limits of Malwa with geological homogeneity in the area extends up to parts of Sagar district in the east and parts of Guna district in the north. State boundary of M.P. by and large, is the western boundary of the region. Some parts of Jhabua district have different geological formation but because of contiguity have been included in the region. Thus more or less the physiographic region overlaps the geological region of Malwa except that the Deccan trap extends beyond Narmada even in the State of M.P., in the south.

Cultural Traits

Language is one of the basic traits of culture and it may well be considered as one of the important variables in delineating the cultural regions. Not only the physical characteristics but also culturally the region Malwa is separate entity because of land-scape and historical reasons.

Malwi is dialect of Hindi and an identified language of the

Malwa region. The Malwi dialect also forms a well defined region separated from other parts of the state and from other surrounding states. This becomes more important variable in regionalisation as the cultural traits die hard and transformation process is very slow. Over time, the region emerges automatically with distinguished cultural traits.

Linguistically Upadhyay[2] defines the extent of Malwa on the basis of Malwi language which includes 12 districts of M.P. These are :

Shivpuri, Guna, Bhilsa, Rajgarh, Shajapur, Dewas, Indore, Ujjain, Mandsaur, Ratlam, Jhabua and Dhar. He further states that Bhopal state has been a non controversial part of Malwa whereas Hoshangabad being a part of Bhopal state also partly comes under the Malwa region. He also includes the areas of south of Vindhyan hills and north of Satpura—the Narmada valley – culturally as a part of Malwa region whereas some parts of Mandsaur district has been excluded from Malwi culture with an argument that it constitutes a part of Mewar. Besides this, some parts of Kota and Jhalawar district of Rajasthan come under the cultural boundaries of Malwa.

Cultural traits are, by and large, bounded by physical barriers. This is because physical barriers like rivers, mountains etc. increase the friction of space and produce basic constraints in cultural interaction of communities. This is to argue that the Malwi region also overlaps the geological and physiographic region of Malwa. Thus the eastern boundary is formed by Betwa river which separates Malwa from Bundelkhand. Along the Narmada river in south from Onkareshwar Mandhta to Udaipura of earlier Bhopal state, the river constitues the southern boundary of the region—River Chambal and Parwati separate the Rajasthan areas from Malwa in the north and in west river Mahi separates Malwi from Banswara district of Rajasthan. Jain and Tiwari[3] give the linguistic boundary of the region as Indore in the south-west, Bhopal and parts of Hoshangabad in south east, Guna in the north-east and Neemuch in the north-west. Furthermore, they also include some parts of Gwalior district of M.P. and parts of Kota, Jhalawar and Chittorgarh districts of Rajasthan. Pure Malwi language speaking region is confined to Indore, Dewas and Ujjain districts.

Boundaries of The Region

On the basis of three criteria discussed above, the region emerges clearly with clear well-defined physiographic, geological and linguistic boundaries. The super-imposition of the three maps reveal that the region constitutes 13 districts of north west Madhya Pradesh viz. Ratlam, Dewas,Shajapur, Rajgarh, Sehore, Bhopal, Raisen, Shajapur, Rajgarh, Mandsaur, Dhar, Jhabua and Indore. Sagar and Guna districts are not included in the Malwa region because of their being on the fringe considered from all the three criteria. Only small parts of these two districts come within the region under study. The malwi language even does not have much influence over there and partly the geology and physiography of districts is also not contiguous to the region. Geologically some parts of Jhabua district present different features than Deccan trap but they are ignored bacuase most of the district has the same geology which Malwa has and it is, therefore, included in the limits of the region.

Location of The Region

The region Malwa is located between 12° 55′ to 25° 2′ north latitude and 4° 5′ to 78° 48′ east with a general altitude of 500 metres above the mean sea level. The region is well connected by two main broad gauge lines joining Delhi-Madras which passes through Vidisha, Bhopal and Raisen districts and Delhi-Bombay via Ratlam and Mandsaur districts. Two national highways Nos. 3 and 12 also pass through the region. The region is well connected with rail and road transport with the rest of the country. Internally the region has higher connectivity level with different areas and major towns of the region, Bhopal-Ratlam-Indore broad gauge railway line connects eastern parts with western parts of the region.

Topography

Malwa region is a plateau known after its name and constitutes a part of Deccan trap. Topographically, the whole region is covered by table lands and small hillocks. The north of Narmada basin Vindhya ranges form a cliff and from here towards north there is a gentle slope. On an average, the height of Vindhyan ranges and Malwa plateau is 500 meters from the mean sea level. Amidst the plateau topography there are erected hills with even 600 metres height, south of Mhow being the highest point with 850 metres. The height of Vindhyan ranges lowers down towards Hoshangabad. Just in the north of this lies the Vidisha plateau and in the east there is Sagar plateau.

Drainage

Malwa plateau is drained mainly by river Chambal and its tributaries at the right bank. Kali Sindh, Parvati Sindh, Betwa, Kshipra and Dhaan are the main rivers which flow from the region from south to north. Among these, the Chambal river is the biggest river. All the rivers originate from Vindhyan Kaimur and Bhander ranges and join Chambal and fianlly Yamuna. All the rivers flow in deep eroded villages which are still busy in cutting base of rivers. Base erosion confirms the rejuvenation of the region. Present drainage system emerged after the deposition of Cretaceous period of Deccan trap and rift valley of Narmada. With the origin of Himalayas, the erosion rate has increased in the region. The rivers at places have waterfalls but, by and large, they flow in deep eroded channels. Southern parts of the region are drained by small tributaries of Narmada which joins at the north bank of the river. These tributaries are small as after covering very small distance they join Narmada. These small tributaries flow in the southern parts of Dhar, Indore. Dewas and Sehore districts.

Soils

The entire region is almost homogeneous in soil quality. The region is covered by black soil with the lowest variability. The black soil region is formed by Deccan trap of Basaltic igneous rocks and with the weathering effect, the rocks are converted into black soil. The pH value of this soil varies between 7.5 to 8.5. The black soil uniformly covers the entire region with slight variability in the thickness. The 13 districts of Mandsaur, Ratlam, Jhabua, Dhar, Indore, Dewas, Sehore, Bhopal, Ujjain, Shajapur, Rajgarh, Vidisha and Raisen are covered fully by uniform soil quality.

Climate

The latitudinal location of the region being on tropic of cancer, has fairly high temperature throughout the year and altitudinal variations, the region has high variability in rainfall. In general the climate is moderate and on the whole healthy. Satpura and Vindhyan ranges have marked influence over the climate. The region experiences three seasons, cold season from October to February, hot season from March to June, and rainy season from July to September. The temperature starts rising from February and continues till May which is also the hottest month in the region. Occasionally temperature touches 45°c marks in summer. During May temperature varies spatially between 35° c and 42° c with a diurnal range of 15°c. With the outburst of monsoon in June, temperature falls to about 8°c on an average, monthly till September. Following the withdrawal of monsoon, the region experiences improvement in temperature. During rainy season temperature varies between 33.15° c in June 25.9° c in August. Temperature begins to fall again from October and continues till December which marks the coldest month in the region. Occasionally with cold waves experienced in January, the region has a range of 16°c of temperature.

Land-Use Pattern

The Table 3.1 presents land-use pattern in different districts of Malwa region in 1979-80.

Land use pattern of a region is determined by its geoclimatic, socio-economic and institutional factors. In the Malwa region, more than 50% of the total geographical area is put to cultivation. Only Raisen district has 47.6% of total geographical area as sown area. In Dewas district also the percentage is comparatively low (49.8%). The highest percentage of net sown area was to be found in Ujjain (68.8%), followed by Indore (67.2%). In the state as whole, net sown area constituted 41.6% of total geographical area. In all the districts comprising the Malwa region, the percentage of net sown area is higher than the state average. The region having better geo-climatic conditions has higher percentage of net sown area than the state average. Area sown more than once is less in the eastern

TABLE 3.1

Land-use Pattern (1979-80)
(000 hectares)

District	Geographical area	Forests	Land not available for culti-vation	Other unculti-vated land except fallow	Culturable waste land	Fallow land	Net sown area
1	2	3	4	5	6	7	8
Indore	381.1	52.2 (13.5)	28.6 (7.5)	33.1 (8.7)	8.3 (2.2)	3.4 (0.9)	257.5 (67.2)
Dhar	819.6	75.2 (9.2)	152.9 (18.7)	59.4 (7.2)	25.0 (3.1)	15.5 (1.9)	491.6 (60.0)
Jhabua	679.2	113.8 (16.9)	141.9 (20.9)	51.0 (7.5)	11.0 (1.6)	26.9 (4.01)	334.6 (49.3)
Ujjain	611.6	7.7 (1.3)	42.3 (6.9)	77.1 (12.6)	18.5 (3.0)	9.7 (1.6)	456.3 (74.6)
Mandsaur	946.4	10.7 (11.3)	198.7 (21.0)	56.3 (5.9)	54.6 (5.8)	7.8 (0.8)	522.0 (55.6)
Ratlam	486.5	35.0 (7.2)	57.2 (11.8)	41.4 (8.5)	43.0 (8.8)	8.7 (1.8)	301.2 (61.9)

1	2	3	4	5	6	7	8
Dewas	700.3	20.4 (29.1)	45.3 (6.5)	90.0 (12.8)	6.1 (0.9)	6.1 (0.9)	348.6 (49.8)
Shajapur	617.8	2.9 (0.5)	95.0 (15.4)	66.3 (10.7)	32.4 (5.2)	7.8 (1.3)	413.4 (66.9)
Bhopal	270.8	39.0 (14.3)	27.0 (10.0)	35.8 (13.6)	15.1 (5.6)	1.8 (0.71)	152.1 (56.2)
Sehore	647.0	156.8 (25.6)	37.2 (5.7)	36.1 (5.6)	53.4 (8.3)	4.9 (0.8)	349.6 (54.0)
Raisen	848.6	336.2 (39.6)	39.1 (4.6)	34.6 (4.1)	27.1 (3.2)	7.5 (0.9)	404.2 (47.6)
Vidisha	730.2	105.2 (14.4)	47.2 (6.5)	41.9 (5.7)	24.1 (3.3)	9.5 (1.3)	502.3 (68.8)
Rajgarh	611.6	13.0 (2.1)	66.8 (10.9)	94.8 (15.5)	30.5 (5.0)	11.6 (1.9)	394.9 (64.6)
M.P.	44201	14128 (36.2)	4517 (10.2)	3014 (6.8)	1914.4 (4.3)	2227 (5.1)	18399 (41.5)

(Figures in brackets indicate the percentages of total geographical area in each district)

(Source : Agricultural statistics 1980—Directorate of Agriculture—M.P.)

four districts as compared to the rest of the Malwa region. These four districts covering Raisen, Sehore, Bhopal and Vidisha, have the least irrigation facilities in the region. The area under forests is the highest in Raisen district, (39.6%) followed by Dewas (29.1%) and Sehore (25.6%) and the lowest Shajapur district (0.5%) followed by Ujjain (1.3%). Only Raisen district has higher percentage area under forests than the state average (36.2%). Land not available for cultivation as percentage of total geographical area in the district was the highest (21.0%) in Mandasur district, followed by Jhabua (20.9%), Shajapur (15.4%) Ratlam (10.8%) and the lowest in Raisen (4.6%) followed by Sehore (5.6) and Vidisha (6.5%). The three categories of land use, land not available for cultivation, other uncultivated land excluding fallow land and cultivable waste land, taken together constitute the highest percentage of total geographical area in Shajapur (31%), followed by Rajgarh (30%) and Dhar, Jhabua and Bhopal (19% each) and the lowest in Raisen (12%) followed by Vidisha (15%). Cultivable waste land which can be brought under the plough varies between 0.9% in Dewas to 8.8% in Ratlam.

Intensity of Crops and Cropping Pattern

Cropping intensity in Madhya Pradesh as such is very low due to meagre irrigation facilities. Cropping intensity is the highest in Mandsaur district, being 147%, followed by Ratlam (128%) Ujjain (117%) and the lowest in Raisen (102%) followed by Bhopal (104%). In six out of 13 districts of the region, cropping intensity is less than the state average (113%). The entire Bhopal division and also Dewas district have cropping intensity lower than the state average. This is mostly due to scanty irrigation in these areas.

Area under food grains occupies the major portion of total cropped area in the region. The area under foodgrains covers more than 60% in the region but is as high as 89% in Vidisha, closely followed by Raisen (83.86%), Bhopal (82.52%), and Jhabua (81.48%). The lowest percentage area under foodgrains was found to be in Dewas (61.68%), followed by Dhar (66.93%) and Shajapur (68.3%). This may be linked with the quality of land and irrigation facilities. Eastern part of the region has more area under foodgrains than cash crops.

Wheat, Jowar and Maize are the three major cereals and Gram, Tur and Urad are the main pulses which cover most of the area under foodgrains. Wheat occupies the largest percentage area in Vidisha (56.2%), Bhopal (45.7%), Raisen (36.3%) and Sehore (33.1%). Whereas maize is predominant crop in Rajgarh, Ujjain, Shajapur and Dewas. Area under wheat is the lowest in Jhabua district, predominantly tribal district. Area under gram in the region is higher than the state average. Mandsaur, Ratlam, Raisen and Vidisha have more than 20% area under gram. Urad is more popular, accounting for fairly high percentage of area in the western districts of the region, while tur is grown throughout the region. Area under oilseeds varied from 3 to 15%. South western parts of the region covering Dhar, Indore, Dewas, have nearly 14 to 15% of gross sown area under oilseeds. Among the oil seeds, groundnut covers substantial area. Other crops like sugarcane, cotton, chilies, spices and condiments are grown in the region but the area under these crops is very small.

One interesting feature which emerges from comparison of 1971 and 1981 data is that there has been a substantial shift of area from foodgrains to cash crops or from inferior to superior grains. There has been significant increase in area under wheat followed by decline in area under maize and jowar. There is also increase in area under gram and oil seeds. This shift of area under superior crops or cash crops from millets shows increasing commercialisation of agriculture in the region.

Irrigation

Irrigation facilities throughout the region are scanty. The Table 3.2 presents the percentage of gross irrigated area to gross cropped area.

In 1960-61 only one out of 13 districts in the region, had percentage of gross irrigated to gross cropped area higher than the stage average (5.2%), in 1970-71, the number of such districts increased to 2 (Mandsaur and Indore), the state average being 7.4% and the number remained the same both in 1974-75 and 1979-80. In the region, Mandsaur district has the highest percentage of gross irrigated area (13.53%) followed by

Indore district (9.72%) in 1974-75. In 1979-80, the highest percentage of gross irrigated area to cropped area was found in Indore district (14.1%), followed by Mandsaur (11.26%). The eastern part of the Malwa region covering the districts of Bhopal, Raisen, Rajgarh, Vidisha and Sehore, have lower percentage of area irrigated.

TABLE 3.2

District	1960-61	1970-74	1974-75	1979-80
Bhopal	—	—	5.9	8.3
Raisen	0.7	1.63	2.31	2.1
Rajgarh	4.5	4.37	5.81	4.7
Sehore	3.3	4.50	4.49	6.6
Vidisha	0.2	0.55	0.82	1.6
Indore	3.1	8.17	9.72	14.1
Dhar	3.5	5.49	5.53	10.4
Jhabua	2.3	2.50	2.40	5.3
Dewas	1.7	3.38	4.57	9.6
Mandsaur	9.3	11.29	13.53	11.2
Ratlam	5.2	7.05	8.82	7.6
Shajapur	3.7	5.84	6.86	7.5
Ujjain	1.0	3.55	4.95	8.4
M.P.	5.2	7.11	8.30	10.7
India	18.31	23.32	23.20	—

Irrigation, is by and large, confined to wheat, gram, and sugarcane only. Whereas wheat has the highest percentage irrigated area, almost 50% area of gross irrigated area which even increased to 83.82% in Raisen district. Western districts of the region have switched over to cash crops to a large extent. In these districts, area irrigated under gram, sugarcane, and even cotton is higher than eastern districts of the region.

Well irrigation is the largest single source of irrigation in the region. More than 70% area is irrigated by this source. Only two districts, Raisen and Vidisha, which have very poor irrigation facilities, have lower share irrigated by wells. In these districts, more then 50% of the total irrigated area is irrigated by canals and other sources.

The percentage share of this region in the total foodgrain production of the state has gone down from 37% in 1977-78 to 32% in 1979-80. The region contributes nearly 1/3rd of the total foodgrain production in the state, though its share is declining.

Area Under High Yielding Variety Seeds and Consumption of Fertilizers

The percentage of net sown area under high yielding variety seeds varied between 20% in Vidisha to 32% in Mandsaur districts in 1979-80. The area under HYV has not shown any marked increase between 1977-78 and 1979-80. In the state as whole, the percentage area under HYV has come down during this period. The Malwa region as a whole, accounted for 21% of total area under HYV in 1977-78 in the state, whereas in 1979-80, this percentage has gone up to 29. This increase in percentage is not due so much to increase in area under HYV in this region, as to decline in area under HYV in the state as a whole.

Area under HYV seeds was mostly accounted for by two crops, namely, wheat and Jowar. In most of the districts, it was under jowar but in the districts of Bhopal, Sehore and Raisen, it was mostly under wheat. Lower percentage area under HYV is due to scanty irrigating facilities in the region.

The Table 3.3 persents use of fertilizers per unit of cropped area (kg./hect.)

Fertilizer consumption per hectare in the state as a whole is very low, only 7.67 kg. per hectare in 1979-80. Fertilizer consumption, by and large, depends upon the use of HYV and availability of irrigation facilities. In 6 out of 13 districts, per hectare consumption of fertilizer is below the state average of 7.67. The consumption of fertilizer was found to be the highest in Indore district, more than 3 times the state average, followed by Ratlam, Ujjain, Dhar and Dewas districts and the lowest consumption was recorded in Rajgarh district. The consumption was comparatively lower in Bhopal division, because of lesser percentage of area under irrigation. Ratlam district accounted for the highest area under HYV and also the second highest consumption of fertilizer. Districts with lower area under HYV recorded lower per hectare consumption of fertilizer. The western part of the Malwa region has higher consumption of fertilizer than the eastern. This is because fertilizer consumption is always linked with irrigation and area under HYV seeds.

TABLE 3.3

District	1977-78	1978-79	1979-80
Indore	20.50	23.45	24.82
Dhar	11.05	13.37	15.26
Jhabua	2.77	3.07	3.48
Ujjain	10.72	16.72	13.61
Mandsaur	12.00	20.81	13.61
Ratlam	15.25	21.85	17.45
Dewas	9.22	12.52	15.35
Shajapur	5.05	5.66	5.23
Bhopal	9.47	12.32	8.85
Raisen	6.60	8.06	3.18
Sehore	5.69	5.54	4.92
Vidisha	3.0	3.79	4.04
Rajgarh	2.35	2.78	2.08
M.P.	7.39	8.36	7.67

Farm Implements and Machinery

The farm implements in the region, by and large, are traditional and agricultural operations are mainly carried on by wooden ploughs and bullock-carts, driven by animal power. The use of modern farm implements and machinery is very low. Not even one tractor is available for 1000 hectares of land except in Vidisha, Raisen, Bhopal and Mandsaur districts.

The availability of oil and electric pumps is much higher io western districts of Dhar, Dewas, Ujjain, Mandsaur and Ratlam where irrigation facilities are comparatively better. The eastern districts have lesser number of pumps per hectare of land. Sugarcane growing districts have more crushers for production of gur and Khandsari sugar.

Yield per Hectare

The variability in the yield of different crops is very high among the districts as well as between crops. In the state as a whole, yield per hectare has been declining over time. In respect of rice, not a single district had yield per hectare higher than the state average. This is due to the fact that the region is not rice producing area of the State. Only in 4 districts of the region, yield per hectare registered an increase in 1978-79 over 1970-71.

Wheat, jowar and gram are the major crops of the region, which are grown in wheat-gram combination in the eastern districts and wheat-jowar with cotton combination are grown in western districts. Wheat has greater percentage share of total population of the districts in the eastern part of the region than the western part. Vidisha and Ujjain are the main wheat producers, accounting for 61.63 and 51.21% of the total production of the districts. Rajgarh has the minimum share in wheat which has greater share of jowar 54% of total production. The share of gram in total production is high in the eastern districts. More than 70% of the production is accounted for by food grains. Other crops in the region are sugarcane, cotton, groundnuts, pulses like tur, urad. Production of linseed, rapeseed, mustard, soyabean is very less. The region has also the production of spices and condiments along with narcotics and drugs but none of these commodities accounts for more than half per cent of total production. Areas adjacent to Rajasthan also grow maize and bajra.

The average yield per hectare of jowar is higher than the state average in Dewas, Shajapur, Rajgargh and Ujjain districts of maize in Shajapur, Mandsaur, Vidisha, of wheat in Jhabua, Mandsaur, Ujjain, Ratlam, Shajapur, Indore and Ragihar districts.

The money value of agricultural production has increased appreciably in all the districts, mainly due to rise in prices. But the money value is considerably reduced when presented in terms of per capita. The gains of money value of prodnction per hectare are considerably reduced when money value of production per capita is taken into account. This may be due to increase in population which might have swallowed the gains in money value due to increase in production. The money value of agricultural product per hectare was the highest in Shajapur district in 1974-75, followed by Bhopal, but per capita value of products was the highest in Dhar district followed by Ratlam and Ujjain districts.

TABLE 3.4

District	Money value of agri-products per hectare (Rs.)			Money value of agri-products per capita (rural population)		
	1960-61	70-71	74-75	1960-61	1970-71	1974-75
Bhopal	—	—	1507	—	—	—
Raisen	319	643	1495	254	478	1011
Rajgarh	272	613	1398	179	438	934
Sehore	405	495	1218	332	390	979
Vidisha	385	607	1575	356	535	1254
Dhar	350	641	984	277	451	621
Indore	365	928	1412	272	668	1042
Jhabua	251	435	693	156	256	495
Dewas	344	702	1497	261	499	972
Mandsaur	319	731	1497	236	564	1126
Ratlam	336	701	1414	242	519	986
Shajapur	329	776	1631	231	287	1089
Ujjain	325	786	1341	286	680	1032
M.P.	341	685	1294	224	433	698

The region contributed nearly 25% to the gross agricultural product in the state in 1970-71 as well as in 1980-81. At current prices, gross agricultural output in the region has more than doubled between 1970-71 and 1980-81 but at constant prices (1970-71), there has been a very small increase, about 10%, or less than 1% per annum on an average. There appears to be no major break-through in agriculture in the region as revealed by gross value of agricultural produce.

Size of Holdings

There seems to be greater degree of concentration of land holdings in the region under study compared to the state, as evidenced by the fact that 34% of holdings are small and marginal in 1976-77 and 35% in 1980-81, accounting for 6.2% and 7% respectively of the area in the two periods. On the other hand, large holdings accounted for 13% of total number of holdings but 44.4% of the total area in the region in 1976-77 and 12% of number and 42.5% of the area in 1980-81. In the state as a whole, large holdings accounted for 7.5% of number and 34% of the area. Semi-medium and medium between 2 and 10 hectares, accounted for 52.6% of total number of holdings in 76-77 and 50.3% in 1980-81 but 49% of the area in 1976-77 and 50.3% in 1980-81. Thus the majority of holdings are semi-medium and medium, accounting for little more than half of the number as well as area of holdings in the region. There seems to be no marked decline in the area and number of large holdings in the region. The Malwa region belonged to former princely states characterised by feudal relations of production. The remnants of feudal society still continue. Because of loopholes and ineffective implementation of land reforms, there has been no material change in size and pattern of land holdings in the region. Even the data in respect of land distribution is questionable as correct land records are not being maintained. A number of farms which in fact, are large farms have been shown to be split up into small farms in different names to evade the ceiling legislation though the ownership continues to be vested in the hands of large farmers.

In Dewas district, in 1980-81, large holdings accounted for 17.4% of number and 53% of total area, whereas small and marginal holdings accounted for 30.6% of number but only 4.6% of the total area. In Ujjain district also, a little more than 50% of area is held by 17% of total of holdings belonging to the category of large holdings. Small and marginal holdings accounted for 30.4% of number and only 4.8% of area. In Vidisha district, the distribution is equally skewed where large holdings accounted for 19% of number but 57.2% of area. On the other hand, small and marginal holding taken together accounted for 28% of number but only 3.8% of total area of these holdings. Other districts where more than 50% of total area was held by large holdings are Ujjain, Bhopal, Sehore Indore and Raisen districts. The lowest concentration seems to b: in Mandsaur district, where large holding accounted for only 5.4% of number and 22.8% of area, followed by Jhabua district, with 6.3% of number and 23.7% of area.

The Co-efficient of variation in area held by large holdings in different district increased from 23.9% in 1976-77 to 25.12% in 1980-81 but CV of number of holdings remained more or less the same. There has been a marked decline in CV in respect of small holdings both in number and area. On the whole, there appears to be no marked change in the pattern of land holding in the region which continues to have a large proportion of large holdings compared to the state as a whole, with not very wide variations among distritcts. Semi-feudal or feudal relations continue to prevail in the region which before independence was dominated by princely rulers.

The average size of agricultural holdings is comparatively larger in the region compared to the state as a whole, because of the presence of higher percentage of large holdings. In every district, the average size of holding is higher than that of the state. There seems to be no marked decline in the size of holdings between 1976-77 and 1980-81. The highest average size of holding was in Vidisha district, 6.7 hectare followed by Sehore, (6.2) and the lowest in Jhabua and Ratlam districts (3.8 hect. each).

The Malwa region accounted for 17.5% of total holdings in the state in 1980-81 and 25.2% of the area held by these holdings. Whereas the region as a whole accounted for 18.6% of total land holdings in the state in 1976-77, the percentage declined to 17.5% in 1980-81, but the area held by these holdings inereased from 24.9% to 25.2% in the same period.

Table 3.5 shows average size of holdings and the percentage of number and area of the whole state.

TABLE 3.5

District	Average size of holdings (in hect.)		Percentage of the state Number		Area	
	1976-77	80-81	1976-77	80-81	1976-77	80-81
1. Indore	6.1	5.5	0.8	0.8	1.3	1.3
2. Dhar	5.5	5.0	1.6	1.7	2.4	2.4
3. Jhabua	4.0	3.8	2.5	1.5	1.7	1.7
4. Ujjain	5.9	6.0	1.5	1.4	2.4	2.4
5. Mandsaur	3.7	5.0	2.5	2.4	2.5	2.5
6. Ratlam	4.0	3.8	1.4	1.4	1.6	1.6
7. Dewas	6.3	6.0	1.1	1.1	1.9	1.9
8. Shajapur	4.8	4.8	1.6	1.6	2.2	2.2
9. Bhopal	6.4	5.7	0.5	0.5	0.8	0.8
10. Sehore	6.6	6.2	1.0	1.0	1.8	1.8
11. Raisen	6.3	5.8	1.1	1.2	2.0	2.0
12. Vidisha	7.0	6.7	1.3	1.3	2.5	2.5
13. Rajgarh	4.5	4.4	1.7	1.6	2.1	2.1
M.P.	3.5	3.3				
Total			18.6	17.5	24.9	25.2

Industrial Development

The existing structure of towns of this region is the result of constant growth over a long period. The growth of industrialisation has accelerated the pace of urbanisation in the region.

Though the region has a larger share in industrial development, most of the industries are concentrated at few places. It is because of four or five industrial centres in the region that the percentage share of the region in industrial development of the state is comparatively higher than other regions. Indore is regarded as the industrial capital of M.P. and has a large number of industrial units belonging to different lines of manufacturing, though textile and engineering are the two important industries. Bhopal, the capital seat of M.P. has Heavy Electricals and a few other industries, but the city does not have a diversified industrial structure. Ujjain has textile and chemical industry, Ratlam, Dewas, Nagada are other industrial centres in the region. In the State as a whole, there is the dominance of five or six industries, such as electrical equipment, generation and distribution of power, textiles, cement, paper and iron and steel.

M.P. has rich deposits of a number of mineral resources, most of which are located in the eastern and inland eastern region of the State. There are at present industries for production of aluminium (from bauxite), aluminium sulphate, superphosphate and sulphuric acid (from limestone), copper (from copper ore), steel (from iron ore), refractories (from fire clay) etc. There are a few other industries consuming minerals, such as caustic soda and ceramics. Further, there are coal washeries in the state. Of the existing mineral-based industries in M.P., only one cement unit, is located at Nayagaon in Mandsaur district of Malwa region. Since the region under study does not have any mineral resources worth the name, mineral based industries which are tied to raw materials due to very high material index, are mostly located in eastern and inland eastern sub-regions of the state. In the last few years, these two regions of the state have witnessed a high rate of industrial growth and consequent high rate of urban growth. Though the level of urbanisation is the highest in Malwa region, the rate of growth of urban population has been the highest in eastern region, where a number of mineral-based industries and thermal plants have come up in the last 10 or 15 years.

The socio-economic milieu in Malwa region is essentially rural, much as it had been before the advent of industrial ethos. The Malwa region has mostly the traditional industries in the nature of agro-based industries like textiles and sugar, though a number of engineering and chemical and other industries on modern lines, came to be set up in the region during the planning period.

Table 3.6 shows the number of workers per lakh of population in different districts of Malwa region.

In six districts, the number of workers per lakh of population is much below the average of the state. The average of the state is just half of the average for the whole country. These six districts which have very low number of workers in industrial units are Raisen, Rajgarh, Vidisha, Jhabua, Mand-

TABLE 3.6

Number of workers per 1 lakh of Population in Registered factories in Malwa region

District	1961	1966	1971	1972	1973	1974	1975
1. Raisen	Negli-gible	Neg.	Neg.	Neg.	Neg.	Neg.	Neg.
2. Rajgarh	212.81	172.68	177.71	174.87	171.87	172.06	175.41
3. Sehore	1020.27	1695.66	1965.99	1923.46	1864.08	1590.27	1573.75
4. Vidisha	40.88	52.98	72.14	70.03	68.74	70.98	70.40
5. Dhar	217.46	271.30	303.30	295.92	297.48	281.43	325.91
6. Indore	3343.95	3317.91	3446.35	3430.25	3340.70	2991.54	3073.56
7. Jhabua	116.64	102.32	113.66	115.44	112.61	60.53	59.93
8. Dewas	514.66	580.72	604.07	593,06	587.59	649.54	753.20
9. Mandsaur	531.84	386.56	386.53	282.29	275.54	250.82	265.47
10. Ratlam	972.08	1055.12	792.02	778.75	764.15	677.72	758.28
11. Shajapur	437.18	216.92	270.19	267.72	263.02	259.11	265.90
12. Ujjain	2508.69	2038.11	2634.55	2678.98	2615.02	1852.99	1817.00
M.P.	465.21	480.57	508.52	509.28	502.48	455.66	454.75
India	887.94	953.45	992.45	950.63	954.15	968.38	956.04

(Sehore district included Bhopal also)

saur and Shajapur. In these six districts, the number of workers per lakh of population has declined in 1975 over 1960. The largest number of workers per lakh of population was recorded by Indore district, followed by Sehore which at that time included Bhopal also and Ujjain and the lowest number of workers was to be found in Raisen, followed by Jhabua and Vidisha. Most of the districts of the region are industrially less developed. In the state as a whole the number of workers to one lakh population has declined from 465.21 in 1960 to 452.75 in 1975, whereas in the country as a whole, the number has gone up from 887.94 to 956.04 in the same period. Considered from this angle industrial development in the Malwa region continues to be concentrated at few urban centres in a few districts. The concentration of economic activities leads to concentration of population at few urban centres. The rate of growth of Class I cities with the exception of Bhopal has started decelerating since 1971. This may be due to the fact that further concentration of industries at these centres has slowed down. The decadal rate of growth of population of Indore, Ratlam, and Ujjain has decelerated as shown by 1981 census. The process of industrial growth at these centres has slowed down.

Looking to the ASI data, we find that five districts of the region, viz. Indore, Bhopal, Ujjain, Dewas and Ratlam, accounted for nearly 14% of fixed capital, 38.5% of workers, 32.4% of output and 30% of value added by manufacture, in 1977-78, in the entire ASI factory sector of the state. These percentages have shown a decline compared to 1970, indicative of the growth of other industrial centres in the state. The state does not have a diversified industrial structure, as revealed by the fact that six dominant industries accounted for 81.29% of total value added by manufacture in the state and there seems to be no marked change in this percentage over time. Of the five districts which account for a large proportion of fixed capital, employment, output and value-added, Bhopal accounts for 5.28% of total fixed capital in the state, mostly bacause of the location of Heavy Electrical plant, followed by Ujjain district due to location of textiles and chemicals and Dewas due to engineering industry. Indore district accounted for 16.5% of the total employment in the industrial sector of the state, mostly due to textiles and engineering units. Bhopal contributed the highest percentage of value added to the state total, 13.12% in 1974-75, followed by Ujjain, 6.23% but the gap between the two is very large. Other districts of the region account for less than 1% each to the value added in the manufacturing sector in the state. Of all the districts of Malwa region, Indore district has more diversified industrial structure and larger employment in the industrial sector. Most of the industries that have come up in the region have poor linkages with the regional economy, the exceptions being agro-based industries.

Of the 18 no-industry districts in M.P. in 1982, three, namely, Dhar, Jhabua (tribal districts), and Rajgarh, belong to Malwa region. Of the 36 industrially backward districts in the state, the following 9 belong to the Malwa region :

Dewas, Dhar, Jhabua, Mandsaur, Rajgarh, Raisen, Ratlam, Sehore, Vidisha.

Of the 57 industrial licences issued between 1978 and 1982, 30 have been for the Malwa region, the largest number (9) for Bhopal district, 9 for Dewas, 3 for Indore. This shows little dispersal of units. For future industrial units, most of the letters of intent have been issued for metallurgieal industries, chemical, paper products, cement and electrical equipment, most of which are likely to be located in the eastern region which is the mineral belt of the State. But Malwa region has considerable potential for the location of food processing, vegetable oil and vanaspati, drugs and pharmaceuticals, textiles, sugar, leather and leather goods, engineering industries and electrical equipment.

A recent survey conducted on behalf of Madhya Pradesh Audyogik Vikas Nigam (M.P.A.V.N) holds immense potential for setting up industrial units in the state which may attract a total investment of Rs. 430 crores, 300 crores in mineral based and 130 crores in other industries. Whereas almost all the mineral based industries will be located in eastern and inland eastern regions, there is scope for locating other industries in the Malwa region.

Of the 130 crores of proposed investment in units other

than mineral-based, a sum of Rs. 39.5 crores is proposed to be invested at Mandideep in Raisen district, Makshi in Shajapur district and Dewas. Nearly 45% of the proposed investment in the whole state is likely to be invested in units located at three places in the Malwa region. These three industrial centres are located on the rail route and are within the proximity of large cities, Mandideep near Bhopal, Makshi near Indore and Ujjain and Dewas near Indore. The M.P.A.V.N has also visualised further industrial development at three centres in the region. The process of urbanisation is likely to increase at a fast rate at these centres which are already showing fast rates of growth. But the pressures of these centres will increase on large cities within their proximity. The M.P. Audyogik Kendra Vikas Nigam has identified the following centres in the region as growth centres :

Name of Centre	*District*
Dewas	Dewas
Cawla	Dhar
Makshi	Shajapur
Meghnagar	Jhabua
Pithampur	Dhar
Mandideep	Raisen

We do not know on what basis these centres have been identified and why these centres are confined only to a few districts. The Survey conducted on behalf of the AVN (Audyogik Vikas Nigam) has identified potential industries at only three centres. Unless growth centres are identified in all the districts and detailed survey of resources conducted, the industrial potential cannot be known. The policy of incentives and concessions is leading to concentration of industrial units at such centres which are within the proximity of large cities. A much larger number of growth centres has been identified in the eastern and inland eastern regions than in the Malwa region.

Makshi which is emerging as an important industrial centre and where large investment has been proposed, is in Shajapur district, one of industrially backward districts of the region. It is at a distance of 37 km. from Ujjain and 70 km. from Indore, on the Agra-Bombay national highway and also a railway junction on Ratlam-Bhopal broad gauge line. The Indore-Dewas-Makshi region is increasingly becoming popular with the industrialists, has the maximum concentration of industries—textilies, leather, engineering. With industrial growth having reached a saturation point at Indore, the focus of new projects has turned to Makshi. Moreover, Makshi falls in category 'C' backward district and hence the new units are eligible for more incentives and concessions. Some of the important industries set up at Makshi are cement, soya products, steel castings, leather board, proteins, and soyabean oil extraction plant. Makshi will have greater linkages with the neigbouring areas because of a number of agro-based products.

The other important emerging industrial centre where large proportion of investment has been proposed is Mandideep located in one of the most industrially backward districts, Raisen. For all practical purposes, Mandideep is a satellite town of Bhopal, located at a distance of 22 km. away from the city and connected by broad gauge railway through Bhopal with all important cities of India—Delhi, Bombay, Madras. The national highway passes through the town. In this complex, 8 units have already gone into production in 1982 and 122 more units would be coming up in the near future. Major industrial units at this centre are Hindustan Electro-graphite, M.P. United Pesticides and chemicals, M.P. Forest industries, pipes and poles and castings. Units which are expected to come up will produce high tension insulation, soyabean oil, biscuits, fabrication, low tension switchgears. Mandideep is putting pressure on Bhopal city as most of the employees reside in Bhopal and commute daily between the two centres. It has poor linkages with the regional economy. In the name of backwardness all sorts of concessions have been obtained by the industrialists but the place is within the proximity of Bhopal on the rail and road route, having little linkage with Raisen town, the district headquarters.

Small-Scale Industrial Units

Small units are generally assumed to be more labour intensive and dispersed in nature. The Malwa region has 25.6% of number of units, 32% of investment and 28% of total employment in the small scale registered units in Madhya Pradesh in 1981. The following table presents district-wise position of small scale industrial units in Malwa region.

TABLE 3.7

District-wise registered small scale units in Malwa region 1982

District	Units (Number)	Investment (lakhs of Rs.)	Employment (Number)
1. Bhopal	1949	938.7	10,542
2. Dewas	1577	628.5	8307
3. Dhar	1705	659.1	7033
4. Indore	3855	1596.4	22923
5. Jhabua	1226	230.8	3736
6. Mandsaur	3330	552.6	8889
7. Raisen	994	119.9	3744
8. Rajgarh	2160	241.4	7654
9. Ratlam	1850	894.4	8115
10. Sehore	1647	207.2	3802
11. Ujjain	3424	524.1	12955
12. Shajapur	1341	139.9	3907
13. Vidisha	1352	278.4	4047
Total Malwa region	26430	7011.4	105654
Total M.P.	103260	21689.7	376495
percentage in region	26.6	32.3	28.0

Like large scale industrial units, small scale units are also concentrated in few districts : The five districts, Indore, Bhopal Ujjain, Mandsaur and Dewas, taken together account for 54% of all units, more than 60% of total investment as well as employment in small scale sector in the region, indicating high degree of concentration of units which were supposed to have been more dispersed. The type of small scale units which have come up do not have much linkages with local economy and their impact, therefore, has been not so high as we expected. Their location is mostly at such centres where already large units have been set up. They are getting incentives and concessions from the Government, irrespective of their line of manufacture, value added by manufacture and linkages with the local economy. Only smallness is sufficient to make these units eligible for assistance. The result is distorted and lop-sided industrial structure. This is happening not only in this region but in the whole state. Integration between agriculture and industry is lacking.

Economic Activities in the Region

In 1980, an economic census of non-agricultural enterprises and agricultural enterprises other than crop production and plantation, was undertaken in the state, by the Directorate of Economics and Statistics. For the purpose of economic census, an enterprise is defined as an undertaking engaged in production and/or distribution of goods and or services not for the sole purpose of consumption. Thus the census covered all entrepreneurial activities of non-agricultural sector and some specified activities of agricultural sector excluding crop production and plantations.

The economic census shows that 25% of all enterprises in the state were located in Malwa region, with an equal percentage of agricultural and non-agricultural enterprises (25% each). Of the total persons employed in these enterprises, 27% were in Malwa region. The region accounts for 21% of the total enterprises in rural area with 20% of total employment and 36% of total enterprises in urban areas with 34% of total employment in all enterprises in urban areas of the state. The percentage of total enterprises in the state in rural areas is comparatively less in proportion to rural population of the state in the region, but the percentage share of urban enterprises of the region in the state is higher than the share of the region in total urban population.

Of the total 3,36221 enterprises in the region, 55% were

located in rural areas and 45% in urban areas as against 64.6% and 35.4% respectively in the state as a whole. A higher percentage of enterprises compared to the state were located in urban areas. This is due to location of 4 Class I towns in this region and higher percentage of urban population living in urban areas in the region compared to the whole state. Of the total enterprises in the region, 7% were agricultural and 93% non-agricultural, of the total non-agricultural enterprises, a little more than 51% were rural and 49% urban. Of the total employment in non-agricultural enterprises, 38% were employed in rural areas and 62% in urban areas as against 46.3% and 53.7% respectively in the state as a whole. Bhopal and Indore are the two districts where a small percentage of total enterprises are located in rural areas, 11% in Bhopal and nearly 20% in Indore. More than 60% of total enterprises in the region are concentrated in five districts, viz. Indore, Bhopal, Mandsaur, Ratlam and Ujjain, with more than 60% of total employment in the region.

This analysis shows that rural economy of the region is less diversified, as indicated by lesser percentage of non-agricultural enterprises located in the region. Higher percentage of total enterprises in urban areas is mostly due to concentration in four Class I towns.

Infrastructural Development

Building up of adequate infrastructure facilities is an important pre-requisite to sustain and support all kinds of developmental effort in the state. In respect of different indicators of infrastructure development, like per capita consumption of electricity, net irrigated area, length of railways and roads per unit of area, literacy, skilled manpower and availability of banking facilities, the state fares poorly. In fact, the level of infrastructure development as constructed by the Commerce Research Bureau, shows that state index was only 64 in 1979-80 against the base of 100 for all-India and 212 in Punjab, 156 for Haryana and 156 for Tamil Nadu. Some of the components of infrastructure have been discussed in this chapter. We would now focus on some important indicators of infrastructure.

Power Development

The region does not have coal reserves. Henee most of the thermal plants are located in the eastern and inland eastern regions of the state. The main reliance of Malwa region is on hydal plants and power generated in other regions but supplied to Malwa region. In many districts, the region has poor power facilities. The following table presents the percentage of villages electrified by March 1983, in different districts of the region.

TABLE 3.8

Table showing percentage of villages electrified and per capita consumption of electricity

District	percentage of villages electrified (March 1983)	per capita consumption of electricity (1981-82) in kwh.
1	2	3
1. Rajgrah	36.89	18.41
2. Sehore	65.52	35.38
3. Vidisha	30.93	18.02
4. Raisen	29.18	97.54
5. Bhopal	66.79	201.15
6. Mandsaur	98.16	78.64
7. Ratlam	58.62	121.96
8. Jhabua	35.90	11.60
9. Ujjain	100.00	214.52
10. Dhar	54.24	45.18
11. Dewas	72.17	121.48
12. Indore	99.69	203.45
13. Shajapur	55.87	29.52
M.P.	46.33	95.24

(Source : Statistics of power development—M.P. Electricity Board –1981-82)

There are four districts where the percentage of villages electrified is lower than the state average (46.33%). Districts like Vidisha, Jhabua had less than 40% villages electrified and districts like Dhar, Shajapur, Ratlam, Sehore, Bhopal had less than 70% villages electrified. Only Ujjain district has 100% villages electrified, followed by Indore (99.69%) and Mandsaur (98.16%).

Per capita consumption of electricity in the state as a whole increased from 45 kwh. in 1970-71 to 95 kwh. in 1981-82. Only five districts namely Indore, Dewas, Ujjain, Ratlam and Bhopal, have higher per capita consumption of electricity compared to the state average and these are relatively industrialised districts of the region. The lowest per capita consumption of electricity was found in Jhabua district, followed by Vidisha, Shajapur and the highest in Ujjain, followed by Indore districts.

The Table 3.9 presents enegry consumed per consumer in kwh. in different districts of Malwa region.

Electricity consumed per consumer in 1981-82 in the state was 2598 kwh. The highest consumption per consumer was in eastern region (7226 kwh.) where most of the mineral based industries are located. BALCO alone at Korba consumes about 10% of elecitricty generated in the state. Surprisingly, the consumption of electricty per consumer is the highest in Raisen district which is one of the most backward districts of the region. This is mainly due to the fact that a few industrial units consuming very high quantum of power, are located at Mandideep which though within the proximity of Bhopal city, is located in Raisen districts, where all concessions are being given by state and central Governments and the financial institutions.

The consumption of electricity per consumer was the lowest in Jhabua district (542 kwh.) followed by Shajapur (647). Only in two districts Raisen and Ujjain, per consumer consumption was higher than the state average. Judged by this criterion, the region is relatively less industrialised and agriculturally less modernised.

Analysing the disaggregated data, we find that per consumer consumption of electricity for commercial purposes and domestic purposes is very low in majority of the districts ; for industrial purposes it is the highest in Raisen district, followed by Ujjain, Bhopal and the lowest in Rajgarh and Vidisha

TABLE 3.9

District	All categories	Commercial	Domestic	Industrial	Irrigation	Street light
1. Rajgarh	608	462	274	4592	582	3543
2. Sehore	822	522	268	11041	882	3340
3. Vidisha	739	478	365	4857	712	8261
4. Raisen	4383	682	264	90530	912	3456
5. Bhopal	2173	903	438	76934	1484	20,888
6. Mandsaur	1027	413	237	29612	646	3134
7. Ratlam	1685	528	296	49098	1090	5016
8. Jhabua	542	337	179	6330	662	4091
9. Ujjain	3028	665	354	90459	929	4822
10. Dhar	962	450	203	15779	1162	3360
11. Dewas	2152	670	275	56575	987	5238
12. Indore	1912	808	408	41893	1491	12414
13. Shajapur	647	509	237	5525	688	4032
Madhya Pradesh	2598	660	330	65405	1034	3974

(Source ; Statistics of power development-MPEB 1981-82, pp. 120-126)

districts. In only 3 districts, per capita consumption of electricity for industrial purposes is higher than the state average. For irrigation purposes, it is the highest in Indore district, followed by Bhopal and the lowest in Raigarh district followed by Mandsaur.

By percentage of electricity consumed in rural areas, the number of consumers using electricity for irrigation purposes, number of pumps and power used in irrigation. But in respect of industrial uses of electricity, the region lags much behind the eastern region, though ranking next to this region.

Transport and Communications

Because of inadequate network of railways, roads form the backbone of the state transport system. The state has been endowed with hilly terrain and black cotton soil area in abundant measure which have created problems for road construction. The sheer size of the state requires road length of larger magnitude to serve the people which may not be necessary to that extent in a smaller state, with high density of population. In Malwa region, black cotton soil, through which state highways pass necessitated extra strengthening of the crust of roads and also widening at many stretches. The density of road length worked out to be only 14.9 km. per 100 sq. km. of area.

Because of Madhya Pradesh's central location in the country, state highways and national highways have to bear the major brunt of traffic heavily loaded vehicles. There are 4 national highways, Agra-Bombay, Nagpur-Raipur, Rewa-Nagpur and Rewa-Allahabad. Only the first one Agra-Bombay passes through Malwa region.

As regards provision of roads in villages, the situation is unsatisfactory. At the end of 1981-82, of the 70,883 villages in the state, only 20.8% were connected by surface roads, whereas 79.2% remained unconnected.

The Table 3.11 gives the length of roads per 1000 sq. km.

Road development in relation to area appears to be the lowest in Raisen district, followed by Vidisha and the highest in Indore, followed by Dhar and Jhabua. In the two tribal

TABLE 3.10

Villages connected with surfaced roads in M.P.

Population group	total number of villages	March end 1983 percentage of total villages connected with roads
Above 1500	2990	71
1000—1500	4347	45
less than 1000	63541	17
Total	70,883	20.8%

TABLE 3.11

Length of Roads per 1000 sq. km.

District	1965-66	70-71	74-75
1. Raisen	—	7.36	6.74
2. Rajgarh	6.28	6.17	10.51
3. Sehore	3.08	8.49	10.16
4. Vidisha	6.10	6.36	7.67
5. Dhar	7.42	9.90	14.71
6. Indore	13.57	16.89	20.65
7. Jhabua	4.13	9.17	13.61
8. Dewas	5.12	6.10	8.23
9. Mandsaur	7.35	7.27	9.61
10. Ratlam	8.09	8.43	9.42
11. Shajapur	5.07	6.76	8.60
12. Ujjain	6.19	8.70	9.79
M.P.	5.72	6.84	8.98
India	6.81	8.04	9.51

districts, road development is higher in relation to area. This is because of funds received under tribal development schemes from the Central Government.

Railway development has remained neglected in the state. Over the past 25 years, there has been insignificant increase in railway route length from 4891 km. in 1955-56 to 5732 km. in 1981 which worked out to be only 11 km. per 1000 sq. km. of area in 1955-56 and 13 km. in 1981, as against all-India average of 19 km. The level in M.P. is unfortunately one of the lowest in the country.

The future development of railways has been mainly proposed in eastern and inland eastern regions to exploit the mineral resources of the state.

Most of the towns in the region do not lie on the rail route. Even 4 district headquarters, Dhar, Jhabua, Raisen and Shajapur, are not connected by rail. District of Jhabua, Dhar Raisen, Mandsaur, Shajapur, are poorly served by railways. Indore is connected with Bhopal by slow moving trains.

Post-Offices

In respect of area and population served per post office, the situation is not very comfortable. Among the districts of Malwa, the lowest area served by each post office, on an average, is in Bhopal, followed by Indore and the highest in Vidisha, followed by Dhar. The average population per post office was the lowest in Raisen district, followed by Sehore and the highest in Indore, followed by Bhopal.

Regulated Markets

Regulated markets play an important role in getting fair prices to the cultivators of their products. At the end of March, 1982, there were only 256 principal regulated produce markets in the state. The area per regulated market is very high and there are wide disparities among the districts in this respect. The area served by each market on an average was the highest in Jhabua, followed by Raisen and the lowest in Rajgarh followed by Shajapur districts, the two predominantly agricultural districts of the region. The growth of urbanisation in such districts is due to agricultural development. The growth of regulated markets can help in increasing the flow of marketed surplus from rural areas to urban markets and thereby increase interaction between the two.

TABLE 3.12

Showing average area served per regulated market (1981-82)

	District	No. of principal markets	Average area per market (sq. km.)
1.	Bhopal	2	1386
2.	Dewas	6	1170
3.	Dhar	6	1359
4.	Indore	4	975
5.	Jhabua	4	1696
6.	Mandsaur	8	1224
7.	Raisen	5	1693
8.	Rajgarh	10	615
9.	Ratlam	5	972
10.	Sehore	5	1316
11.	Shajapur	9	688
12.	Ujjain	7	870
13.	Vidisha	7	1053
	Malwa region	78	1078
	M.P.	256	1732

Compared to the state as a whole, regulated markets serve lesser area on an average in Malwa region. Little more than 30% of total regulated markets in the state are located in Malwa region which is better served compared to other regions.

Banking Development

There are large variations in banking development in the region. In 5 out of 13 districts, banking offices per lakh of population were less than the state average in 1981. The largest number of bank offices per one lakh of population was in Bhopal (9.3), followed by Indore (9.1), Ujjain (5.9) and the lowest in Rajgarh and Mandsaur (3 each), followed by Jhabua and Vidisha (3.5 each).

On the whole, the region is better served by banking facilities than other regions of the state.

TABLE 3.13

District-wise bank offices

District	per lakh of population 1961	1971	1981
1. Bhopal	—	—	9.3
2. Dewas	1.2	1.7	4.0
3. Dhar	0.5	1.3	4.2
4. Indore	4.1	5.2	9.1
5. Jhabua	0.3	1.0	3.5
6. Mandsaur	0.8	2.0	5.7
7. Rajgarh	0.7	1.0	3.0
8. Ratlam	1.7	2.3	5.3
9. Sehore	1.4	2.2	3.6
10. Ujjain	1.9	2.2	5.9
11. Vidisha	0.7	1.0	3.5
M.P.	0.8	1.4	4.2

The Malwa region as a whole accounts for 37% of total number of accounts and 50% of outstanding bank credit in the state. However, there are wide variations among the districts. Five districts, Bhopal, Indore, Ujjain, Ratlam and Mandsaur account for a little more than 50% of total accounts in the region and 78% of total outstanding bank credit, showing a marked degree of concentration of bank credit in relatively more developed districts of the region.

The shares of districts like Dhar, Jhabua, Raisen, Rajgarh, Sehore and Vidisha, are comparatively lower in total bank credit.

Occupational classification of outstanding credit shows that of the outstanding credit to industry in the state, 60% is accounted for by the Malwa region. Nearly 33% of accounts are in this region. The degree of concentration of bank credit to industry within the region is evident from the fact that 64% of total number of accounts and 90% of outstanding credit to industry is accounted for by five districts, viz. Bhopal, Indore, Ujjain, Ratlam and Dewas.

In respect of advances to agriculture, 31% of all accounts and 36% of outstanding credit is accounted for by the Malwa region. Agricultural credit is more equitably distributed among different districts than credit to industry.

The region accounts for 38% of total accounts and 38% of total outstanding advances to trade and 26% of total account and 39% of total credit to transport, 38% of accounts and 40% of credit to services, 30% of accounts and 51% of credit to trade in the whole state. Outstanding credit to transport is concentrated in two districts, Bhopal and Indore, accounting for more than 80% of credit to this sector in the region.

This analysis shows that Malwa region has larger share in total bank credit in the state. But there are wide variations in banks credit among different districts, relatively developed districts claiming a larger share. The concentration of bank credit to industry is much greater than bank credit to agriculture. The flow of bank credit to industry has followed more or less the pattern of industrial development in the region.

The Malwa region accounted for 33.7% of total loans and 36% of total amount disbursed by the DLDBs in M.P. in 1978-79. But within the region, the disbursement is highly skewed as evidenced by the fact that three districts, viz. Indore, Dhar and Dewas accounted for nearly 50% of both loans and amount disbursed by these banks in the region. The shares of districts like Bhopal, Sehore, Vidisha, Rajgarh, Jhabua and Shajapur are particularly very low in total disbursements of loans.

One redeeming feature of these loans is that 37% of total number of loans and 35% of total amount disbursed has gone to small and marginal farmers in the region, with holdings up to 2 hectares. If we add medium size holdings in the range of 2—4 hectares, than 66% of loans and 73% of amount disbursed by the banks is accounted for by holdings up to 4 hectares.

Conclusion

The region has poor infrastructure but has an edge over other regions in respect of infrastructure for agricultural development in terms of irrigation, power consumption in agriculture, pumpsets, roads, communications and banking development. The infrastructure in the eastern region is mainly for industrial development. Malwa region is better served by different functions and facilities, but this does not mean that the region has adequate infrastructure both for industrial and agricultural development. The infrastructural facilities are concentrated in few cities of the region. The better performance of the region is mainly due to the fact that 4 Class I cities, viz. Bhopal, Indore, Ujjain, Ratlam, are located in this region. Bhopal being the capital seat of the State and Indore being an industrial city, known as the commercial capital of the state, have well-developed infrastructure. The rest of the region and the hinterland of the towns remains under-developed.

REFERENCES

1. Spate—OHK et al (1971) India, Pakistan and Ceylon — The Regions, Mathuen and Co. London, Pub., Bombay pp 621-22.
2. Upadhya CM (1964)-Malwi Lok Geet Eik Vivechanatmake Adhayan, Mangal Prakashan, Jaipur.
3. Jain D.C. & Tiwari K. (1922) Hindi, Eivm Uski Vividh Bolian—M.P. Hindi Granth Academy, Bhopal.

CHAPTER 4

URBANISATION IN MALWA REGION

Against the background of physical features, determining the delineation of Malwa region, let us now capture the process of urbanisation that the region has witnessed. The growth of towns is not so much a function of size as of their location, their economic base and can be explained by national and regional factors, operating through economic, demographic, social, political and institutional factors.

The Malwa region that we have delineated include 13 districts of Madhya Pradesh. Of these, 9 districts constitute part of western region which has a total of 11 districts and remaining 4 are part of inland western region which consists of 9 districts. The Malwa region is thus carved out of two NSS sub-regions, mostly western and partly inland western regions, having 13 geographically contiguous districts.

Share in Population and area of the State

According to 1981 census, Malwa region supports over 22% of the total population of M.P., distributed over 13 districts. Indore district has the highest population of 14 lakh and Sehore district, the lowest of 6.6 lakhs, other districts have population of 7-8 lakhs. The region is basically rural with two exceptions of Bhopal and Indore districts which have higher ratio of urban to total population, the rural population in Indore being 34.08% and in Bhopal district 23.74%. Ujjain and Ratlam districts also have lesser rural population compared to other districts, the percentages being 62.53 in Ujjain and 69.2 in Ratlam districts. Remaining districts are less urbanised, with more than 80 per cent rural population. Jhabua and Raisen have the lowest level of urbanisation, with less than 10% population living in urban areas.

The Malwa region has 22.8% of total population, 26.6% of total rural population and 32% of total urban population of the State in 1981. The region accounts for nearly 19% of the total area of the state. A smaller percentage of area is maintaining a higher percentage of population of the state and a much higher percentage of total urban population. Districts like Indore, Ujjain and Bhopal are maintaining a much larger proportion of population of the State, compared to their percentage shares in area of the state. Dewas, Vidisha, Raisen, Sehore have higher percentage of area of the State compared to their percentage share in total population of the State.

The Following table presents these facts :

TABLE 4.1

Percentage share of districts of Malwa region in total population and area of the state

District	Share of population	Percentage share of area of state
1. Indore	2.70	0.88
2. Mandsaur	2.42	2.22
3. Ujjain	2.14	1.37
4. Dhar	2.03	1.84
5. Bhopal	1.72	0.62
6. Rajgarh	1.54	1.39
7. Jhabua	1.53	1.53
8. Dewas	1.52	1.56
9. Ratlam	1.50	1.10
10. Vidisha	1.50	1.66
11. Raisen	1.36	1.91
12. Sehore	1.26	1.48
13. Shajapur	1.61	1.40
Malwa region	22.83	18.98

Table 4.2 shows that Malwa region is comparatively more urbanised than the state and the country. Its level of urbanisation in 1981 was 28.52 as against 20.31% in the state and 23.7% in India. Throughout the period between 1901-81, the level of urbanisation in the region has been higher than that of the state as well as of the country as whole. The region has experienced lesser temporal variations in the level of urbanisation over the period 1901—1981 than the state, as evidenced by CV which was 29.22% for the Malwa region and 33.52% for M.P. and 28.9% for India.

The region accounted for nearly 1/3 of total urban population and 26.4% of Rural population of the State in 1981. The higher proportion of urban population may be due to the fact that out of 14 Class I cities in the State, 4 are located in this region and out of a total number of 303 towns in the State, 84 (28%) are located in this region. The percentage share of Malwa region in total urban population of M.P., has gradually come down from 39.08% in 1901 to 32.06% in 1981. This may be due to slow growth of urban population in the region and faster growth in other regions of the State.

TABLE 4.2

Level of urbanisation in Malwa region

Year	Malwa	Madhya Pradesh	India	% of total urban population of state in Malwa region
1901	17.12	8.65	10.84	39.08
1911	11.91	6.68	10.29	34.64
1921	12.79	7.51	11.48	34.71
1931	14.62	8.30	11.99	35.80
1941	17.01	9.81	13.86	35.26
1951	20.09	12.02	17.29	34.94
1961	22.92	14.29	17.79	34.45
1971	24.64	16.29	19.90	33.41
1981	28.52	20.31	23.70	32.06
CV	28.22	33.52	28.90	—

Table 4.3 presents the growth of urban population in the Malwa region since 1901. Whereas total population in the region has increased by little more than 3½ times between 1901—1981, rural population also by the same multiple, the urban population has recorded an increase of more than 6 times and this spurt has been more rapid since 1951 when urban population increased by more than 3 times. Thus whereas urban population has nearly doubled in 50 years between 1901—1951, it has increased more than 3 times in 30 years between 1951-81.

The decennial growth rate of urban population in the region has been the highest between 1971-81 (49.71%) as against 56.07% in the State as a whole, of total population 29.37% as against 25.17% for the state, and of rural population 22.71% as against 19.16% of the state as a whole. The rate of growth of urban population has been lower in the region compared to the urban growth in state since 1941. But higher rates of growth recorded by total population in 1961 and 1981 in the region compared to those of the State, have been due to higher rates recorded by rural population in the region (Table No. 4.3). This is the only region of the State where urban population has recorded rates of growth lower than the state average, although the region is the highly urbanised region of the state. This means that other regions are urbanising at faster rate and the disparities in the levels of urbanisation between different sub-regions of the state, are gradually narrowing down.

The region with well distributed urban settlement system, is agriculturally more developed than other regions of the state. In 1981, the highest urban growth was recorded by inland eastern region (61.03%) as against 49.7% in Malwa region. The eastern and inland eastern have low level of urbanisation but has greater potential for the emergence of new towns and accretion of population to existing towns, because of increasing industrialisation in the mineral and forest belt of the State. The URGD in the Malwa region has been all through lower than the state since 1911, with the exception of 1931. In 1981, the URGD in the region was 27, the highest recorded so far since 1901 as compared to 36.98 for the whole

TABLE 4.3

Growth of Urban Population in Malwa region of Madhya Pradesh

Year	Population			Decadal growth rate			URGD	Level of
	Total	Urban	Rural	Total	Urban	Rural	decadal	urbanisation
1901	3327623	569753	2757879	—	—	—	—	17.12 (8.65)
1911	3776304	449890	3326414	13.48 (15.3)	—21.04 (—10.9)	20.61 (17.78)	−41.65 (—28.69)	11.91 (6.68)
1921	3907663	499912	3407750	3.48 (—1.38)	11.12 (10.87)	2.45 −(2.26)	8.67 (13.13)	12.79 (7.51)
1931	4338362	634287	3704075	11.02 (11.39)	26.88 (23.03)	8.70 (10.45)	18.18 (12.58)	14.62 (8.30)
1941	4877726	829635	4048091	12.43 (12.34)	30.80 (32.78)	9.29 (10.49)	21.51 (22.29)	17.01 (9.81)
1951	5447912	1094752	4353160	11.69 (8.67)	31.96 (33.16)	7.54 (6.01)	24.42 (27.15)	20.09 (12.02)
1961	6954308	1594187	5360121	27.65 (24.17)	45.62 (47.70)	23.13 (20.95)	22.49 (26.15)	22.92 (14.29)

(Figure in parentheses indicate percentages of State as a whole)

1971	9199365	2267016	6932349	24.40 (28.67)	41.21 (46.63)	29.33 (20.68)	12.88 (20.95)	24.64 (14.29)
1981	11900840	3393870	8506970	29.37 (25.17)	49.71 (56.07)	22.71 (19.16)	27.00 (36.98)	28.52 (20.31)
CV for the Region				51.88	79.09	58.11	179.13	28.22
CV for the State				(40.93)	(68.65)	(59.88)		(33.52)

(Figures in parentheses indicates percentages of State as a whole)

state, as against 12.88% for the region and 20.95% for the whole state in 1971.

It would be interesting to study the factors accounting for the slow growth of urban population in the Malwa region compared to the state as a whole. Partly it can be explained by the growth rate of different size class of towns and partly by factors like the economic bases of the towns in the region.

Table 4.4 gives disaggregated picture of urbanisation in the Malwa region at the district level.

The total number of towns in the region has gone up from 68 in 1961 to 70 in 1971 and 84 in 1981. The region has nearly 28% of all towns in the state but nearly 1/3 of total urban population.

The largest number of towns in the region is in Mandsaur district (12), followed by Shajapur (9), Dewas and Rajgarh (8 each) and the lowest number in Bhopal district (2). There has been no increase in the number of towns since 1961 in Mandsaur, Ujjain, Jhabua, Vidisha and Bhopal districts. The highest percentage increase in the number of towns has taken place in Raisen district which has also recorded the highest growth rate of urban population in 1971-81. The increase in the number of towns largely depends upon the administrative decision of the State Government which has the power to declare any settlement as urban, by creating urban local bodies, even though the place may have a population of less than 5,000 and may not have urban characteristics.

Of the 13 districts comprising this region, Bhopal district has the highest level of urbanisation (76.26%), followed by Indore (65.29%), mainly due to location of cities in these districts, and the lowest in Raisen district (9.77) as against 28.5% in the region as a whole and 20.31% in the state. The lowest increase in the level of urbanisation has taken place in Mandsaur district.

Of the 13 districts comprising the region, only 5 districts have level of urbanisation higher than the level of urbanisation of the region as well as of the state in all the three censuses 1961, 1971 and 1981. The level of urbanisation in all districts in the region has been continuously rising since 1961, except in

TABLE 4.4

Spatial pattern of Urban Population in Malwa region

Name of District	No. of towns			Level of Urbanisation			Urban population growth		
	1961	1971	1981	1961	1971	1981	1961	1971	1981
1. Mandsaur	12	12	12	21.21	20.23	20.26	38.24	21.94	31.47
2. Ratlam	5	5	6	28.63	28.93	30.81	23.26	30.93	33.19
3. Ujjain	6	6	6	32.45	35.55	37.47	21.83	42.80	36.43
4. Shajapur	5	6	9	10.08	11.47	14.84	52.53	46.67	60.25
5. Dewas	7	7	8	15.08	15.96	18.71	101.20	40.80	56.69
6. Jhabua	6	6	6	32.45	35.55	37.47	21.83	42.80	36.43
7. Dhar	6	6	8	10.33	10.17	12.60	54.96	28.82	55.26
8. Indore	4	5	5	59.99	62.71	65.92	25.39	42.21	44.16
9. Rajgarh	5	5	8	9.48	9.59	13.08	19.12	26.03	69.73
10. Vidisha	4	4	4	13.14	14.11	16.97	48.92	44.49	43.15
11. Bhopal	2	2	2	61.65	68.62	76.26	119.86	71.32	77.99
12. Sehore	3	3	4	10.52	11.07	13.13	56.96	32.77	54.63
13. Raisen	3	3	6	5.31	5.56	9.97	230.03	40.89	129.79
14. Malwa region	68	70	84	22.92	24.64	28.52	45.62	42.41	49.71

Name of District	Rural population growth			URGD		
	1961	1971	1981	1961	1971	1981
1. Mandsaur	20.63	29.44	31.25	17.61	— 7.50	0.22
2. Raltam	28.09	29.04	21.72	— 4.83	1.89	11.47
3. Ujjain	21.77	24.36	25.55	0.06	18.44	10.88
4. Shajapur	18.74	26.94	14.13	33.79	19.73	46.12
5. Dewas	21.71	31.60	29.30	79.49	9.20	27.39
6. Jhabua	21.77	24.36	25.55	0.06	— 2.53	17.25
7. Dhar	25.21	31.09	21.95	29.75	— 2.27	33.71
8. Indore	25.38	26.78	25.34	0.01	15.43	18.82
9. Rajgarh	21.09	24.52	19.59	— 1.97	1.51	50.14
10. Vidisha	23.92	33.09	15.00	25.00	11.40	28.15
11. Bhopal	20.60	25.96	18.44	99.26	48.36	59.55
12. Sehore	32.79	34.03	25.35	24.17	— 1.26	29.28
13. Raisen	26.19	34.05	22.21	203.84	6.84	107.58
14. Malwa region	23.13	29.33	22.71	22.49	12.88	27.00

Mandsaur district. In 1981, of the 13 districts, 7 districts have shown growth rates of urbanisation higher than the regional growth rate (49.71%) as against 4 in 1971 and 7 in 1961. The highest rate of growth of urban population was recorded by Raisen district (129.79%), followed by Bhopal (77.91%), and the lowest by Mandsaur district (31.47%). There has been decline in urban growth rate in 1981 compared to 1971 in Ujjain, Jhabua and Vidisha districts, where the number of towns has remained constant, and slow growth in Ratlam and Indore districts. The fastest rate of growth has been recorded by Raisen district which is one of the backward districts of the State, where the number of towns has gone up from 3 to 6 between 1971—1981. The rate of growth of Bhopal has slackened compared to 1961. The fastest growth of Bhopal in 1961 was due to rapid increase in population consequent upon its becoming the capital of the state in 1956.

Rural population growth rates have been higher than the region as a whole, in 6 out of 13 districts, the highest growth rate was recorded by Mandsaur district (31.25%), followed by Dewas district (29.3%) and the lowest by Sahajpur district (14.13%). The region as a whole has shown a decline in rural population growth rate from 29.33% in 1971 to 22.71% in 1981, which of course is higher than the rate of rural growth in M.P. as a whole. This decline is mostly due to very low rates of growth of rural population in districts like Sahajpur, Vidisha Rajgarh and Bhopal.

The URGD for the region has been 27.0% in 1981 as against 36.8% for the state as a whole. The URGD has shown wide variations between different districts, the highest being in Raisen district, followed by Bhopal district and the lowest in Mandsaur district (0.22).

Table 4.5 presents the number of towns in different size-classes and growth rates of population by size-class of towns.

The total number of towns has gone up from 36 in 1901 to 84 in 1981, the increase has been very rapid in 1961 compared to 1951, but it slowed down in 1971, again to increase faster in 1981. The change in the concept of urban in different censuses and the frequent administrative decisions of the

Government to create municipalities, leading to conversion of rural settlements into urban, have vitiated comparability of data over time. The number of Class I towns has increased in 1981. The largest number of towns in this region, (65 cut of 84) is of such towns which have population of less than 20,000 each.

The growth rate of Class I towns in the region has decelerated from 67.12% in 1971 to 52.15% in 1981. In 1951, the decadal rate of growth of Class I towns was the highest mainly due to increase in the number of towns in this class from one to 3. The Class II towns have shown the highest growth rate, 177.94% in 1981 as against 97.35% in 1971. The number of Class II towns has increased from 3 to 7 and this fact accounts for faster rate of growth of this class of towns. The Class III towns in the region has shown a negative rate of growth, partly because of the decline in the number of towns from 10 to 8. Next to Class II towns, the highest rate of growth was manifested by Class IV towns (61.84%), partly due to increase in number of towns from 21 to 30 partly due to graduation of next lower class of towns to this class, and partly due to increase in population of existing towns due to expansion of trade and commerce. Class V towns had registered a growth rate of 30.37%, This is the highest rate of growth recorded by this class of towns. This is due to comparison with a very low rate of growth manifested in 1971 (2.28%) on account of decline in number of towns from 31 in 1961 to 29 in 1971. The number increased to 35 in 1981. The region did not have a single Class VI town in 1981, though there were three such towns in 1971 and 7 in 1961. The rate of growth of population of this class of towns, has fluctuated with changes in number of towns.

Of the 84 towns in the region, 73 are small towns with population of less than 50,000 each and 7 medium towns, in the population range of 50,000 and less than one lakh.

There has been a lot of size-growth debate in the field of urbanisation and generally we believe that because of higher efficiency of large towns, there is migration from rural and urban areas to these cities and rapid growth of urban population. Kundu[1] has rightly observed :

TABLE 4.5

Corrected and uncorrected rates of growth by size-class of Towns

Census Year/ Size class of towns	I Population Growth			II Population Growth			III Population Growth		
	No. of towns	Uncorrected	Corrected	No. of towns	Uncorrected	Corrected	No. of towns	Uncorrected	Corrected
1	2	3	4	5	6	7	8	9	10
1901	—	—	—	2	—	—	6	—	—
1911	—	—	—	2	36.88	36.88	3	45.66	—22.06
1921	1	—	—	—	—	36.30	4	55.42	8.97
1931	1	35.33	35.33	2	—	—	3	—40.45	22.31
1941	1	42.92	42.92	2	35.28	35.28	7	115.71	17.15
1951	3	166.58	52.61	1	—59.49	48.34	7	5.97	5.97
1961	3	40.34	40.34	1	37.96	37.96	8	34.62	18.78
1971	4	67.12	51.48	3	97.31	36.33	10	16.97	35.78
1981	4	52.15	52.15	7	117.94	37.09	8	—19.67	40.23
CV		74.21	15.06		169.13	42.27		180.47	121.90

Census	IV Population Growth			V Population Growth			VI Population Growth		
Year	No. of towns	Uncorrected	Corrected	No. of towns	Uncorrected	Corrected	No. of towns	Uncorrected	Corrected
	11	12	13	14	15	16	17	18	19
1901	6	—	—	15	—	—	7	—	—
1911	6	12.05	+12.05	18	22.55	– 1.35	6	—26.67	0.71
1921	7	13.71	— 3.99	16	—12.65	—16.6	8	2.40	—23.39
1931	8	8.34	8.02	18	11.84	8.68	12	72.90	23.93
1941	7	—20.90	28.88	23	23.85	14.98	8	—34.49	15.48
1951	8	22.03	19.95	24	12.61	17.40	0	—	51.40
1961	18	112.50	21.62	31	18.52	22.11	7	—	—
1971	21	17.86	27.88	29	2.28	28.20	3	—55.38	27.10
1981	30	61.84	29.94	35	30.37	31.67	0	—	72.62
CV		143.55	66.06		99.72	121.61		735.27	145.09

"Theoretical and empirical investigation into relationship between the size of an urban centre and its growth has unfortunately got clouded due to strong normative predispositions of scholars and inappropriateness of and inadequacies in their methods of analysis."

To get a relatistic picture of the growth rates of urban centres by size class categories, it is necessary to re-calculate the growth rates, by keeping the towns in each category the same as in the base year.

It has been rightly argued by Jain (1977), Kundu and Raja (1980), Rakesh Mohan and Pant (1982) that the computation of the growth of population in cities on the basis of the population in respective censuses has raised a false alarm. They have computed the growth rates for different categories of towns by taking the population at the two census point only for those towns that belonged to that category in the base year. It is, however, important to note that in computing the rates, they had excluded the declassified towns from both the time points. They may give a bias in the growth estimates for the lower categories of towns for which the number of declassified towns is likely to be large.

We have also attempted to follow the above technique to estimate the corrected rate of growth of different classes of towns, by keeping the number of towns in each class constant at two points. Since the number of Class I towns remained the same in 1971 and 1981 censuses, there is no difference in the corrected and uncorrected rates of growth. But there is wide divergence between the two rates in all such years when the number of cities has changed. The co-efficient of variation of Class I towns between 1931 and 1981, was 74.21% in respect of uncorrected rate and only 15.06% in respect of corrected rate. In respect of Class II towns, the corrected rates of growth do not show much variations in different census years. The uncorrected rate was 117.94 between 1971-81, while the corrected rate was only 37.09%, the CV for the period 1911 to 1981 was 169.13% in the case of uncorrected rate and 42.27% of corrected rates. If we take corrected rates of growth of different size class of towns, we find that the highest rate was registered by Class I cities in 1981, followed by Class VI and

Class III towns. There is no doubt that Class I cities have exhibited a significantly high rates of growth compared to the lower order urban centres during the 50s, 60s and 70s. But the growth rates of cities obtained after making adjustments in the terminal year, population growth rates exceed those of lesser order towns by a much smaller margin than what was suggested by the census approach based on unadjusted population figures in different size of categories in different censuses.

Table 4.6 shows the predominance of Class I cities in the total urban population of Malwa region. This fact is evident from the data that 4 Class I towns accounted for 57% of total urban population in the region in 1981 as against 56.3% in 1971. The percentage of population living in Class II towns has gone up from 7% in 1971 to 14% in 1981 and of Class III towns declined from 14.8% to 7.7% in the same period. There has been a marginal increase in percentage share of class IV towns and marginal decline in the share of Class V towns. There was no Class VI town in the region in 1981. The table shows that the percentage shares of class I, Class II and Class IV towns in total urban population of the region, have increased. The percentage share of small towns has gone down from 36.7% in 1971 to about 29% in 1981 and of intermediate towns has gone up from 7 to 14% in the same period. The co-efficient of variation in growth rates in different size classes of towns has gone down from 199.06% in 1971 to 126.05% in 1981, indicating narrowing down of variations among growth rates of different size class of towns.

The percentage distribution of urban population in the region among different size class is more skewed than the state. This is because of location of 4 Class I cities in the region.

Table 4.7 provides some clues to the differential growth rates of different size-class of towns in the region.

Of the four Class I towns, two have recorded grawth rate higher than the growth rate of urbanisation in the state and 2 lower than the average. Of the 7 Class II towns in 1981, 3 exhibited higher growth rate than the state average, of the 8 Class III towns, only one had registered higher rate, of the 29 Class IV towns only 4 and of the 21 class V towns not a single

TABLE 4.6

Decadal growth rate of population by size class (1971 and 1981) and percentage distribution of urban population among different size class of towns

Size class	No. of towns		Population		Decadal growth rate (%)	
	1971	1981	1971	1981	1971	1981
I	4	4	1273603	1937768	67.12	52.15
			(56.3)	(57.0)	(69.12)	(62.23)
II	3	7	172593	479702	92.31	177.94
			(7.0)	(14.1)	(83.05)	(177.83)
III	10	8	323435	259813	16.93	—19.67
			(14.8)	(7.7)	(41.06)	(— 3.60)
IV	21	30	272894	441656	17.86	61.84
			(12.3)	(13.0)	(30.4)	(64.30)
V	29	35	210918	274932	2.28	30.37
			(9.1)	(8.2)	(1.88)	(68.60)
VI	3	—	13573	—	55.38	0.00
			(0.5)	—	(—56.97)	(—54.75)
All Classes	70	84	2267016	3393870	41.21	49.71
			(100)	(100)	(46.63)	(56.07)
CV	85.60	95.71			199.06	126.05

Note : Figures in brackets of decadal growth rates relate to the whole state and figures in brackets under population indicate the percentage of total urban population.

TABLE 4.7

Number of towns with decadal growth rate increasing, declining and constant

Size elass of towns	Increasing		Declining		Constant		Not available		Total		Number of towns having growth rate higher than state growth rate of urbanisation	
	1971	1981	1971	1981	1971	1981	1971	1981	1971	1981	1971	1981
I	4	4	0	0	0	0	0	0	4	4	2	2
II	3	7	0	0	0	0	0	0	3	7	1	3
III	10	8	0	0	0	0	0	0	10	8	4	1
IV	20	29	1	0	0	0	0	1	21	30	1	4
V	27	21	0	0	0	0	2	14	29	35	0	0
VI	2	0	1	0	0	0	0	0	3	0	0	0
Malwa region	66	68	2	0	0	0	2	15	70	84	8	10

town had growth rates higher than the state average. This analysis provides some explanation to the higher growth rates shown by Class I, II and IV towns and negative or slow rates of growth of other classes of towns in the region.

Of the four Class I towns in the region, two have shown growth rates higher than 5% per annum in 1981, whereas only one town was in this category in 1971. Class II towns have shown the fastest growth rate, partly because of the fact that of the 7 towns in this category in 1981, three had experienced growth rate higher than 5% per annum, whereas in 1971, not a single town of this class belonged to this range. Class III towns have manifested negative growth rate in 1981, because only one out of 8 towns in 1981 was in the range of more than 5% per annum, whereas in 1971, two towns belonged to this range, and two belonged to the range of 4-5%, In 1981, not a single town of this class was in this range of 4 to 5% growth rate. Class IV towns recorded higher growth rate in 1981 compared to 1971, because there were 4 towns in the range of above 5% growth rate in 1981 compared to only 2 in 1971. Class V towns registered negative growth because of downward mobility of some towns from higher range of growth rate to lower range and also because of the emergence of new towns in this class whose growth rate could not be compared with 1971.

Table 4.8 presents growth rates of individual Class I cities in the Malwa region. Of the four Class I towns in this region, only Indore has shown consistent increase in decadal growth rate since 1961, but the rate of growth of this city has been less than average growth rate of Malwa region and also of the state. In 1981, only Bhopal has manifested a growth rate higher than the average for the region and also for the state. Ratlam has shown a continuous deceleration in growth rate since 1961. The decadal growth rate of Bhopal city has come down from 117.87% in 1961 to 72.62% in 1971 but marginally increased to 72.69% in 1981. The spurt in growth rate of Bhopal in 1961 was mainly due to abnormal increase in its population, consequent upon its becoming the capital seat of Madhya Pradesh in 1956. The rate of growth of Class I cities as a whole in the region has decelerated from 67.12% in 1971 to 52.15% in 1981, and also in the State from 73.52% in 1961 to 69.12% in 1971 and to 62.23% in 1981. As already observed, the whole region has a well-distributed urban settlement system centred around certain large cities such as Bhopal, Indore, Ujjain, Ratlam, and surprisingly enough, long established cities are growing at a slow rate than the new ones, like Shahdol, Sidhi, Katni, Durg-Bhilai, Hoshangabad, Itarsi and Dewas. In the state, urbanisation is following the generation of new economic activity and the location of major and medium industries in backward regions. The pressures exerted by growing rural population with no adequate avenues of employment in rural areas, are not the major factors giving impetus to urban growth in the State.

TABLE 4.8

Growth of Class I towns in Malwa region

City	Population Growth rates (Decadal)		
	1961	1971	1981
Indore	27.05	42.03	47.44
Bhopal	117.87	72.62	72.69
Ujjain	11.05	44.66	35.15
Ratlam	37.96	36.33	31.23
Malwa region	40.34	67.12	52.15
State	73.52	69.12	62.23

Table 4.9 presents the growth of number and population of small towns in Malwa region since 1901.

The number of small towns with population of less than 50,000 each, has more than doubled between 1901 and 1981, with nearly three-fold increase in population in small towns. The sudden spurt in number of small towns may be due to definitional changes adopted in 1961. The State Government has also played an important role in increasing the number of small towns by creating urban local bodies in a number of settlements. There seems to be no consistency in the growth of number of small towns in the region. This is due to lot of

TABLE 4.9

Number and Population of small towns in Malwa region with population below 50,000 (1901 to 1981)

Census year	Number of small towns	Population of small towns	Average town population	Percentage of number of small towns to total settlement (urban)	Percentage of population of small town to total urban population
1901	34	394926	11615	94.44	69.32
1911	33	339545	10289	94.29	75.47
1921	35	294595	11274	97.22	78.93
1931	41	376076	9173	93.18	59.29
1941	45	469440	10432	93.75	56.58
1951	39	488340	12522	90.70	44.61
1961	64	744655	11635	94.12	46.71
1971	63	820820	13028	90.00	36.31
1981	73	976400	13375	86.90	28.77

discretion given to the census authorities to designate areas as urban, more particularly in the pre-1961 census period. The average population of small town in the region has not shown much increase in the period 1901-1981, being 11,615 in 1901 and 13,275 in 1981. The average size has been less than 15,000 population. The percentage of number of small towns to total number of towns in the region has declined from 94.44 to 86.9% and the percentage share of population in small towns to total urban population in the region has declined appreciably from 78.93% to 28.77% between 1901 to 1981.

The average size of a town in the region is larger than the whole state in each of the three census years, and has increased from 23,444 in 1961 to 40,403 in 1981. Taking the mean size of towns by size class we find that Malwa region has higher mean population than the state in every size-class of town in 1981, though in earlier censuses the mean size of some class of towns was marginally higher in the state compared to the Malwa region. There has been consistent increase in the mean size of population of Class I towns, Class IV towns and Class IV towns since 1961. But the mean size of towns belonging to other class of towns, has shown no consistent increase in the three census years. There does not appear to be much difference in the size of population of Class IV, V and VI towns in the region and the State.

Table 4.10 presents the growth of small and intermediate towns in different districts of Malwa region in 1981.

The table shows that there are 80 small and medium towns in the region in 1981, of which 14 were added in 1981. The region has only 4 Class I cities and the number has remained unchanged since 1971.

The highest rate of growth of small and medium towns in the region was shown by Raisen district, followed by Dewas district and the lowest in Indore district, followed by Ratlam district. The range of variati on in corrected rates of growth is not very wide.

The annual average rate of growth of urban population was higher than the rate of urban growth in the region in Raisen, Sehore, Bhopal, Rajgarh, Dhar, Dewas and Shajapur districts. The rate of growth of urban population was lower

TABLE 4.10

Growth of small & medium Towns in Malwa Region (1981)

Name of District	No. of cities	No. of small and medium towns	New towns added	Annual population growth rate of cities	Annual population growth rate of small & medium Towns	
					Correted	Un-corrected
1. Mandsaur	0	12	0	—	3.147	—
2. Ratlam	1	5	1	3.12	2.862	3.695
3. Ujjain	1	5	0	3.52	3.643	—
4. Shajapur	0	9	3	—	2.804	6.026
5. Dewas	0	8	1	—	4.709	5.669
6. Jhabua	0	6	0	—	3.559	—
7. Dhar	0	8	2	—	5.358	5.526
8. Indore	1	4	0	4.74	2.168	—
9. Rajgarh	0	8	3	—	3.050	6.973
10. Vidisha	0	4	0	—	4.315	—
11. Bhopal	1	1	0	7.47	3.936	—
12. Sehore	0	4	1	—	4.188	5.463
13. Raisen	0	6	3	—	5.352	12.979
Malwa	4	80	14			4.97
M.P.						5.60

Name of Districts	Population Growth		URGD	Mean population of small & medium towns	Level of urbanization
	URBAN	RURAL			
1. Mandsaur	3.147	3.125	0.022	21313	20.26
2. Ratlam	3.319	2.172	1.147	16976	30.81
3. Ujjain	3.643	2.555	1.088	27285	37.47
4. Shajapur	6.025	1.413	4.612	13850	14.84
5. Dewas	5.669	2.930	2.739	18582	18.71
6. Jhabua	3.559	1.788	1.771	11033	18.32
7. Dhar	5.526	2.195	3.331	16623	12.60
8. Indore	4.416	2.534	1.882	24934	65.92
9. Rajgarh	6.973	1.959	5.014	13107	13.08
10. Vidisha	4.315	1.500	2.815	33239	16.97
11. Bhopal	7.399	1.844	5.555	10845	76.26
12. Sehore	5.463	2.535	2.928	21867	13.31
13. Raisen	12.979	2.221	10.758	11783	9.97
Malwa	4.97	2.27	2.7	13375	28.52
M.P.	5.60	1.91	3.6		20.31

than the state average in Mandsaur, Ujjain, Jhabua, Indore and Vidisha districts. In all these districts, the rates of growth of rural population were higher than the average growth of the region. The URGD was the highest in Raisen district (10.75%), followed by Bhopal (5.55%) and Rajgarh (5.0%) and the lowest in Mandsaur district (0.022%) followed by Ujjain (1.88%). The districts where new towns were added in 1981 have registered higher rates of growth with the exception of Bhopal which has witnessed a high rate of growth, despite no addition to the number of towns. The corrected rates of population are much lower in all the districts where new towns have been added in 1981, than the uncorrected ones. Raisen district has recorded the highest annual rate of growth (12.9%) of urban population between 71-81 but the corrected rate of growth has come down to 5.55%. Similarly uncorrected rates of growth are higher than corrected rates in Shajapur, Rajgarh and Dhar districts due to increase in the number of towns in these districts.

The table also shows that the level of urbanisation was the highest in Bhopal district (76.26%), followed by Indore (65.92%), Ujjain (37.47%) and Ratlam (30.81%) and the lowest level in Jhabua district (8.32%), followed by Raisen (9.9%), Dhar (12.6%) and Rajgarh (13.08%). Of the 13 districts comprising the Malwa region, 9 districts had levels of urbanisation much lower than those of the region as well as the State.

Only 4 districts in the region have urban growth rates higher than the state average, but 9 districts out of 13 had higher rates of rural population compared to the state average. The rate of urban growth in the region (4.97% per annum) has been lower than the state as a whole (5.6%). But despite low rate of growth of urbanisation, the region is the highly urbanised region of the state. This is mostly due to location of 4 Class I cities in this region. Nine out of 13 districts have very low level of urbanisation. This implies concentration of population in a few districts where Class I cities are located.

Table 4.11 presents the locational factors of small and medium towns in the region along with their growth rates.

Of the 73 small towns in the region, the highest decadal

TABLE 4.11

Percentage variation in population of small towns classified by locational factors (1971-81)

	Locational factor	No. of towns	Percentage variation in population
A. Type of road	1. National highway	9	36.11
	2. State highway	12	26.71
	3. District and branch roads	75	34.43
B. Rail route	1. Yes	15	31.49
	2. No	58	33.53
C. Road link with the nearest city	1.. National highway	9	36.11
	2. State highway	12	26.71
	3. District highway	52	34.43
D. Rail link with the nearest city	1. Yes	15	31.49
	2. No	58	33.53
E. Distance from the nearest city	1. below 25 km.	1	37.19
	2. 26-50 km.	8	34.21
	3. 51-100 km.	28	29.21
	4. 101-200 km.	33	34.40
	5. 201 km. and above	3	47.11

growth rate (47.11%) was recorded by 3 towns located at a distance of more than 200 km. away from the nearest city, 33 towns located at a distance of 101-200 km. had a growth rate of 34.4%. Although no positive relationship can be established between growth rate and increase in distance from the nearest city, the fact emerges that of the 73 towns, 36 located at a distance of above 100 km. from the nearest city, had registered higher rates of growth than others, though one town located within 50 km. of the nearest city has achieved higher rate of growth and those also which are located at a distance of more than 100 km. But the number of such towns within distance of 50 km. is much smaller, only 9 out of 73 compared to 66 towns located at a distance of above 100 kms. from the nearest city.

Towns which are located on national highways have registered higher growth rates compared to those located on state highways or district and branch roads.

Of the 73 small towns, 15 are located on the rail route and have lower growth rate than such towns which are not located on the rail route. Of the 73 towns, 15 have direct rail links with the nearest city, 58 have no such links.

The analysis shows that the largest number of small towns are located on district or branch roads, have no railways, are not connected with the nearest city by rail and are located at a distance of more than 100 km. from the nearest city. Such towns have, by and large, exhibited higher rates of growth compared to such towns which are located on state highways, are located at a distance of 25 to 100 kms. from the nearest city.

Table 4.12 presents rural population and area served on average by a town in the region :

TABLE 4.12

District	rural population served per town		area served per town (sq. km.)	
	1971	1981	1971	1981
1. Mandsaur	63916	83888	816	816
2. Ratlam	89061	90335	972	811
3. Ujjain	92652	116328	1015	1015
4. Shajapur	100096	79494	1033	688
5. Dewas	71352	90724	1003	878
6. Jhabua	103165	121606	1130	1130
7. Dhar	126125	115355	1359	1019
8. Indore	76450	95820	780	780
9. Rajgarh	116513	87087	780	780
10. Vidisha	141388	162598	1843	1843
11. Bhopal	89764	106321	1386	1386
12. Sehore	152066	142378	2193	1645
13. Raisen	174086	106379	1822	1416
Malwa region	99033	101273	1202	1002
CV	29.57	22.48	42.35	32.69
M.P.		137128		1463

Rural population served on an average by each town comes to 10, 12, 73 in the region as a whole as against 137128 in the state. The town-rural population ratio is the lowest in Shajapur district (79494), followed by Dewas (80724) and the highest in Vidisha (162598) followed by Sehore (142378). The rural population served by a town has declined in all such districts where the number of towns has increased in 1981 over 1971, with the exception of Ratlam district, where despite increase in the number of towns by one, rural population served by a town, has increased and of Mandsaur where it has increased without change in the number of towns.

Area served per town in sq. km. in the region has declined from 1202 sq. km. in 1971 to 1002 km. in 1981 and has declined in all such districts, where the number of towns has increased. In 1981, the lowest area served by a town was in Shajapur district (688 km.), followed by Rajgrah (769 km.), Indore (780 km.) and the highest area served was in Vidisha district (1843 km.) followed by Sehore district (1645 km). The CV in respect of rural population served by towns and area served per town, of different districts in the region, has declined in 1981 compared to 1971, indicating narrowing down of disparities. But the number of towns in relation to population and area served, remains inadequate.

Sex Ratio

Sex ratio in urban areas in the region is higher than that of the state as well as the country. This may be due to the fact that cities like Bhopal, Indore, Ujjain and Ratlam, have gradually reached that stage where male migrants have brought their families with them. It is generally in newly emerging industrial towns and in project towns, that sex ratio is low in the initial period. The cities in the region have passed through that stage and now are well established.

The sex ratio in different size class of towns is indicated in Table 4.13.

In 1971, the sex ratio was the lowest in Class I towns and with decline in population size of towns, the ratio goes on increasing. But sex ratio registered an increase in Class I towns from 858 in 1971 to 884 in 1981, from 862 in 1971 to

TABLE 4.13

Size class	sex ratio	
	1971	1981
I	858	884
II	862	873
III	873	876
IV	920	907
V	912	922
VI	910	—
Malwa region	872	890

873 in 1981 in Class II towns. This shows that gradually the sex ratio in large towns get improved. In 1981, sex ratio was the highest in Class V towns, followed by Class IV towns. By and large, this ratio tended to increase with decline in the population size of towns. The inverse relationship between the size of population of town and its sex ratio is reflection of male selective migration into large cities. In small towns with greater interdependence with local economy, there has been higher sex ratio compared to larger towns.

There is not a single town in the region which has a sex ratio in the range of 600-700, 700-800 and above 1000. All towns in the region are placed in two ranges of sex ratio 800-900 (32 towns) and 900-1000 (59 towns). In the state as a whole, there are some towns in the lower ranges of sex ratio and also in the higher range of above 1000. Even Class I cities, with the exception of Bhopal (886) which are supposed to have low ratios have higher sex ratios than the state average, Indore (887), Ujjain (905), Ratlam (906). These are all well established towns with the exception of Bhopal which had a big spurt in its population since 1956, the sex ratio has tended to stabilise and improve. Industrial centres and mining towns and project towns have generally low sex ratios. Since the region is predominantly agricultural and has well-settled urban system, sex ratios have been improving over time. The lowest sex ratio was observed in the case of Mhow (814) which is a cantonment town, followed by Jhabua (945) which is located in tribal area and where some people from outside do not bring their families. Out of 84 towns in the region, 52 have sex ratio in the range of 900-1000 and 32 in the range of 800-900. Only 21 towns have sex ratio lower than the average of the region (890). Of these, two are Class I towns, 6 Class II towns. Nagada is a developing industral centre. Mhow and Neemuch are cantonment towns, Vidisha is an educational centre with large student population without families and Sehore, a town within the proximity of Bhopal. exhibit low sex ratios.

The Primacy Ratio

The primacy ratio is defined as the ratio of population of the largest city to the combined population of second, third and largest cities in the region/state.

The primacy ratios for the region and different regions of M.P. and the country are presented in the following table :

TABLE 4.14

Primacy Ratios

Country/Region	Index of primacy	
	1971	1981
1. India	0.56	0.46
2. M.P.	0.42	0.43
3. Malwa region	0.78	0.74
4. Eastern region	0.60	0.80
5. Inland eastern	2.70	2.9
6. Inland western	1.4	1.8
7. Northern	2.8	2.8
8. Western region	1.3	1.4

The primacy ratio in Malwa region is higher than the state as well as the whole country, but has declined from 0.78 to 0.74, whereas in the state, it has marginally gone up from 0.42 to 0.43. Of all the sub-regions of the state, Malwa region has the lowest primacy ratio in 1981. This is because of the fact that no other region has 4 Class I cities as this region has. The ratio is the highest in the inland eastern region where it has gone up from 2.7 to 2.9 between 1971-81. Similarly the ratio is also very high in northern region, (2.8).

Density of Population

The Malwa region has higher density of population compared to the state as a whole. The increase in density between 1971 and 1981 in the region has been much greater compared to the state. The CV of density among different districts of the region has increased from 43.64% in 1971 to 51.35% in 1981. The density has increased in every district of the region in 1981 compared to 1971. In 1971, density of population was lower than the state average in 4 districts out of a total of 13 districts comprising the Malwa region ; in 1981, five districts belonged to this category. Jhabua district had density higher than the state average in 1971, but in 1981, its density was marginally lower than the state average, other districts having density lower than the state average, were the same, in the two censuses viz. Dewas, Vidisha, Sehore and Raisen. In 1971, 9 disiricts had density lower than the average of the region in 1981, the number of such districts remained the same, indicative of increase in concentration of population. The CV reveals this fact. Indore district has the highest density (361) followed by Bhopal (323) and Ujjain (183), indicating a wide gap between the level of density of Indore and Bhopal on the one hand and that of Ujjain on the other. The lowest level of density was found in Raisen district, with density of only 84 in 1981, followed by Sehore (100) and Vidisha (106). The gap between the maximum level of density in the region in 1981 was more than 3 times, whereas in 1971 this gap was nearly 4 times. The higher the level of urbanisation, the higher the level of density, though there are exceptions to this. Indore having the second highest level of urbanisation in the region, had recorded the highest level of density in 1981. Bhopal district had the highest level of urbanisation in the region, with second rank in density of population. Raisen, Jhabua and Sehore districts had lower levels of urbanisation in the region and also lower levels of density. Districts which had higher density level but lower levels of urbanisation are: Shajapur, Dhar and Rajgarh.

Higher density level and higher urbanisation level generally go together in all cases.

Table 4.15 presents the data relating to levels of density and levels of urbanisation.

Literacy Rates

Malwa region being comparatively more urbanised, has higher percentage of literacy (29.19%) compared to the state (27.82%) in 1981. The literacy ratio has gone up from 24.36% in 1971 to 29.19% in 1981. The male literacy ratio has gone up from 33% in 1971 to 40.40% in 1981 female rate from 13.18% to 16.06% in 1981, compared to 39.38% for males and 15.53% for females in the State as a whole. The male literacy rate in urban areas was 64.9% as against 44.5% of female literacy rate in 1981.

Of the 13 districts, the highest literacy rate was found in Indore districts, 48.98% in 1981 as against 43.45% in 1971 and the lowest rate in Jhabua district, 10.99% for the total population and 15.54% for males and 6.78% for females, followed by Dhar district, the two tribal districts of the region.

In urban areas, the literacy rate was the highest in Indore district, 60.05% for total population, 68.94% for males and 50.7% for females, followed by Bhopal district, with 56.47% for total population 63.87% for males and 47.94% for females. Both these district are highly urbanised. The lowest literacy rate in urban areas was found in Raisen district, 45.91% for total population, 56% for males and 34.12% for females.

In rural areas, the lowest literacy rate was recorded in Jhabua district (7.01%) followed by Rajgarh (13.97%) and highest rate was found in Indore district (26.9%) in 1981.

The Table 4.16 shows the number of districts in different ranges of literacy rates in the two census years, 1971 and 1981.

The table shows that there has been slight mobility of districts from low literacy range to high literacy range in respect of rural population. In 1981, 2 districts were in the lowest literacy range of 0—15% in respect of rural population, whereas in 1971, 6 districts belonged to this category. With

TABLE 4.15

Density of Population and level of Urbanisation District-wise

District	Density of population		Level of urbanisation	
	1971	1981	1971	1981
1. Mandsaur	99	129 (7)	20.23	20.26 (5)
2. Ratlam	129	161 (4)	28.93	37.81 (4)
3. Ujjain	142	183 (3)	35.55	37.47 (3)
4. Shajapur	109	136 (5)	11.47	14.84 (8)
5. Dewas	85	113 (9)	15.96	18.71 (6)
6. Jhabua	98	117 (8)	7.31	8.32 (13)
7. Dhar	103	130 (6)	10.33	10.17 (11)
8. Indore	262	361 (1)	62.71	65.92 (2)
9. Rajgarh	105	130 (6)	9.59	13.08 (10)
10. Vidisha	89	106 (10)	14.11	16.97 (7)
11. Bhopal	207	323 (2)	68.62	76.26 (1)
12. Sehore	82	100 (11)	11.07	13.31 (9)
13. Raisen	66	84 (12)	5.56	9.97 (12)
Malwa region	110	141	24.64	28.52
M.P.	94	118	16.29	20.31
CV of the region	43.64	51.35	—	—

(Figures in brackets indicate ranks)

TABLE 4.16

Literacy range	1971			1981		
	Rural	Urban	Total population	Rural	Urban	Total population
0—15%	6	—	2	2	—	1
15 to 25%	7	—	6	9	—	5
25 to 35%	—	—	3	2	—	4
25 to 50%	—	10	2	—	5	3
above 50%	—	3	—	—	8	—
Total	13	13	13	13	13	13

regard to urban literacy rates, there has been considerable mobility from lower range to higher range. In 1981, 8 districts belonged to the range of above 50% whereas the number of districts in this range in 1971 was only 3. In 1981, 5 districts were found in the literacy rate range of 25-50%, but in 1971, 10 districts belonged to this category. Because of slow upward mobility of districts in respect of rural population, there has been slow upward mobility of districts in respect of total population. The number of districts in the lower range of 0 to 15% was reduced from 2 in 1971 to one in 1981, in the range of 15-25% also reduced by one, from six to five and in the range of 25-35 and 35-50 there has been increase of one district each. Not a single district was found in the literacy rate of above 50%, in respect of total population, though there were 8 districts in respect of urban population and only 3 districts in respect of rural population. Lesser number of districts in the higher range of literacy rate in the rural population has dampened down the literacy rate of the total population.

Occupational Characteristics of Working Force

The Table 4.17 presents the distribution of main workers in different districts of Malwa region.

Of the 13 districts comprising the Malwa region in 8 districts, the percentage share of cultivators in total workers, has increased, in two districts, viz. Jhabua and Dhar, the increase

TABLE 4.17

District	Cultivators 1971	Cultivators 1981	Agricultural workers 1971	Agricultural workers 1981	Total workers 1971	Total workers 1981	Workers in Household industries 1971	Workers in Household industries 1981	Other Workers 1971	Other Workers 1981
Mandsaur	63.12	61.86	15.81	16.80	78.93	78.66	2.58	2.33	18.49	19.01
Ratlam	53.19	53.10	18.80	17.67	73.99	70.77	3.25	3.04	24.76	26.19
Ujjain	41.61	41.28	24.40	23.18	66.01	64.46	3.51	3.47	30.48	32.07
Shajapur	48.54	50.73	32.10	29.40	80.64	80.13	4.18	3.05	15.18	16.82
Dewas	46.69	46.41	32.40	29.55	79.09	75.96	4.34	3.05	16.57	20.99
Jhabua	80.60	83.10	8.53	6.99	89.13	90.09	1.84	1.33	9.03	8.51
Dhar	58.11	62.23	26.85	24.32	84.96	86.55	3.15	2.17	11.89	11.28
Indore	20.08	19.34	16.22	16.53	36.30	35.87	3.12	2.86	60.58	61.27
Rajgarh	57.38	59.81	23.93	21.19	81.31	81.00	3,92	3.26	14.77	15.74
Vidisha	46.72	48.35	36.70	28.09	83.40	76.44	2.40	2.66	14.18	20.90
Bhopal	19.42	17.43	14.13	10.74	33.55	28.17	2.60	4.86	63.85	66.94
Sehore	47.91	49.06	34.12	30.87	82.03	79.93	4.24	3.51	13.43	16.56
Raisen	40.53	41.22	39.27	27.72	79.99	68.94	4.34	3.98	15.85	17.08
Malwa region	—	45.5	—	22.40	—	77.94	—	3.10	—	29.00
M.P.	52.86	52.10	26.56	24.17	79.42	76.27	3.84	3.80	16.94	19.93
Malwa region as % of M.P.	—	18.00		19.00				16.00		27.00

has been accompanied by decline in the percentage shares of all other categories of workers in four districts, Shajapur Rajgarh, Vidisha, Sehore and Raisen, at the cost of percentage share of agricultural labourers and workers in household industries. There has been marginal increase in the percentage share of household workers only in one district, Bhopal. In all other districts the percentages have declined. The largest percentage of total workers engaged as "other workers" was recorded in Bhopal district, nearly 67% in 1981 as against 64% in 1971, followed by Indore district (61.27%), and Ujjain (32.07). These are three relatively industrialized districts of the region. The lowest percentage of "other workers" was found in Jhabua district (8.58%), followed by Dhar district, the two tribal districts in the region. There has been decline in the percentage share of agricultural labourers in total workers between 1971-1981, with the except ion of two districts, Mandsaur, from 15.81% to 16.8% and Indore district from 16.22% to 16.53%. There appears to be no major shift in working force from agriculture to non-agricultural occupations. The only 2 districts, where non-agricultural workers predominate are Bhopal and Indore.

Malwa region is predominantly agricultural with 7 out of 13 districts having more than 76% (the state average) of main workers engaged in agriculture in 1981, as against 9 districts in 1971. The highest percentage of main workers engaged in agriculture was found in Jhabua district (90.09%), followed by Dhar district (86.55%), the two predominantly tribal districts of the region and the lowest in Bhopal district (28.17%), followed by Indore (35.87%), the two highly urbanised districts of the region. The percentage of workers in agriculture increased in Jhabua and Dhar districts between 1971 and 1981, but the decline is just marginal in Mandsaur, Shajapur, Rajgarh, Sehore and Ujjain districts. The decline is sharp in districts like Bhopal, Raisen, Vidisha, Dewas and Ratlam, where there has been increase in the percentage of "other workers" to total main workers.

No major change seems to have taken place in the occupational pattern of working force in the region. With the exception of Bhopal and Indore districts which are more urbanised, where more than 60% of workers are "other workers", in all other districts, majority of workers are engaged in agriculture. The pace of industrialisation in the region seems to be slow. In the last 20 years or so, much of industrial development in the state has taken place in the eastern and inland eastern regions which are minerally rich and where a number of mineral-based industries have come up. Malwa region has mostly agro-based industries, like textiles, sugar, edible oil, food products and chemicals, engineering and a few other footloose industries, like electrical equipment, plastic goods etc.

Scheduled Caste and Scheduled Tribe Population

The two districts, viz. Jhabua and Dhar are predominantly tribal, with 83.5% of total population being tribal in Jhabua and 52.06% in Dhar district in 1981. The other two districts where tribal population accounted for more than 10% of respective population of the districts are Raisen (15.5%) and Ratlam (22.6%). In other districts, the tribal population accounts for less than 1 to 7%. The 3 districts with sizeable population of SC population are Ujjain (24.00%), Shajapur (22.0%), Vidisha (20.5%). In other districts, SC population varies between 10 to 20% of total population of respective districts, with the exception of Dhar (7.00%), Jhabua (3.27%), the two predominantly tribal districts of the region. With the exception of these two tribal districts, SC population constituted a sizeable proportion of total population, varying between 13% to 24% of total population of the respective districts. In Malwa region scheduled castes constituted 14.10% of total population higher than the state average and scheduled tribes 16.0%, less than the state average.

Migration

Migration constitutes the very foundation of the process of urbanisation and is considered chief mechanism by which urban centres continue to grow. The population growth in an urban area depends partly on natural rate of growth of population (excess of births over deaths) and partly on migration from other areas-rural and urban. Prof. V.L.S.P. Rao[1] had distinguished between four types of migration zones along with their characteristics. These four zones are (i) distressed areas with small villages with no infrastructure and limited resource endowments and hence less developed. These settlements are the main source of out-migration (ii) Zone consisting of areas with resource potential and with some development but with limited infrastructure and with large villages. (iii) More developed but with low order infrastructure and small towns. Both large villages of zone and small towns have the potential of becoming "rurban" centres (iv) Highly developed and resource rich areas with cities and high order infrastructure. This is the zone of maximum pull from all the three zones. The migrant cities have strong industrial base with a developed tertiary sector. Zones (ii) and (iii) are potential areas for reverse migration, infrastructure and resource endowments are developed. First two are migration-source areas and the other two migration-receiving areas, two less developed and two more developed. It may be mentioned that clear-cut zonation gets blurred, as the different zones are drawn into the spiral of development through development planning and policy intervention.

Malwa region may conform to the third Zone which is comparatively more developed but with low order infrastructure under-developed districts also, with outmigration from rural and urban areas to bigger cities. The region has four Class I cities, Bhopal, Indore, Ratlam, Ujjain, which have been attracting people not only from rural areas but also from urban areas of the state, as well as outside the state. Agriculturally, the region is comparatively more developed than other regions of the state. The industrial centres in the region are Indore, Dewas, Ujjain, Nagada, Makshi and Ratlam. Bhopal being the headquarters of the state, is predominantly an administrative city and in that capacity, attracts migrants from all parts of the state. The eastern region which has the deposits of mineral ores and also forests and where metal based industries have come up, has recorded the highest rate of migration in the state. Bhilai, Korba, Satna, Katni, Sarni, were small rural centres but with the opening of mines, location of industrial units and thermal plants, these centres have become large urban centres with high rates of population growth, mainly because of migration. Taken as a whole, there seems to be no nexus between urbanisation and industrialisation in the state. Being predominantly agricultural state M.P. is a state of small towns, with strong tendency of migration from rural areas to these small and medium towns. The factor score on urban-industrial factors was negative in the case of M.P. (-0.509) and the state had 10th rank.[2]

Much of industrialisation is taking place in the eastern and inland eastern regions which are the mineral and forest zones of the state. Any development thrust in this region through highly capital intensive industries, may pull migrants from other areas. The industrial nuclei dominated by migrants, stand as enclaves of prosperity amidst poverty, contributing more to national development than to regional or local development.

The Malwa region accounted for only 18.8% of total rural migrants and 30.45% of total urban migrants in the State, according to 1971 census. The higher percentage of migrants of urban areas is mainly due to higher percentage of urban migrants to Indore (8.22%), Sehore (which included Bhopal at that time) 7.11% and Ujjain (4.16%). These three districts of the region are relatively more urbanised and industrialised. Of the 30.45% of total urban migrants of the state to this region, nearly 19% is accounted for by these three districts and remaining districts accounting for 11% of the total. Rural migrants to the region seem to be more well distributed among different districts of the region than the urban migrants. The largest percentage of rural migrant to the region is accounted for by Mandsaur district (2.14%) and the lowest by Indore district (1.04%). The pull of rural areas due to varied rural development appears to be very little in the region. The pull of urban areas appears to be more marked in respect of migrants to Indore, Bhopal, and Ujjain districts.

Classifying all the migrants in the region into rural and urban migrants, we find that 70.60% of all migrants to this region were of rural migrants and 29.4% urban, compared to 79.64% and 20.36% respectively in the state as a whole.

Of the total migrants in Malwa region, 45.6% were from rural to urban and 53.74% from urban to urban, as against

54.34% and 45.74 respectively in the state as a whole, indicating a higher percentage of urban to urban migrants in the region compared to the state. In districts like Dhar, Dewas, Shajapur, Rajgrah, Vidisha, Raisen, the percentages of rural to urban migrants were higher compared to other districts. In districts like Sehore, Indore, Ratlam, Ujjain, which are relatively more urbanised, a higher percentage of total migrants are accounted for by urban to urban migrants. This may reveal mobility of rural people to small towns and subsequently to bigger cities. Each of the four districts which accounted for higher percentages of urban to urban migrants have Class I city to which most of the migrations from urban areas take place.

Of the total rural migrants to urban areas in Malwa region, 65% are accounted for by short-distance migration, that is, within the district of enumeration, whereas this percentage in respect of urban to urban migrants was 33.5%. In the state as a whole, a much higher percentage (76.25%) is accounted for by migrants within the district of enumeration. In districts like Dhar, Dewas, Shajapur, Vidisha and Raisen, more than 70% of rural to urban migrations are, in the nature of short distance.

In the Malwa region, 65.37% of total migrants from urban to urban and 33.5% of migrants from rural to urban were accounted for by medium-distance migrants. In most of the districts, a small percentage of total migrants from rural to urban belong to the category of medium-distance migrantion. A much higher percentage of urban to urban migration belongs to the category of medium-distance migration. Migrants from rural to urban areas are mostly in the nature of short-distance but from urban to urban areas in the nature of medium-distance migration.

It is the urban pull that operates over medium and long distances. Short distance migration may be partly marriage migration, as the marriage market unlike the employment market is limited to adjacent areas.

Migration to Class I Cities in Malwa region

Let us now discuss some of the characteristics of migrants

to each of thefour Class I cities in Malwa region. The data relate to 1971 census. The pattern of migration to Class I cities follows more or less the pattern obtainable in the country.

In 1971, 49.1% of the total population of Bhopal city consisted of migrants, whereas migrants constituted 37.4% of Ujjain, 37.9% of Indore and 38.73% of population of Ratlam.* Bhopal being the capital seat of the State, has the largest percentage of its total population as migrants, where a large number of Government servants belonging to other places are posted and where also workers and employees from outside are working in Heavy Electrical plant and other industrial units.

In Bhopal city, male migrants accounted for 27.26% and female migrants 21.75% of the total population of the city. Of the total migrants to Bhopal, 55.63% were males and 44.37% females. Excess of males over female migrants has been the general pattern of migration to Indian cities. But surprisingly, in Ratlam and Ujjain cities, females exceeded the male migrants. In Ratlam, of the total 38.73% of population as migrants, 17.9% of total population were males and 20.83% females. In Ujjain male and famale migrants constituted 17.79% and 19.61% respectively of total population. Of the total migrants to Ratlam city, 46.22% were males and 53.78% females. In Ujjain 52.44% of total migrants were females and 47.56% males. In Indore city, male migrants accounted for 19.64% of population and females 18.29%. The percentage of male migrants to total migrants was 55.63 and of female migrants 48.22%. Only in Bhopal and Indore male migrants out-numbered females. The fact that a little more than 50% of female migrants in Ratlam and little more than 48% in Ujjain are non-workers, shows that female migrants are, by and large, dependent upon male migrants

* Migration to Class I Cities in India accounted for 38% of total population of these cities (1971). The million cities have 42% of the population as migrants, half a million cities have 31%, while the percentage increased to 39% for cities with less than half million population.

and have accompanied the male bread-earner to these cities. In Bhopal and Indore, where male migrants exceed female migrants, the percentages of non-worker females were 41.1% and 44.6% respectively. Another reason for higher percentage of female migrants in Ratlam and Ujjain may be the necessity to supplement income of families living in rural areas or smaller towns. The male members may stay in villages engaged in agricultural operations and females may migrate to the cities to eke out a living. In Ratlam 1.30% of female migrants and in Ujjain 1.76% were engaged in production activities. These percentages are higher than those of other two cities, where male migrants outnumber females.

The city migration stream is dominated by young adults, in Indore, 30.7% of total migrants belonged to the age-group of 15-29 and 45% to the age-group of 30-59. Both these age-groups which constitute the labour force, taken together accounted for 75.59% of total migrants to Indore. These two age-groups accounted for 73% of total migrants in Ujjain as well as Ratlam, but 65% in Bhopal. In Bhopal comparatively lesser percentage of migrants belonged to this age-group of labour force, may be due to the fact that a number of retired people have settled here and a large number of Government servants who constitute a large population of city population, after retirement settle down at Bhopal where they have built houses with the help of Government financial assistance.

Making occupation-wise analysis of the migrants, we find that a large proportion of migrants are non-workers in each of the four cities, non-workers accounting for 68% in Ratlam, 65% in Ujjain, 61.81% in Indore and 61.49% in Bhopal. Disaggregating non-workers into male and females, we find that in Ratlam, of the total migrants who are non-workers, 50.24% are females and only 18.7% males in Ujjain 48.12% females and 17.09% males. In Indore 44.65% females and 17.6% males and Bhopal 41.10% male and 20.4% males. Male non-workers in the age-group of labour force, may be indicative of unemployment in these cities. In Ratlam, the percentage of male non-workers in the age-group of 15-29, taken together comes to 6.31%, in Ujjain, the percentage was

7.42, in Indore 7.26% and in Bhopal 8.20%. The percentage of unemployment among male migrants was the highest in Bhopal (8.2%) and the lowest in Ratlam (6.3%). A large proportion of non-workers among the total migrants implics high dependency load of workers. Nearly 20 to 22% of total migrants to these cities categorised as non-workers belong to the age-group of 15-29 years. The percentage of non-workers exceed that of workers. This may be due to migration of children, females and old people along with the workers. These cities with the exception of Bhopal, have higher sex ratios compared to the sex ratios of all class I cities in the state (873). The fact that female non workers are more or less evenly distributed in the two age-groups, shows that most of the female migrants are accompanying their husbands.

Of the total migrants to Bhopal city, 14.07% were engaged in production related work including transport, followed by clerical and related activities (7.6%), service workers (4.83%), professions (4.47%). In Ratlam. 11.97% of total migrants were engaged in production related activities including transport, followed by clerical and related activities (5.7%) and service workers (3.64%). In Ujjain, 15.6% of total migrants were working in production related activities, followed by clerical related work (4.34%) and service were (3.27%). Indore being the industrial and commercial centre of the region has somewhat different occupational pattern of the migrants. Nearly 17% of the total migrants were engaged in production activities, followed by clerical and related work (4.35%) service workers (4.21%), sales workers (4.18%) and professions (3.46%).

The above analysis shows that migration stream of the cities of Malwa region is dominated by young adults, mostly illiterate, with a large proportion of non-workers which include married females, children, old people and also unemployeds. The incidence of unemployment appears to be quite high among the migrants as revealed by the percentage of non-workers in the age groups of labour force. In Ratlam and Ujjain, female migrants exceed the male migrants. This may be partly due to marriage migrations, partly to migration of educated females from rural and semi-urban areas to these cities in search of employment and partly due to rural female migrants in search of employment in urban areas. The urban economies of these cities have not expanded to the desired extent as to absorb all the migrants. The propensity of migration has increased with growing education. The location of large number of degree colleges in small towns has further increased the propensity to migrate. The principle of threshold has not been adhered to by the Government in the location of functions and facilities, with the result that a number of anomalies have crept into the location of these facilities. The poors are pushed out of the villages while the rich are pulled into the cities. Majority of the migrants to these cities are educated people, though the percentage of illiterate migrants may be in the range of 35% to 40% of the migrants.

The existence of four Class I cities in the Malwa region has led to large migration of people, particularly the educated ones from rural areas and small towns. The richer sections of the community like to migrate for reason of greater security in the cities. The pull of these four cities on rural population is considerable. Some of the small towns have been losing population in favour of these Class I cities. But 1981 census has revealed an interesting phenomenon that the rate of growth of these cities with the exception of Bhopal, has started decelerating. The publication of migration data of 1981, may reveal some significant facts relating to migration to these cities.

Conclusions

The following facts emerge out of the analysis of urbanisation trends in Malwa region :

1. The Malwa region has nearly 19% of area of Madhya Pradesh but 22.8% of total population, 26.6% of total rural population and 32% of total urban population of the state.
2. The region is comparatively more urbanised than the state as a whole as well as the country, the level of urbanisation in 1981 being 28.52% as against 20.3% in the state and 23.7% in India. Out of 14 Class I

cities in the state, the region accounts for 4, and out of a total number of 303 towns in the state, 84 are located in this region.

3. The decennial growth rate of urban population in the region has been the highest in the decade 1971-81 (49.71%) as against 29.17% of total population and 22.71% of rural population in the region. The rate of urban growth in the region has been lower than that of the state (56.07%). Though the region is comparatively more urbanised, the rate of growth of urban population in 1971-81 has been lower compared to other regions. This fact has led to convergence in the levels of urbanisation of different regions.
4. The region has well distributed urban settlement system and is agriculturally more developed than other regions, but not to the extent that it may yield a very high rate of agricultural growth.
5. There are wide variations in the levels of urbanisation in different districts comprising the Malwa region. Of the 13 districts, Bhopal district has the highest level of urbanisation (76.26%), followed by Indore (65.92%), Ujjain (37.47%) and Ratlam (30.8%) in 1981. Each of these four district contains a Class I city. The lowest level of urbanisation was in Raisen district (9.77%). In 1971-81, 7 districts have recorded growth rate of urban population higher than the regional growth rate. The highest rate was recorded by Raisen district (129.8%), a district with the lowest level of urbanisation. Next to Raisen, Bhopal district has recorded the highest rate of growth of urban population (77.9%), though the rate has slackened compared to the previous decade. There has been decline in urban growth rate in 1971-81 decade compared to the 1961-71 decade in Ujjain, Jhabua and Vidisha districts, where the number of towns has remained constant and slow growth was recorded in Ratlam and Indore districts. Raisen recorded the highest growth rate mainly due to increase in the number of towns from 3 to 6.
6. The growth rate of Class I towns has decelerated from

67.12% in 1971 to 52.15% in 1981. The Class II towns have manifested the highest rate of growth (177.9) in 1981 as against 97.36% in 1971. Partly this may be due to increase in the number of towns from 3 to 7.

To eliminate the impact of change in the number of towns on growth rate of population, we have attempted to present corrected rates of growth and found a wide divergence between the two corrected and uncorrected rates. In respect of Class II towns, the uncorrected growth rate of population between 1971-81 was 117.9% but corrected rate was only 37.09%. The co-efficient of variation between 1901-81 was 15.6% for corrected growth rate of Class I towns as against 74.2% for uncorrected rate 42.27% for corrected and 169.13% for uncorrected growth rate of Class II towns. Similarly CV for corrected and uncorrected growth rate of Class III towns was 66% and uncorrected growth rate of Class III towns was 66% and 143% respectively.

7. The predominance of Class I cities in the total urban population of the region is evident from the fact that 57% of total urban population in 1981 was living in 4 Class I towns. The percentage of population living in Class II towns has increased from 7 in 1971 to 14% in 1981. The percentage share of Class III towns has gone down and there has been only marginal increase in the percentage share of Class IV towns and a marginal decline in the share of Class V towns in the region. The average size of population of a town in this region is larger than the state as a whole and rural population is better served by towns compared to other parts of the state, though the position in this regard is inadequate.
8. The sex ratio in urban areas is higher than of the state as well as the country. This may be due to fact that cities have gradually stabilised and reached a stage when male migrants have brought their families with them.
9. The density of population in urban areas is higher than

the state and is generally higher in such districts where the level of urbanisation is higher.

This region being comparatively more urbanised, has higher literacy rate (29.2%) compared to the state (27.8%). Literacy rates increased in districts according to levels of urbanisation.

10. No major change has taken place in the occupational structure of working force in the region. With the exception of Bhopal and Indore districts, where more than 60% workers are "other workers" in all other districts, the majority is engaged in agriculture.

11. With increase in population size of towns, the percentage of male workers engaged in agriculture and household industries tends to decline and of non-household industries increases.

12. The Malwa region accounted for 30.45% of total urban migrants and 18.8% of total rural migrants in the state. The highly urbanised districts of the region, Bhopal, Indore and Ujjain, taken tagether accounted for 19% of the total urban migrants in the state and the remaining districts only 11% of the total. Rural migrants to the region are more well distributed than urban migrants. The pull of rural areas due to rural development appears to be very little in the region. Of the total migrants to Malwa region, 45% were from rural areas and 55% from urban areas and most of the urban migrants are medium distance. Rural migrants are mostly short distance migrations.

    Migrant population constitutes a large proportion of total population of four Class I cities in the region, 49.1% of Bhopal, 37.4% of Ujjain, 37.9% of Indore and 38.7% of Ratlam in 1971. The migration stream is dominated by young adults, mostly illiterate with a large proportion of non-workers. The incidence of unemployment appears to be quite high among the migrants, as revealed by the percentage of non-workers in the age group of labour force.

REFERENCES

1. Amitabh Kundu—Theories of city size distribution and Indian urban structure—EPW July 30, 1983.
2. V.L.S.P. Rao—Urbanisation in India-spatial dimension—p. 55-56.
3. V.I.S. Prakas Rao—Urbanisation in India-spatial dimensions—page 55-56.
   Factor scores of Maharashtra being 2.126, of Gujarat 1.631, of Punjab 1,244, T.N.O. 0.779 & of West Bengal 0.774.

CHAPTER 5

THE ECONOMIC BASE OF TOWNS

Towns and their Location

In the present study, five towns of Malwa region have been selected for detailed investigation. These towns are Dewas, Shajapur, Badnagar, Alot and Depalpur. These five towns are taken to be representatives of towns in the region, being located in the thick of the region under study. We have avoided taking towns located on the outer limit of the region because of frequent controversy regarding the boundaries of the region.

Of the five towns, Dewas has emerged as an industrial centre within the proximity of Indore and Ujjain. The other four towns are mainly market towns serving their respective hinterlands. Sahjapur and Dewas are the district headquarters, Depalpur is a tehsil headquarter in Indore district, Badnagar a tehsil town in Ujjain district and Alot also tehsil town in Ratlam district. Four of the five towns are located in such districts which have one Class I city each. Shajapur district does not have any class I city. In 1981, Dewas was a class II towns, Sahjapur and Badnagar class III towns, Alot a Class IV town and Depalpur a class V town. Thus towns, selected for this study belong to different size-classes. All the towns have urban local bodies in the form of municipal committees.

This size-class status of these five towns have undergone changes over time since 1901. Dewas was a Class IV town till

1931. It became a class III town in 1941 and remained so till 1961 census. It was in 1971 census that it attained the status of Class II town—a status which it continued to enjoy in 1981 census also. Increase in its population has been phenomenal since 1971. The status of Shajapur was improved from Class V town in 1901 to class IV in 1941 and class III in 1981, and that of Badnagar has fluctuated between Class IV in 1901, V in 1911 and 1921 and again reverting to class IV in 1941, remaining unchanged till 1971. In 1981, it became a Class III town. Alot attained the status of a town in 1931 census as a class VI town, but improved its status to class V town in 1941 and to class IV in 1981 census. Depalpur attained the status of a town in 1961 only as class VI town but improved its size to Class V town in 1971—a position which it continued to enjoy in 1981 census.

(1) **Depalpur**

Depalpur is located in such a tehsil of Indore district as has the lowest level of urbanisation, hardly 5 to 6% with a very low rate of growth of urban population, 38.6% during 1971-81, though the district in which the town is located, is one of the highly urbanised districts of the region as well as of the state. The Indore district where this town is located has the highest level of urbanisation, 66% in 1981 and recorded a decadal rate of growth of urban population of 44.1%. The higher level of urbanisation in the district is mainly due to Indore tehsil (85.5%) and how tehsil (46%). The other two tehsils of Indore district, viz. Depalpur and Sawer have very low level of urbanisation (between 5 to 6%). The number of villages in the tehsil increased from 174 in 1961 to 175 in 1971, and 181 in 1981. The town presents a case of an urban settlement located in the least urbanised tehsil but highly urbanised district of the region. Depalpur is the only town in the whole tehsil. The rate of the growth of total population of the tehsil is less than that of district. The town belongs to the category of class V towns, with a population of 8,343 in 1981. Earlier to 1961, the settlement was not a town. The nearest railway station is at a distance of 20 km. and the nearest city is Indore at a distance of 41 km.

TABLE 5.1

Location of Towns

S. No.	Name of the town	Name of Tehsil & Head-quarter	Name of districts & Districts H.Q.	No. of Villages in the Tehsil			Distance of towns from		The nearest city	Distance from the nearest city in km.	Nearest Railway station	
				1961	1971	1981	Teh. H.Q. in km.	Dist. H.Q in km.			Name	Distance in km.
1.	Dewas	Dewas	Dewas	241	243	243	0	0	Indore	35	Dewas	0
2.	Shajapur	Shajapur	Shajapur	362	362	362	0	0	Ujjain	60	Bercha	17
3.	Alot	Alot	Ratlam	195	195	195	0	82	Ratlam	82	Alot	0
4.	Depalpur	Depalpur	Indore	174	175	181	0	41	Indore	41	Gotampura	20
5.	Badnagar	Badnagar	Ujjain	192	193	193	0	50	Ujjain	50	Badnagar	0

TABLE 5.2

Location of Towns and their growth rate of population along with growth rate of population of Tehsils and districts

	Town	Tehsil/ Distt. location	Decennial growth of population of town 1971-81	TEHSIL					DISTRICT				
				% of urban to total population		Decennial growth rate 1971-81			% of urban to total population		Decennial growth rate of population		
				1971	1981	T	R	U	1971	1981	T	R	U
1.	Dewas	Dewas/ Dewas	60.7	32.3	35.8	44.8	37.1	60.7	15.9	18.7	33.7	39.3	56.7
2.	Badnagar	Badnagar/ Ujjain	19.3	15.99	15.55	22.6	23.2	19.3	35.5	37.5	29.4	25.5	36.4
3.	Shajapur	Shajapur/ Shajapur	34.8	11.19	15.12	26.0	20.5	70.3	11.4	14.8	23.8	14.1	60.2
4.	Alot	Alot/ Ratlam	42.0	16.55	17.59	23.98	19.5	34.7	28.93	30.81	25.3	21.7	33.2
5.	Depalpur	Depalpur/ Indore	38.6	5.73	6.3	26.3	25.5	38.6	62.7	65.9	37.1	25.3	44.1

TABLE 5.3

Change in Classification of towns (1901—1981)

Size-Class of Town

Town	1981	1971	1961	1951	1941	1931	1921	1911	1901
1. Dewas	II	II	III	III	III	IV	IV	IV	IV
2. Shajapur	III	III	IV	IV	IV	V	V	V	V
3. Badnagār	III	IV	IV	IV	IV	IV	V	V	IV
4. Alot	IV	IV	V	V	V	VI	—	—	—
5. Depalpur	V	V	VI	—	—	—	—	—	—

TABLE 5.4
Growth of Population
1901 to 1981

Town	1901	1911	1921	1931	1941	1951	1961	1971	1981
TP	15403	15285	14970	16810	22949	27879	34577	51866	83356
Dewas	—	– 0.77	— 2.06	12.29	36.52	21.48	24.03	50.00	60.71
PG									
TP	9953	8876	7894	7766	10757	13832	17317	25189	33968
Shajapur									
PG	—	—10.82	—11.06	11.62	38.51	28.69	25.20	45.46	34.85
TP	10856	8634	8543	10531	11985	15219	17177	20057	23923
Badnagar									
PG	—	—20.47	— 1.05	23.27	13.81	26.98	12.87	16.77	19.28
TP	—	—	—	4691	5678	8125	8343	10134	14394
Alot									
PG	—	—	—	–	21.04	43.10	2.68	21.47	42.04
TP	—	—	—	—	—	—	4673	6018	8343
Depalpur									
PG	—	—	—	—	—	—	—	28.78	38.63

TP : Total Population
PG : Population Growth

(2) Dewas

Dewas town is a fast growing industrial centre within the proximity of Ujjain and Indore on Ujjain-Indore road as well as rail-route. Of all the five towns, it has recorded the fastest rate of growth of population between 1971 and 1981. It is the only town in the whole tehsil. In the district as a whole, Dewas tehsil is the most urbanised, with a level of urbanisation of 35.8% in 1981, much higher than the level of urbanisation of the district (18.7%). Other tehsils in the district have level of urbanisation varying between 10 to 15%. The growth rate of urban population in the tehsil (60.7%) was higher than that of the district, solely due to growth of Dewas town which is the only town in the tehsil. The tehsil also recorded higher rates of growth of total and rural population than the district. Dewas has improved its status in the urban hierarchy from Class IV town in 1901 when its population was only 15,403 to Class II town in 1981 when its population was 83,356. Between 1901-1961, it was slow growing town, but since 1961, its growth has been phenomenal, its population has more than doubled between 1961 and 1981, mostly due to its rapid industrialisation. Being the seat of district administration and also located on the national highway and rail route, the tertiary sector has also grown at a fairly higher rate.

Dewas town was the headquarter of a small princely state till its merger in Madhyabharat—a "B" state, in 1952. In 1956, it became a part of new state of Madhya Pradesh. Since then its growth has been substantial. Between 1971-81, the number of towns in the district has increased from 7 to 8. Dewas presents a case of a growing industrial city sandwitched between two class I cities, Indore and Ujjain, having more linkages with these two rather than with its hinterland. Because of variety of concessions a number of industrial units have come up in the town which has an advantage of being located near to Indore, hardly 35 kilometres away.

(3) Shajapur

It is a small town of 33,968 population, having district headquarters, not connected by rail, but is on the national highway-Agra—Bombay road. The nearest railway station in

Bercha, at a distance of 17 km. Till 1931, it was class V town, with population declining between 1901 and 1931. It attained the status of class IV town in 1941, became a class III town in 1971, a status which it continues to enjoy in 1981. It is typically a slow growing town in the region. The rate of its population has decelerated from 45.46% during 1961-71 to 34.85% in 1971-81. The town had recorded negative rates of growth in 1911, 1921 and 1931 and slow rates of growth subsequently. The town is located in one of the least urbanised tehsil (15%) as well as district (14.8%), but with slow growth rate of rural population and very fast growth rate of urban population, indicative of high rate of rural to urban migration. The number of towns in the district increased from 6 in 1971 to 9 in 1981. This may be another factor accounting for higher urban growth rate in the district. The hinterland of the town is predominantly rural. Of all the 5 tehsils where selected towns are located, Shajapur tehsil has the largest number of villages, 362 in each of the three censuses.

(4) Badnagar

Badnagar is another slow growing town in the region. It is located in Ujjain district, one of the most urbanised districts of the region. It is located on the national highway and also on rail route and is the seat of tehsil headquarters. Its population has just more than doubled in 80 years between 1980-81. It is the slowest growing town included in the study. Between 1971-81, it registered a decadal growth rate of 19.28% and between 61-71 a rate of growth of 16.77%. Till 1921 it has manifested a negative growth rate. It is located in one of the least urbanised tehsils but highly urbanised district. The tehsil has recorded a higher growth rate of rural population compared to that of urban population as well as total population. The nearest city is Ujjain, at a distance of 50 km.

(5) Alot

Alot town is located in Ratlam district which has Ratlam as a class I city. It attained the status of a town in 1931 when its population was only 4,691, a class VI town. It became a class V town in 1941 and remained to till 1961. In 1971 it became a class IV town and continued to remain so in 1981 when its population was 14,394. The town has shown a comparatively faster growth rate during 1971-81 decade, when it recorded a growth rate of 42% as against 21.5% in the earlier decade. It lies on Ratlam-Kota rail route and is connected with Ujjain by a fair-weather road. The level of urbanisation in the district is fairly high (30.8%), mainly because of Ratlam tehsil (50%) in which Ratlam, a Class I city is located. Alot tehsil has a level of urbanisation of nearly 18% with a rate of growth of rural population of 19.5% and of urban population of 34.7% in the decade 1971-81. The tehsil presents a case where the rate of growth of rural population is very slow compared to both total and urban population. The hinterland of the town has very slow growth of population. The number of towns in the district has increased from 5 to 6. The number of villages in the tehsil has remained the same, 195 in each of the last 3 censuses. The town is located at a distance of 81 km. from Ratlam, the district headquarters.

Five towns selected for detailed investigation belong to different size-class of towns in different districts, some of which are highly urbanised, other are least urbanised, some of which are growing at faster rate, others manifesting a very slow growth rate.

Dewas presents a case of a fast growing town on account of industrial development, Alot and Depalpur are very small towns with less than 10,000 population each, but growing at a fairly fast rate. Shajapur is a town with district headquarters but its growth rate has decelerated during 1971-81 and in the period earlier to that has been fluctuating. Badnagar is a very slow growing town in the Ujjain district. Three towns are located in districts which are comparatively more urbanised, each with one Class I city but are located in such tehsils which have very low levels of urbanisation. Dewas tehsil has higher level of urbanisation than the district. Shajapur is located in the least urbanised district of the region.

Sex Ratio

Table 5.6 presents sex ratios for the five towns. Of the five towns, Dewas has shown the lowest sex ratio of 886 in

1981. Being an industrial town, the sex ratio has shown a decision from 899 in 1971 to 886 in 1981. The sex ratio tends to increase with decline in the population size of town, indicatting the fact that very small towns have higher sex ratios Depalpur which has the lowest population size among the towns included in the present study, has the highest sex ratio-935. The sex ratios in these towns conform to the general pattern obtainable in the state.

Literacy Rate

The literacy rates in these towns ars higher than the state. These rates tend to decline with decline in size population of the towns. It is the lowest in Depalpur (41.06%) and the highest in Dewas (51.94%). The male literacy rates are much higher than the female literacy rates, though female rates are increasing faster than male rates. The lowest rate of increase in male literacy rate has taken place in Badnagar, from 58.01 to 58.84 in 1971.

The Occupational Structure

With the exception of Dewas, other towns have fairly large proportion of working force engaged in primary activities as cultivators and agricultural labourers. With decline in population size of the towns, the percentage of workers engaged in primary occupations, goes on increasing. Small towns belonging to class IV and V are outgrown villages where urban local bodies have been created by the State government and, therefore, these settlements have attained the status of urban areas, though most of the characteristics of population are rural in character. In Depalpur which is the smallest town in the present study, nearly 42.3% of total working force is engaged in primary occupations. In Shajapur, Badnagar and Alot also, more than 20% of working force was reported to be engaged in primary sector. There is predominance of "other workers" in toal working force in these towns. These "other workers" include workers engaged in tertiary activities, administration, trade and commerce, transport and professional services.

TABLE 5.6

Sex Ratio

Town	Size Class	1971	1981
Dewas	II	899	886
Shajapur	III	887	903
Badnagar	III	901	906
Alot	IV	952	931
Depalpur	V	939	235

These towns are either block/district headquarters and in that capacity Government functionaries are posted at these towns. Moreover, these towns with the exception of Dewas, are playing the role of market towns for their respective hinterlands.

Even a casual visit to these small towns shows that they do not have many of the urban characteristics. They become urban because of the administrative decision of the state Government to create municipalities in these towns. These towns are functionally too weak to support even the natural increase in population. The phenomenon of rural functions invading these towns is manifest almost everywhere, leading to a new pattern of rural-urban relations and interactions. The economic base as we shall see later on, is weak. The production-oriented functions are few. The tertiary sector provides the maximum employment and within this sector informal sector predominates.

Apart from the roadsides, all vacant spaces are invaded and occupied for rural land uses. In these vacant spaces, one finds buffaloes, cows and goats. The excreta of cows and buffaloes are converted into cakes for cooking. In most of the localities, not all the houses have latrines. Old and young, males and females defecate outside their houses. The pigs come from time to time clean up the defecation but in turn release their own excreta which remains there to be spread around by men and animals passing that way. Thus judged by all standards, these small towns are mostly outgrown villages, with a few urban functions.

The Economic Base

Urban centres irrespective of their size, cannot be studied in isolation from their hinterlands, because they constitute a part of the whole system of settlements, and therefore, are considered an organic part of the system. This considrration leads to the space relationships of the towns. Mark Jafferson observed that the growth of town took place in response to the demand of services and functions from other places when he stated, "Cities do not grow of themselves. The countryside sets them up to do tasks that must be performed in central places."[1]

Christaller developed the idea on scientific lines in his Central Place theory. Edward Ulman introduced Christallers' work of central places to the English speaking world in 1944. "The essence of central place theory is that a certain amount of productive land supports an urban centre. The centre exists because essential services must be performed for the surrounding land."[2] These linkage are not only service type but the city also looks back for its needs towards the surrounding countryside.

The array of functions, services and other economic activities constitute the economy of the region or of the urban centre. It is possible to disaggregate these functions and economic activities into various groups which may well be referred to as the sectors of the regional or city economy. But this classification of economic activities leaves many questions unanswered, such as where the services and products are consumed and how the consumers are distributed over space. It is possible that services and goods produced at the region or in the city, may not be entirely consumed there. A part may get consumed within the territories of production and another part may be consumed by the consumers living outside the territorial limits of the city or the region. This implies that a certain part of goods and services supports local population and the other part supports non-local population.

Therefore, there exist two sectors in the economy in relation to space relationships between location of producer and location of consumer. By and large, in every city, a portion of the economic effort is supported by non-local demands. The difference between these two sectors of the economy is of fundamental importance, because the former brings money into the city and constitutes city foundation. Jafferson termed these two sectors as basic and non-basic, whereas the former brings income and forms the economic base of the city, the latter, serves the city people and simply involves exchange of money within the city.

The concept of city's economic dichotomy has been recognised as early as in 1921 by Aurousseau[3] as primary and secondary occupations. The New York Regional Planning Committee prepared a regional survey of New York in 1927 and termed the activities as primary and ancillary. Later Hartshorne[4] in 1932 used external functions and internal functions of similar break-up of economic activities. Homar Hoyt in 1939 used urban growth and urban services and later in 1947 regional and local markets by Dickinson for the basic and non-basic-activities. The basic concept remained the same that of division of the urban economy into two sectors, one which brings inflow of income to the city other which serves the city.

Methods for Base Identifications

A number of methods has been employed for the identification of the basic and non-basic sectors of the ecoeomy of the city. The simplest arbitrary method applied to the base identification is that of assuming all the primary and manufacturing activities as basic and all service industries regarded as non-basic. In such a classification, export and local consumption are not considered.

The second method of location quotient (LQ) having greater relevance, is the ratio of employment of the region to the national employment. If the ratio is greater than unity it is taken as basic activity and the workers more than unity are surplus workers producing for exports only.

Homar Hoyt[5] (1939) was perhaps the first who gave a scientific method of measuring the basic non-basic work force by developing a residual method. In this method, the basic activities work force is exclusively identified and subtracted from the total. The remaining workforce is considered occupied in basic and non-basic activities into 1 : 1 ratio, and the residual is assigned to the basic.

Another method of base identification is known as "macro cosmic method" where the local percentage shares in each occupational group are compared with national percentage shares. Any surplus more than national average is considered as basic activity with an assumption that equivalent percentage to the national average is sufficient for city serving only and surplus is engaged in the production for exports.

An additional method of identification of local economic structure is "sales employment conversion method". In this method, the sales of all industries are divided into local and non-local and the employment of the industries is also considered in the same ratio to find basic employment against exports or non local sales, non-basic as the local consumption or local sales.

Still another method was developed by Alexanderson[6] (1959) where after arranging the percentages in a particular industry for all the towns in ascending order, the 5th percentile item from the upper end of the array is considered the minimum requirement to extend the services to the local population. Percentage crossing this minimum requirement is considered basic employment of the city. The same method was further developed by Ullman and Dacey[7] by calculating the minimas by the least square method.

Mattila and Thompson[8] proposed an index of surplus workers which can be used both for classification of cities and for the identification of their economic base on the basis of surplus workers engaged in different activities.

The economic base of a town or region is not only associated with the work force but also reflects the regional character. Thus considering the regional economy, the land use and cropping pattern diversification of agriculture and specialisation with specific crop-mix, would give insight into understanding the small towns because they are basically the collection centres of surrounding areas producing agricultural goods.

Basic Identification of Malwa Towns

Considering Malwa region as predominantly an agricultural region, the problem is considered in the regional context and at the local level of the town. It has been discussed under the sub-heading (i) regional economic base, where the level of development of the surrounding region to the towns is considered in respect to agricultural production, area under different uses, cropping pattern, intensity of land use and irrigation, technology used in the production process. Regression lines for their growth trends have been drawn with a time series analysis.

(ii) Specialisation and diversification of the agriculture is particularly considered. Diversification is measured with reference to intensity of land use, irrigation, area under superior crops and area under commercial crops. Specialisation of crops of the region have been identified by method of Rafiullah.

(iii) The basic and non-basic activities are identified on the basis of 1971 and 1981 census data for ten occupational groups.

(iv) Lastly, the infrastructural development of the region is also considered as an index of strong regional economic base.

At the town level, the base identification is done on the basis of employment groups provided by 1971 and 1981 census and the functions and services available at the town place.

Regional Economic Base

It is assumed that the level of regional development at the nodal region of the town forms the economic base to the city and the region together. The levels of development measurement exercise is quite difficult as it employed the techniques like factor analysis and the principal component analysis. Since the sample size in the present study is very small (only five towns), it is not possible to employ these techniques. Therefore, selected variables like production, yield and area under different superior and commercial crops have been taken in time series, with a view to finding out whether there is any growth or decline taking place in the surrounding regions of the towns. Pulses constitute the highest percentage share of area under different crops. Badnagar tehsil has 29.74%, Depalpur 29.74%, followed by Dewas 18.63, Shajapur and Alot have lower percentage area under pulses 13.93% and 19.35% respectively. The co-efficient of variation is also high in the areas with lower percentages. This means that pulses are grown more consistently in Badnagar, Depalpur and Dewas. The higher percentage of area under pulses, is followed by wheat. Once again the same rank order is maintained in terms of area under wheat crop, as under pulses. Depalpur, Badnagar and Dewas have higher percentage of area under wheat—29.06%, 20.26% and 20.77% respectively compared to 8.28% in Shajapur and 6.35% in Alot. Alot tehsil has the largest percentage area under fibres and fodder. Shajapur tehsil leads other tehsils so far as the area under oil seeds is concerned (16.03%). By and large, the area put to total fruits and vegetables and oil seeds is very less. None of the tehsils cross the 1 percent level of area under fruits and vegetables and so is the case with oil seeds barring Shajapur. The Table 5.1 shows that regional base of these five towns is food-grain based. A significant area, more than 50% is put to wheat plus pulses in Badnagar, Depalpur and Dewas, the other two tehsils also account for nearly one-third of the gross sown area. Commercialisation of agriculture has not gone to a larger extent. In general, there seems to be consistency among all the tehsils in respect of total fruits and vegetables and the total oil seeds. Area under fibres shows the highest level of variability.

Table 5.7 and 5.8 present intensity of land utilisation for different crops and irrigated area. The intensity is calculated by simple ratio.

$$I = \frac{\text{Gross area sown}}{\text{Net area sown}} \times 100$$

The variables—intensity of cropping and intensity of irrigation may well represent the level of regional development as these represent a number of socio-economic and institutional factors.

TABLE 5.7

Intensity of Cropping

$$IC = \frac{\text{Gross Area Sown}}{\text{Net Area Sown}} \times 100$$

Year Name of Tehsil	Shajapur	Depalpur	Badnagar	Alot	Dewas
1970-71	106.90	107.05	108.09	108.44	105.75
1971-72	109.32	106.40	107.05	110.33	108.44
1972-73	106.53	105.55	106.56	107.78	104.68
1973-74	112.54	106.56	108.39	114.67	108.91
1974-75	108.51	107.14	106.95	113.49	108.77
1975-76	112.33	109.45	109.20	113.63	111.63
1976-77	111.19	110.76	111.93	114.90	112.16
1977-78	111.47	113.76	111.29	114.02	114.68
1978-79	112.50	115.66	113.29	128.30	118.13
1979-80	114.49	118.33	118.27	128.46	115.18
1980-81	NA	115.80	117.22	116.22	115.05
X	110.50	110.59	110.75	115.48	111.22
CV	2.27	3.93	3.52	5.72	3.67

TABLE 5.8

Intensity of Irrigation

$$11 = \frac{\text{Gross irrigated Area}}{\text{Net irrigated Area}} \times 100$$

Year Name of Tehsil	Shajapur	Depalpur	Badnagar	Alot	Dewas
1970-71	108.62	107.50	100.67	103.53	110.80
1971-72	103.85	105.66	101.59	108.73	111.32
1972-73	104.76	102.00	101.65	100.23	108.51
1973-74	102.83	103.33	100.39	131.53	105.97
1974-75	103.26	106.12	100.86	102.36	109.26
1975-76	102.86	101.59	100.73	100.36	107.25
1976-77	102.78	101.49	101.16	102.69	106.67
1977-78	101.71	101.22	100.68	113.88	106.86
1978-79	102.96	101.06	100.64	111.91	105.26
1979-80	103.01	101.02	100.48	113.78	106.14
1980-81	103.13	100.88	100.69	101.13	102.40
X	103.62	102.90	100.86	108.19	107.31
CV	1.67	2.23	0.40	8.28	2.28

Intensity of cropping of all the five tehsils has steadily increased though the increase is not significant. It has increased from 105-75 in 1970-71 to 115.05 in 1980-81 in Dewas, from 106.9 to 114.49 in Badnagar and from 107.05 to 115 in Depalpur during the same period. In all the tehsils, the intensity of cropping, though slowly rising, is not so high as to warrant any significant change in land-use pattern. The co-efficient of variation of intensity of cropping in different tehsils over the period 1970-71 and 1980-81 is very low, 2.5% in respect of Shajapur and 6.6% in case of Alot. .

This analysis shows that hardly 11 to 15% of sown area in these tehsils gives two crops in a year. The intensity of cropping in the whole State was 115 in 1978-79 and for the whole country, it was 123. Punjab has the highest intensity of 159, followed by Haryana (151). This shows how much leeway the region has made to catch up the present levels of Punjab and Haryana and the all-India average.

There has been decline in the intensity of irrigation between 1970-71 and 1980-81 in all the tehsils where towns selected for detailed study are located. There is hardly any increase in area irrigated more than once. In certain years, there has been increase in irrigation intensity in Dewas and Alot tehsils but in Shajapur, Depalpur and Badnagar, there has been only marginal increase in some years. The intensity of irrigation in the whole state is also very low, only 104 in 1978-79. This means that two crops are irrigated only on 4% of the irrigated area. The low intensity of cropping is mainly due to low intensity of irrigation. Extension of irrigation, no doubt, is very important, but it is equally essential to raise the capacity of existing sources of irrigation, with a view to increasing irrigation intensity. From the point of view of both these indicators, viz. cropping intensity and irrigation intensity, the five tehsils seem to have low level of development. Foodgrains account for major area under cultivation and that too is mostly rain-fed. Commercialisation has not taken place to any significant extent, though in recent years there has been increase in area under commercial crops.

Irrigation is mostly used for growing foodgrains. More than 50% of gross irrigated area is accounted for by cereals

TABLE 5.9

Percentage irrigated area under different crops to Gross irrigated Area

Name of the Tehsil	Year	Rice	Wheat	Other	Total food crops	Gram	Other	Total Pulses	Sugar cane	Other food grains	Total food grains	Til-han	Other crops
Dewas	1965-66	0.69	1.46	2.07	4.22	1.31	0.54	1.84	66.13	26.19	98.39	0.00	1.61
	70-71	0.83	57.50	0.72	59.05	7.91	0.91	8.82	16.73	14.38	98.98	0.11	0.91
	75-76	0.01	53.68	0.20	53.90	14.95	0.67	15.61	17.72	12.31	99.54	0.04	0.42
	80-81	0.08	59.56	0.33	59.97	17.61	0.39	18.00	11.20	6.26	99.43	0.05	0.50
Shajapur	65-66	1.72	9.62	0.62	11.95	8.12	1.10	9.22	33.75	38.42	93.34	0.31	5.91
	70-71	0.53	53.40	0.16	54.11	16.43	0.00	18.33	8.37	23.30	97.67	0.08	2.13
	75-76	0.17	59.71	0.09	59.97	23.42	0.00	23.92	7 62	0.00	99.44	0.07	0.29
	80-81	0.06	44.77	0.12	44.95	41.21	0.63	41.84	4.11	0.00	99.23	0.32	0.05
Alot	65-66	0.04	34.87	7.33	42.24	10.37	0.26	10.64	23.56	0.00	94.21	0.04	0.00
	70-71	0.00	39.87	2.41	42.28	3.84	0.22	4.06	12.38	0.00	78.34	0.05	0.00
	75-76	0.00	43.23	1.56	44.97	4.97	0.14	5.11	14.69	13.25	83.31	0.02	6.68
	80-81	0.00	50.15	0.74	50.89	11.81	0.10	11.90	5.61	19.93	88.33	0.17	0.00

Depalpur	65-66	0.15	3.07	2.04	5.26	1.46	1.31	2.77	57.96	29.05	95.04	0.00	4.96
	70-71	0.23	71.68	0.32	72.23	3.01	0.32	3.34	16.08	7.48	99.13	0.12	3.06
	75-76	0.00	95.91	0.35	56.26	21.04	0.42	21.46	12.46	8.57	98.74	0.02	1.24
	80-81	0.01	66.77	0.27	67.05	19.44	0.46	19.90	4.99	5.95	97.88	0.10	0.00
Badnagar	65-66	—	—	—	—	—	—	—	—	—	—	—	—
	70-71	0.03	54.78	1.54	56.36	3.95	1.07	5.02	14.43	18.62	94.44	0.00	5.56
	75-76	0.02	39.65	1.07	40.74	18.88	1.98	20.86	16.57	15.98	94.16	0.27	5.57
	80-81	0.01	43.71	2.02	45.74	22.08	2.44	24.52	4.63	13.93	88.82	0.69	10.48

in all the tehsils, followed by pulses in the range of 13% in Alot to 41.8% in Shajapur in 1980-81. Thus a large part of gross irrigated area is accounted for by foodgrains taken as a whole, as revealed by Table 5.9.

Table 5.10 shows the least square regression equations fitted for finding out the growth rate trends. The least square estimates of regression co-efficients have been calculated on the assumption of linear relationships. The table shows that there is constant steady positive change in area under total fruits and vegetables and area under total pulses. The variability explained by co-efficient of determination (R^2) value is also higher in case of fruits and vegetables. The co-efficient of B values are positive for pulses for all the tehsils but the co-efficient of determination value is very low explaining very less variability.

During the last decade, the area under fibres has declined significantly as the B values are also very low in the inverse direction. This means the area has been shifted from fibres to pulses and fruits and vegetables. Shajapur, Alot and Badnagar show a positive B value for oilseeds while Dewas and Depalpur show a decline in area put to total oilseeds.

Area under wheat also has hardly moved in positive direction. Rather, there seems to be shift of area under wheat to pulses and other crops. Only Shajapur tehsil shows a positive B value which is not all significant. Fodder shows a mixed pattern as Badnagar and Shajapur have shown positive regression co-efficients and other three tehsils show a negative relation and the regression co-efficients.

TABLE 5.10

Area under Superior Crops

FODDER

				r	R^2
Alot	26.2012	−1.9356	Xj	−0.54	0.2922
Badnagar	2.1139	+0.8230	Xj	0.83	0.6909
Depalpur	56.4338	−5.5700	Xj	−0.84	0.7064
Dewas	4.4739	−0.1418	Xj	−0.09	0.0084
Shajapur	−1.9989	+41.8991	Xj	0.74	0.5409

WHEAT

				r	R^2
Alot	9.2716	—0.4283	Xj	—0.33	0.1091
Badnagar	17.8038	—0.4869	Xj	+0.59	0.3500
Depalpur	16.6534	—0.3706	Xj	—0.42	0.1761
Dewas	6.0019	—0.0001	Xj	—0.36	0.1308
Shajapur	5.5869	+0.0411	Xj	+0.08	0.0070

TOTAL PULSES

				r	R
Alot	—1.6649	+0.4090	Xj	0.47	0.2209
Badnagar	1.3432	+0.1441	Xj	0.40	9.1640
Depalpur	—2.1632	+0.2323	Xj	0.35	0.1225
Dewas	0.0283	+0.2130	Xj	0.34	0.1124
Shajapur	—3.5713	+0.5995	Xj	0.73	0.5350

TOTAL OIL SEEDS

				r	R^2
Alot	—9.0274	+20.0608	Xj	0.63	0.3919
Badnagar	2.6007	+0.4354	Xj	0.32	0.1009
Depalpur	6.8571	—0.1117	Xj	0.09	0.0097
Dewas	13.9126	—0.1.1455	Xj	08.3	0.6835
Shajapur	4.9112	+0.0804	Xj	0.07	0.0044

TOTAL FRUITS AND VEGETABLES

				r	R^2
Alot	—9.0274	+120.0608	Xj	0.63	0.3919
Badnagar	—11.9295	+34.2403	Xj	0.92	0.8404
Depalpur	—13.1776	+37.4696	Xj	0.69	0.4769
Dewas	—3.8769	+11.6199	Xj	0.85	0.7183
Shajapur	—12.5998	+38.7766	Xj	0.69	0.4769

TOTAL FIBRES

				r	R^2
Alot	13.9823	—0.7143	Xj	—0.51	0.2602
Badnagar	11.2769	—1.3174	Xj	—0.79	0.6326
Depalpur	9.5659	—2.8800	Xj	—0.83	0.6917
Dewas	8.6514	—1.8048	Xj	—0.89	0.8092
Shajapur	13.0166	—0.6976	Xj	—0.96	0.9156

Thus the variability accounted by time variable has explained the variability among fruits and vegetables and the area under total fibres. The co-efficient of determination of pulses has been very low. It can well be said here that slowly commercialisation is picking up as revealed by increase in area under pulses, fruits and vegetables. During the last decade, wheat is showing very slow decline although insignificant and this area is being shifted to other crops.

The regression equations show that in respect of wheat, there has been a declining trend in area but the decline is marginal as the best fit is not significant for any of the co-efficients. The change in area under fodder is significant in Badnagar and Shajapur in positive direction and in Depalpur negative direction. A significant growth in area under total pulses is apparent in all the tehsils, but Shajapur manifests the highest growth. Area under oilseeds is significant in positive direction in Alot and in negative direction in Dewas.

The positive growth in fruits and vegetables area and clear decline in area under fibres in all the five tehsils, is significant as the R^2 values are quite high for all the tehsils.

Agricultural Specialisation of the Region

Specialisation of agriculture generally means the types of crops grown with specific combinations, the amount of area put and the variety of crops grown. The simple techniques may be used, "ranking of crops" and Rafiullahs' crop combination methods, although a number of other techniques have been deployed for finding such specialisation of functions and crops. Nelson made a rational classification of American cities in 1955 by using simple but useful techniques of mean and standard deviation to compare the local work force with the national norms. He took specialisation to third level by taking mean plus three standard deviation percentage.

Similarly, J C Weaver (1953) used standard deviation and gave a critical combination of crops in which a region specialises. The method extended by Weaver was critically analysed by an Indian Geographer SM Rafiullah (1965) who suggested one improvement to the Weavers' methods. Rafiullah's method is used in this study for finding out the combinations of crops in which the region has specialisation.

The method suggested by him is :

$$6=\sqrt{\frac{\Sigma Dp^2-\Sigma Dn^2}{n^2}}$$

Dp=Sum of positive deviations

Dn=Sum of negative deviations

N is the crops included in the combination.

Ranking of Crops

If the area assigned to the first few crops is ranked and the first three crops are taken, they may well represent the crop specialisation of the region. In case of Malwa, the first three rank crops in 1970-71 were : (See Table 5.11).

The first three ranking crops given in table 5.11 present a very interesting picture. The first rank crop in 1970-71 was wheat in the case of Dewas, Badnagar and Depalpur, while in Alot and Shajapur, jowar ranked first. In 1980-81, the inferior crop Jowar has ranked first in all the tehsils except Depalpur. That means the change-over to rainfed crops is once again taking place in the absence of growth of area under irrigation. The second rank crop, gram at Badnagar is replaced by wheat, jowar is replaced by wheat which ranks first in Dewas in 1981 and the commercial crop cotton which ranked second in Alot and Shajapur is replaced by gram and groundnut in 1980-81.

Jowar, cotton and gram occupy third rank compared to fodder, jowar and wheat in 1970-71. Wheat which occupied third rank in 1970-71 in Shajapur tehsil, does not find any place in the first three ranks. Gram has been relegated to third rank in Dewas, Badnagar and Shajapur in the second period. Wheat has lost its rank to jowar in three tehsils, Dewas, Badnagar and Alot.

Crop Specialisation (after Rafiullah)

The crops in Malwa region are not grown in isolation from each other. The first three crops are predominantly grown in their combinations. The critical combinations also show, by and large, combination of three to four crops grown in com-

VII Trade and commerce	— 44.2	— 69.8 (1.98)	— 527.4	200.9 (2.29)	163.7 (1.88)	260.5 (4.50)	831.5 (8.09)	968.5 (12.44)	—1454.7	—120.1
VIII Transport storage and communication	—248.7	—161.6	— 332.9	— 324.0	—213.8	—237.1	55.5	105.2	— 802.1	—284.3
IX Other service	2352.8	—451.6	4689	471.5	2538.3	2514.9	5361.7	3141.1	1872.8	—354.6
Total surplus										

Formula used : $S = ei \frac{et}{Et} Ei$

Where Total working force of Tehsil
ei=In occupational concerned
et=Total working force of Tehsil in all occupations
Ei=Total working force of state in occupation concerned
Et=Total working force of state in all occupations

TABLE 5.14

Basic, Non-Basic Employment in Towns

	ALOT		SHAJAPUR		BADNAGAR		DEWAS		DEPALPUR	
	1961	1971	1961	1971	1961	1971	1961	1971	1961	1971
I Cultivators	—1604.5	—1001.1	—3176.3	—2852.1	—3106.8	—2173.0	—6429.9	—6120.7	—767.7	525.5
II Agriculture Labourers	— 462.3	— 554.0	— 865.8	— 936.6	— 856.9	—1062.1	—1726.5	—2656.7	—238.9	—204.4
III Livestock Forest Fish Hunting etc.	56.9 (2.75)	25.7 (1.64)	26.7 (0.66)	— 41.1	110.5 (2.79)	—4.2	—76.6	— 102.4	70.8 (7.40)	55.3 (7.47)
IV Mining quarying	—	— 14.1	—	—	—	—	—	— 76.2	—	—
Va Manufacturing process HH Ind. Industries	274.3 (13.27)	222.4 (14.17)	483.7 (11.97)	129.9 (3.35)	789.3 (19.91)	287.7 (8.76)	500.7 (6.08)	970.9 (10.84)	145.2 (15.18)	117.3 (15.84)
Vb Manufacturing process other than HH Ind.	264.3 (12.79)	107.5 (6.85)	373.7 (9.25)	338.3 (8.74)	421.3 (10.63)	611.0 (18.61)	1546.7 (18.79)	1999.2 (22.33)	63.2 (6.61)	63.4 (8.56)
VI Construction	65.4 (3.16)	22.9 (1.46)	234.9 (5.81)	145.2 (3.15)	65.7 (1.66)	55.5 (1.69)	269.9 (3.28)	291.1 (3.25)	38.7 (4.05)	6.6 (0.89)
VII Trade and Commerce	424.2 (20.62)	415.1 (26.45)	341.7 (18.35)	1066.5 (27.54)	935.6 (23.60)	1024.2 (31.19)	1449.6 (17.61)	1339.6 (14.96)	164.7 (17.74)	198.7 (26.83)

VIII Transport Storage & Commerce	68.2 (3.30)	107.8 (6.87)	81.1 (2.01)	189,4 (4.89)	184.2 (4.65)	89.3 (2.72)	432.1 (5.25)	469.7 (5.25)	11.3 (1.18)	23.1 (3.12)
IX Other service	913.5 (44.20)	657 9 (42.56)	2100.2 (51.96)	2002.6 (51.72)	1457.2 (36.76)	1215.9 (37.03)	4034.2 (48.99)	3882.5 (43.37)	462.7 (48.39)	276.3 (37.30)
Total surplus workers										

Formula used : $S = ei - \frac{et}{Et} Ei$

Where

ei=Total working force of Town in occupation concerned

et=Total working force of Town in all occupation (I to IX)

Ei=Total workIng force of State in occupation concerned

Et=Total working force of State in all occupation (I to IX)

pective shares in total basic sector. This surplus labour force becomes further diversified in 1971 by including construction, trade and commerce and livestock, forestry, fishing etc. Badnagar tehsil also has a very similar trend in 1961 but the tehsil got more diversified in the sense in 1971 that though the major share comes from agricultural workers and other services, other sectors also contributed to basic sector of the economy.

In Depalpur also, three sectors in the both the years, 1961 and 1971, constituted equal shares of labour force from agricultural labourers, household industry and other services. In 1971, livestock replaces the "other services." Dewas tehsil is the most diversified in the basic occupational structure and the major share of surplus labour comes from secondary and tertiary sectors. This is mainly due to the fact that Dewas town has emerged as an important industrial centre.

The Economic Base of the Town

The surplus labour index is calculated for the five sample towns with a view to identifying the Economic base of the towns. As expected the contribution of surplus labour force among all the towns comes from all the occupational groups in tertiary and secondary sectors. All the towns of Alot, Shajapur, Badnagar, Dewas and Depalpur, irrespective of their size variability, show that the major share of basic sector or the surplus labour is contributed by "Other services" varying between 36.76% and 37.03% for Badnagar, 52% for Shajapur for the years, 1961 and 1971. This share of surplus labour force from service sector has declined marginally in 1971 compared to 1961.

Trade and commerce rank second in the surplus labour share in all the towns, but the share does not cross the 30% level for both the census years. Other sectors in order of their contribution to the basic labour force are household industry, manufacturing other than household industry, transport and communications and construction. Except Dewas, all other towns have a marginal contribution of livestock, forestry, fishing, hunting etc.

Contribution to the basic sector of all the occupational groups show diversification of the town economy. Almost all categories of economic activities contribute to the town economy. This implies that services and goods produced at the towns are surplus and the towns export outside the territories of the boundaries of their economies.

Dewas being the largest in size and also being the most industrialised town among all the towns, has the highest number of workers as surplus. It has also quite large surplus labour force in manufacturing other than household also. Alot and Depalpur show the minimum surplus labour among all towns. This is obvious because the size of surplus labour in absolute numbers will be the result or will be in proportion to their size continuum. Thus smaller towns have lesser number of workers compared to larger ones.

Urban Functions

An attempt has also been made to identify those functions which have made towns distinct from other settlements. The number and complexity of the functions vary with the size of the towns and with other variables including the nature of areas which they serve. Some of the functions are ubiquitous in all towns of a given size. These towns perform what Christaller terms as "central place functions." We have not applied the central place theory, only some aspects of the theory and the concept of population threshold have been examined. In this context a number of functions has been chosen to examine the central role of the towns in Malwa region.

Of the 5 towns included in the study only one, Dewas, has emerged as industrial node but the functional and occupational character of other towns clearly shows that diversity in functions and specialisation in manufacturing is absent.

Since a number of functions are performed by urban local bodies, let us first examine the role which municipalities are playing in these towns, by way of providing functions and facilities. Local bodies lack financial resources to build up infrastructure, particularly when the size of population is very small. In many cases, the threshold is so small that a number of functions like protected water supply under-ground sewerage, fire brigade, cannot be provided by any of these towns. The civic bodies are not equipped to serve their residents either organisationally, financially or technically. Most of them like to play safe by adhering to customary budgeting and civic practices for combating the problems faced by them. There has been no attempt at improving the services or at creating a new infrastructure. The land-use pattern is the legacy of the past which has today resulted in redundant lanes and bylanes and the inability of main markets to expand.

In the case of small towns, the contribution of commutation spillover in creating "minimum threshold" or minimum sale volume have helped in setting up comparatively large firms producing/selling product for rural communities. In these five towns, it is estimated that commuters constitute nearly 5 to 10% of towns population. In Dewas a Class II town and fairly industrialised nearly 10,000 people are estimated to enter the town daily. The spill over is equal to 10 to 13% of resident population of Dewas. In other smaller towns, commuters may be in the range of 2 to 5 thousand daily. These spillovers offer an assured market for particular products. In short, commuters spillovers have generally contributed to the overall growth of towns by shaping the initial investment size and by generally expanding and diversifying the investment base.

Spillovers in small towns are mostly one-way i.e. to the small towns. Commutations take place from surrounding villages. Unlike in the case of a big city, it is a feature of rural-urban interaction. For selling their produce, buying essential commodities and for sharing a wide range of service and amenties, such as health care, education, recreation and services of the state departments, an extra population may enter daily in the small towns. A unique situtation is created by such spillovers in a poorly provided small town. Ill-built and ill-maintained roads open spaces are crowded by people. There is unauthorised use of roads and public places leading to unhygienic conditions. The wells which are the only source of drinking water in the small towns, are exposed to dust. An enriched rural sector can transmit growth to the private sector in a small town and quickly produce a set of multiplier effects. But the town economy does not improve because of inadequate resource at the disposal of civic bodies.

Shopping Facilities

The number of shops in a town largely depends upon population of the town and of the adjoining areas having linkages with the town, the income level of the people and the functional characteristics of the towns. Dewas is the largest town amongst those included in the present study and has emerged as a fast growing industrial town. Number of shops per 1000, dealing in textiles, grocery, eating establishments, is the largest. In Dewas, the largest number of shops per 1000 of population are in respect of grocery, followed by textiles, kerosene and vegetable oils and eating establishments. This is quite consistent with the daily needs of the people. In Shajapur, the same pattern is obtainable, in Alot, surprisingly, the largest number of shops, followed by textiles and grocery. In Depalpur, grocery shops account for the largest number per 1000 of persons, followed by tea-shops and such shops which deal in vegetable oil. Badnagar has the least number of shops per 1000 population, dealing in textiles.

Warehousing

Warehousing facility is another important function which the towns are expected to provide to the rural areas. The warehousing capacity available in these towns is given in Table 17, Dewas, being the district headquarters and also being the largest town with more than 80,000 population, has the largest storage capacity of 12593 tonnes, followed by Shajapur with a capacity of 2157 and Badnagar with a capacity of 1680 tonnes. Depalpur has the lowest capacity with 417 tonnes.

Greater storage capacity is indicative of greater linkages of rural hinterland with the towns.

Traffic and Connectivity

The connectivity of a town depends upon its location and its transport network with other places. Dewas is located on Agra-Bombay national highway and also on rail-route (Ujjain-Indore). It is connected with Bhopal, Ujjain and Indore by rail and road route. It is a big transport node—a bus junction for a number of routes. Fifty five buses daily originate from the city and an equal number of buses terminate here, out of 260 buses going out of the town and an equal number coming into the city daily. All these buses pass through the town. All buses connecting Indore and Ujjain with Bhopal and towns beyond Bhopal have to pass through Dewas. Shajapur is another big transport centre, daily 79 buses go out of the town and an equal number enter the town, of which 46 terminate or originate from the town.

In other three towns, the number of originating-terminating buses is very small, between 3 to 5 but number of buses passing through the towns daily is quite large, 36 in Alot, 40 in Depalpur and 23 in respect of Badnagar. These towns are on important bus routes, therefore, are well connected with other towns.

Dharmshalas, Hotels and Lodges

Larger the number of people spillover to a town from neighbouring areas for availing of functions and facilities, the greater is the need for hotels and lodging places. Each town has rest house, Dewas 3, Alot 3, Shajapur 2 and Depalpur and Badnagar one each. Rest houses are generally meant for Government officials of different departments coming to the town on official tours. They are not made available to private persons. Dewas and Shajapur have 8 dharmshalas each, Dewas with 250 beds capacity and Shajapnr with 200 feds capacity. Of these five towns, Dewas has the largest capacity in the form of dharmshalas, hotels/lodges and rest houses. This is due to the fact that it is the district headquarter and an industrial town. A large number of people come from outside daily on business. Depalpur is an outgrown village with a population of less than 9,000. It does not have any lodging facility, except a rest house provided by the Government. Villagers from adjoining villages generally do not stay overnight. They leave the town well in time to reach their respective villages before dusk. Badnagar and Alot have two dharmshala each, though Shajapur has a capacity of 200 beds, Alot has a capacity of only 32 feds. Alot and Depalpur do not have a single private hotel or lodge.

Recreational Facilities

Cinema is a function of higher order located where there is threshold population. Generally a population of 30,000 is regarded as threshold for a cinema to make it economically viable. Even if town does not have this much population, it can have a cinema, provided population of adjoining villages avail of this facility. Of the five towns under study, Dewas is the largest. It has 4 cinemas with 1880 seating capacity and the number has gone up from 1 in 1970-71 to 4 in 1980-81. Shajapur is the other town with a population of 24554 which has 2 cinemas with 900 capacity. The town itself cannot provide threshold population for two cinemas but the neigbouring villages must be availing of this function at the town. Badnagar with a population of nearly 24,000 has one cinema with a capacity of 400 seats and Depalpur and Alot one temporary cinema each with a capacity of 400-500 seats. Badnagar and Dewas have 2 playgrounds each, whereas other towns have one each. Badnagar has four libraries, Dewas three and Shajapur and Alot two each and Depalpur one. These are small libraries either run by the municipal committees or by private agencies which give books on hire. Dewas has 3 parks/gardens, Shajapur and Alot two each and Badnagar one and Depalpur does not have a single.

Medical Facilities

Towns being central places of higher order provide medical facilities to their own population and also to the surrounding areas. Since this function is mostly provided by the Government and is non-commercial in nature, the threshold norms have not been adhered to. A higher order central place may have functions of lower order. Dewas has the largest number of medical institutions, one civil hospital, 3 dispensaries, 2 primary health centres, two maternity and child welfare centres, two family welfare centres, 29 private doctors and 160 beds in the hospital. Medical facilities have relationship with population size. Each of the five towns has hospital run by the Government, one dispensary, primary health centre, maternity child welfare centre, the facilities provided by the

Government. But no private practitioner would set up his practice unless the threshold is there. Next to Dewas, medical facilities provided by the private sector are available at Badnagar, followed by Shajapur.

Educational Facilities

Education is another function which is performed at different levels from primary school to post-graduate colleges. A centre of higher order may also have a number of functions of lower order central places. Dewas has 13 primary schools with 4955 students in 1980-81 compared to 12 schools in 1970-71 with 3603 students. These are figures of recognised schools, there may be many more unrecognised schools in the town. The number of middle schools has increased from 8 in 1970-71 to 12 in 1980-81 and of higher secondary schools from 3 to 4 in the same period. Dewas has two post-graduate colleges, one in arts and science and another in education.

Dewas has 12 middle schools, Shajapur 8, Alot 2, Depalpur 3 and Badnagar 6. The number of middle schools does not bear any relationship with the number of primary schools. Each town has higher secondary schools, Dewas has 4, Shajapur 2, Alot one, Depalpur one and Badnagar 2. Shajapur and Badnagar have degree colleges, though the threshold may not be there. Location of functions and facilities in the state has taken place according to the pressures of politicians and not according to economic criteria.

The above analysis shows that five towns of Malwa region do not have adequate functions and facilities to sustain their own population. The financial resources of local bodies are very scanty to make any marked improvement in the civic life of the residents.

REFERENCES

1. Jafferson, M. (1931) "The distribution of the world's city folks : A study in comparative civilisation." Geographical Review Vol. XXI p. 453—1931.
2. Ullman, E.L. "A theory of location of cities" American Journal of Sociology. Vol. 46, 1941, pp-853-64.

3. Auroeesseau M. 1921—The distribution of Population: A constructive problem, Geographical Review Vol. VI p. 574.
4. Hartshorne, R (1936)—New map of manufacturing belt of North America, Economic Geography Vol XII pp. 45-53.
5. Weimer, AM and Hoyt H (1939) Principles of Real Estate—New York.
6. Alexanderson G (1959)—The industrial structure of American cities, Lincoln Nebrasha and Stockholm.
7. Ullman E.L. and Decey M.F. (1960)—The minimum requirement approach to the Urban economic base—Papers and proceedings of the Regional Science Association—Vol 6.
8. Mattila JM and Thompson (1955)—The measurement of economic base of the Metropolitan area, Land Economics Vol. 31, p. 215.

CHAPTER 6

URBAN–RURAL INTERACTION

In this chapter, we present the zone of interaction of each of the five towns selected for detailed study. The hinterland of each town has been demarcated on the basis of linkages as revealed by movement of people for availaing of functions and facilities made available in the towns.

Human settlements are very often distinguished as rural and urban, though this distinction is sometimes blurred and, therefore, appears to be arbitrary. Many of the small towns are outgrown villages and exhibit most of the rural characteristics. There is considerable rural urban interaction, as revealed by the movement of people and goods and services. Despite all this, we classify settlements into rural and urban on the basis of some criteria laid down in the census and then try to identify linkages between the two.

In its economic aspects, urbanisation mainly relates to movement of people out of agricultural communities into non-agricultural communities. It is related to economic development. The urban economy depends upon rural for the supply of foodgrains and raw materials and also provides market for urban produced goods. Similarly the rural economy depends upon urban economy for employment of its surplus labour, for sale of agricultural and other products, for exchange of goods. There are social, cultural and economic linkages between the two. If one economy is injured the other cannot remain healthy.

The urban centres develop in a regional setting, and in the process develop strong relations with the surrounding countryside and competing and complementary urban centres. The interaction arises and intensifies on account of these relationships in a regional setting. The interaction takes place through certain paths. The distance produces the frictional effect on the movement which restricts it to a large extent. In this regard, the effect of distance on movement has been recognised at all levels of development since the work of Ravenstein in England and Andersson in Sweden at the end of the 19th century. Hagerstrand[1] in 1957 and Isard[2] in 1960 discussed relations between distance and volume of migration in details.

As the interaction involves the movement of both people and commodities, it is expected that both consumers and producers keep this movement minimum, other things being equal, the consumers tend to move to the nearest. On this principle of minimum effort Christaller[3] based the Central Place theory, which Loesch[4] later developed as complex economic landscape. Zipf[5] developed this principle scientifically in social sciences as the principle of least effort. Huff[6] has suggested that a consumer's preference for visiting one shopping centre or another varies with his value system and psychological drive, the way the alternatives are perceived. According to him, proximity of facilities does not alone determine consumers' interaction field and people from different social and cultural background have different patterns of spatial behaviour. The conclusion is further supported by Murdie[7], showing how cultural differences may affect interaction fields by considering the differences in shopping behaviour between "modern" and "old" Canadians. Baumol and Ide[8] have suggested that the willingness of consumers to travel various distances is related not only to the cost of travel but also to the difficulty of shopping at various centres. VL Prakasha Rao[9] has studied recently the consumer travel pattern in Morna Block located to the east of Muzaffarpur and showed how some rich consumers skipped over lower order settlements to make purchases from higher order settlements.

Despite all these modifications, the basic principle of Christaller and Losch could not be refuted. The higher order functions at higher level central places do have larger interaction fields than lower order functions, and hence the interaction fields also vary according to the size of settlements.[10] The interaction field of towns though influenced by many factors is mainly influenced by frictional effects of distance. The distance restricts the movement of people and goods. Near the market centres, the interaction will be the highest and as the distance increases, the interaction falls. This is known as the lapse rate and is dicussed at length by Helvig[11] and Zipf.[12] Helvig shows that the number of truck trips is associated with distance.

Dahl[13] found a general fall off of movement with the increasing distance. He mapped movement of population, passenger traffic, telephone traffic, news paper circulation, business contacts, rail trade contacts and goods traffic for town of Vastera (Sweden) with the rest of the country.

The rural-urban interaction is a two way traffic. The city extends its services and functions to the countryside and forms a zone of interaction or the sphere of dominance. In turn, the country-side provides the labour force, the day-to-day requirements of agriculture and dairy products. The rural urban interaction is of considerable interest to both Indian and foreign scholars.

William Skinner[14] in a study of marketing in rural China views rural-urban relations as a link of rural areas with urban economies through a series of market relationships that get mainfested in regional frame. Johnson[15] considers that in a primarily agricultural community, agriculture and trade in agricultural products are the most important factors for the identification of rural urban interaction.

Several methods have been deployed to measure the interaction between rural and urban areas and to delimit the maximum limits of interaction fields. The interaction can best be measured in terms of actual shopping trips made by consumers at various distance. The number of trips made by individuals gives the level of interaction of a settlement with the market place. The interaction fields may be delimited empirically as well as mathematically. The fields of individual functions may easily be plotted on the map and by taking the origin of the consumer at varying distances. Thus the catchment area may be defincd by taking the outermost boundaries of the places from where the consumers are derived. These functions and services may be selected by taking into account the nature of the region and the urban centres. The general interaction field may be taken as outer-most boundaries of all functions together, irrespective of the functions or the medium line of these tributary areas. By taking the central functions and services and possible aspects relating to the interaction, Bracey[16] studies the spheres of influences of centres of Somerset. He circulated a questionnaire to every settlement in Somarset from which it was determined which towns were used for each of the services. Smails[17] argues that the zone of interaction of all services in the city (hospitals, schools, cinemas, etc.) and the trading areas of all the commercial activities have to be considered together at the same time. Green[18] and Carruthers[19] defined the hinterlands of towns of England and Wales on the basis of overall flow of traffic based on the frequency of bus serivce.

The interaction between the market places or urban centres has often been described in mathematical form also to explain the fall off or lapse rates. The models explaining the lapse rates are classified into two types : (i) models which are based on physical analogies and (ii) models which are empirical attempts to generalise the detailed findings in mathematical form. A very good review of such models may be seen in Reif[20] and Haggett.[21]

The most important borrowings from physical science by geographers are the gravity and absorption analogies. The gravitational theory of Newton was taken by Reilly[22] who applied to the market centres and developed the "Law of Retail Gravitation" which is condidered to be the earliest contribution to marketing science. The gravity model suggests that the interaction between two places would be proportional to the product of their populations (masses) and inversely proportionate to the square of distance separating these points. It may be expressed mathemetically as :

$$Mij = P_i P_j \ (Dij)^{-2}$$

Where Mij is the intcraction and $P_i P_j$ are the measure of mass of the two centres (often population) and Dij is the distance separating these centres. Later this model was applied by Steward[23] and Zipf[24] to a wide range of social phenomena with modification to the original formula. To measure the influence or the interaction of an intermediate centre with the nearby higher order centres would be proportionate to the sizes of the two centres and the inverse proportion to the square of the distances from these two centres to the intermediate place. This may be written as :

$$\frac{Ti}{Tj} = \frac{Pi \ (Di^{+2}}{Pf \ (Di)}$$

Ti and Tj interaction of intermediate centres with i and j centres, Pi Pj as defined above and Di and Dj distance of i and j from the intermediate centre. Later this law of retail gravitation was transformed in "Break point" equation by Converse.[25] The Break point from the centre j may be calculated from the formula :

$$Dj = Dij/1 + Pi/Pj$$

Dj gives the breaking point from centre j, Dik, Pi and Pj are defined above. The break points calculated with all the towns in all directions when joined with smooth line give the urban interaction zone of a centre. Later the model was used in various modified forms by using different indicators of mass and distance of the centre.

Another physical analogy used in the interaction lapse rate is that of absorption. Johnson suggested that migration from a centre might be like the rate of light. Light is absorbed in space in proportion to flow per unit of distance and in the same way migrating population may be thought to be absorbed in the areas into which it moves. Curve fitting is still another approach. Kant suggested in study of migration Pareto type formula :

$$M = aD^{-6}$$

a and b are estimated constants with reference to migration and distance.

Hieff[26] later proposed one probability model. The probability contours are drawn for the centres on the basis of probability of visiting a particular centre by a consumer. The probability of a consumer declines for visit with the increasing distance. The contour of equal probability may be taken as the separating point of interaction between two competing centres.

The Case Study of Malwa Region

In the present study five representative towns of Malwa have been selected for the measurement and determination of interaction between the urban centres and the surrounding countryside. The concept of lapse rate or general fall off has been tested by taking a variety of variables in relation to socio-economic stratification of the rural society. The interaction fields have been determined for all the towns empirically and later are compared with the theoretical boundaries, drawn with the help of break point concept discussed earlier.

In the case of identification of rural-urban interaction, it is assumed that the towns particularly the small towns, by and large, do not interact with surrounding countryside. The countryside hardly takes the advantage of functions and facilities available at the centres. The facilities available at these centres are hardly adequate to serve the population of the town itself. The villagers visit these towns only to purchase their household commodities like sugar, oil, grains, clothes, etc. They generally mix these shopping trips with the sale of agricultural produce. When they come to sell their agricultural produce, they make most of the purchases of household needs. Secondly, it is further assumed that the interaction of these towns is lopsided and only a particular section of rich farmers, visits the town or interact with the towns more frequently. The poor peasants or landless labourers hardly interact with these market centres. These small towns hardly provide any employment opportunities to the landless labourers who migrate in search of employment.

There seems to be two clear-cut reasons for this poor rural urban interaction in the towns under study. Firstly, the urban economy of these small and mediume towns, is hardly developed and secondly, the intervening opportunities restrict the interaction to a large extent. We have already seen in previous chapter that municipal expenditure on functions and facilities is deplorably poor.

If we look from the historical perspective at these towns, we find that they were not developed as service centres. These towns were used by the British rulers as instruments of exploitation of their respective regional economies. Either these centres were collection centres of agricultural produce or natural resources like forest or mineral. After independence also the same political economy was pursued and these centres were neglected comparatively in locating the central functions, though these centres have the potentialities of developing interaction with their respective hinterlands. Even today most of the small and medium towns are 'mandi' towns and are acting as collection centres of agricultural produce. Most of these towns are tehsil headquarters and lack basic functions and facilities. If at all we want to develop these towns, necessary conditions have to be created at these centres so as to develop strong regional linkages vertically as well as horizontally.

The second constraint on the development of interaction of these towns with surrounding country-side is the invervening opportunities which the villagers get in the form of "Haat," the periodic markets. Most of the poor class people satisfy their demands in these haats which are held at a fixed interval of time. These haats are held in such a manner that they cover the entire region within a week or fifteen days. Thus, the lower order goods are made available at these periodic markets and only for higher order goods, people move to nearby towns. The rich and the well-to-day by-pass small towns and may go to larger towns to make their purchases. Mostly haats are held at central villages which act as the lowest order market centres in the region.

Trip Making

In the process of interaction two factors are involved in the movement of people and goods. These are distance travelled and mode of transport used by the consumers. The frequency and purpose of trips for obtaining various consumer goods and services is revealed by interview of 51 heads of families coming from different villages in each of five towns included in the study. The majority of the villagers are farmers and they, by and large, come with their bullock carts and use this mode of transport. This is because they come to sell agricultural produce and make purchases also. In Shajapur town about 16% villagers come from a distance of less than 5 kms. and 5 to 10 kms. each, about 55% visit the town from a distance of 10 to 20 kms. 41.4% villagers visiting the town use bullock cart, 17.6% use their tractors and 13.76% use both tractors as well as bus. Only 6% people come on foot and they too from a distance of less than 5 kms. Other modes of transport used are bicycle, bus, bullock cart and bus both. Majority of the people in Alot come from a distance of less than 10 kms. Nearly 66% come on bullock carts. A very similar travel pattern and mode of transport used by villagers may be seen at Depalpur, a very small town. About 50% use bullock carts and come from less than 10 kms. distance. The mode of transportation is similar in Badnagar town, 56% using bullock carts. Dewas being comparatively bigger in size and also being an industrial centre, draws consumers from greater distance. Nearby 70% of the villagers come from more than 10 kms. distance. Lesser percentage come by bullock carts. Nearby 13% use bus service, 18.5% use tractors, 11.1% use bicycles.

The transitional stage in the transformation of agriculture from traditional to modern, is well brought out by the co-existence of different modes of transport. Bullock carts are the most frequently used mode followed by bicycle. Movement by tractors is an innovation, particularly for passenger movement.

The consumers were classified by ownership of land holdings and mode of transport used. This analysis shows that small farmers either move on foot or by bullock carts, whereas large farmers use tractors, buses or bullock carts. The same pattern may be seen in all the five small towns of the Malwa region. Big farmers travel larger distance than small and marginal farmers.

In respect all other five towns, the ownership of assets was found to be positively related to the ownership of land. Farmers with holdings of 5 acres and above, have tractors and electric motors. Farmers with less than 2.5 acres have very little assets other than land.

The purpose of visit to these town markets vary from repair of agricultural implements to use of the function of police station, administrative function, recreation and use of postal function. Of these purposes, the visits for repair of agricultural implements, account for the largest percentage of total visits, followed by use of administrative functions. Larger town like Dewas could attract larger percentage for recreational purpose.

In the present study, the interaction and interaction field of five small towns have been analysed. The interaction of customers with these small towns has been measured in terms of :

(i) number of times a person visits a town,
(ii) the quantum of agricultural surplus he sells in the market,
(iii) his consumption level,
(iv) the level of per capita expenditure,
(v) borrowings from the banks located in the town,
(iv) intervening opportunity available to the cousumer in relation to (a) the distance the consumer covers and (b) the economic status (size of operational holdings).

Interaction Lapse Rate

Interaction declines with increasing distance. Interaction is measured in terms of number of trips a farmer or a consumer makes to the market. This hypothesis is tested with the help of simple linear bivariate regression equations. The number of trips are regressed against distance which the consumer travels. The correlation co-efficients for all the towns are negative, i.e. Badnagar (–0.51), Depalpur (–0.38), Dewas (0.10), Shajapur (—0.28) and Alot (—0.38). The correlation coefficients for Badnagar and Depalpur are significant at 1 per cent level of significance. The least square regression equations are given in the following table. Whereas Y is number of trips and X is the distance travelled.

TABLE 6.1

Regression equation of number of trips and distance travelled

1.	Badnagar	Y=12.74	—0.49* X (3.36)	R^2=0.2609
2.	Depalpur	Y=12.42	—2.42* X (3.06)	R^2=1.1458
3.	Dewas	Y= 9.13	—0.22 X (0.39)	R^2=0.0106
4.	Shajapur	Y=10.69	—0.39**X (2.06)	R^2=0.0788
5.	Alot	Y=13.68	—0.69**X (2.23)	R^2=0.3800

* Significant at 1 per cent
** Significant at 5 per cent

The regression equations in the table also confirm the same hypothesis that with increasing distance, the frequency of trips to the town declines. The regression co-efficients for Badnagar (—0.49) and Depalpur (—0.42) are negative and significant at 1 per cent and for Shajapur (—0.39) and Alot (—0.69) are significant at 5 per cent level of significance. The co-efficient of determination is not very high in all the cases.

Both the correlation and regression co-efficients thus confirm the movement/interaction lapse rate hypothesis.

Intervening Opportunities

Intervening opportunities are those where the consumer is satisfied at lower order central-market place and these centres of lower order act as principal restricting forces. The trips to the market place will only occur for a higher order commodity/goods. To test how far these opportunities restrict the visit, the distance to the town and a consumer in other towns are correlated. This intervening opportunity visit is taken as dummy variable (when the consumer visits the other town, the value I is assigned otherwise zero). In such a situation a hypothesis that "with increasing distance from the town the consumer looks for lower order market and visits that market too" is extended for test. In all the five cases, this hypothesis stands confirmed as the correlation co-efficients for the all towns. Badnagar (0.54), Depalpur (0.69), Shajapur (0.61) and Alot (0.64) and Dewas (0.33) are significant at 1 per cent level of significant at 5 per cent level.

This means that distance produces friction of space and the travel cost increases with the increase in distance. In such cases, it is not economic to purchase all goods from one centre, thus the lower order centres restrict the visits to the market place and the intervening opportunities do restrict the interaction of the town and the hinterland in turn. This also confirms the hypothesis/principle of least efforts.

Number of Trips and Ownership of Land

It is tried here whether the farm size has any relation with the trips. It is often assumed that big farmers/landlords visit market centres more frequently than the poor peasants or the landless. The regression equations relating to the five towns do not show any relationship as the co-efficients for none of the towns are significant. The same is the case of correlation co-efficients. The regression equations are shown in the table No. 6.2 below with Y=number of trips and X as ownership of land.

TABLE 6.2

1. Badnagar	5.88	+0.009 X (0.12)	R^2=0.0044
2. Depalpur	10.34	—0.17 X (0.01)	R^2=0.0656
3. Dewas	5.38	—0.02 X (0.04)	R^2=0.0037
4. Shajapur	4.98	+0.06 X (0.79)	R^2=0.0128
5. Alot	11.41	—0.33 X (1.66)	R^2=0.0837

Sales and Size of Holdings

Total sales of the farm produce are associated with the

size of operational holding, with an assumption that the big farmers sell more than the small farmers. The correlation co-efficient calculated between the two variables comes to be quite high in all the cases, that is, Badnagar (0.41), Depalpur (0.44), Dewas (0.22), Shajapur (0.93) and Alot (0.32). The Table 6.3 shows the regression equations for the five towns when the total sales in rupees are regressed against size of operational holdings :

TABLE 6.3

Sales and size of holdings

1. Badnagar	Y=1112.90	+136.56 X (1.88)	R^2=0.1647
2. Depalpur	Y=1297.95	+373.04* X (3.61)	R^2=0.1917
3. Dewas	Y=3481.91	+104.47 X (1.64)	R^2=0.8682
4. Shajapur	Y=2401.91	+174.84* X (6.53)	R^2=0.8682
5. Alot	Y=2401.91	+658.81* X (3.75)	R^2=0.1042

* Significant at 1 per cent

Regression equation table shows all the co-efficients positive, of which the co-efficients for Depalpur (373.04) Shajapur (174.84) and Alot (658.81) are significant at 1 per cent level of significance. The other two towns, Dewas (104.4) and Badnagar (136.56) also have positive co-efficients but they are not significant. The co-efficient of determination is the highest in case of Shajapur, followed by much lower in respect of Badnagar and Depalpur. The regression co-efficients confirm the hypothesis that the big farmers sell more in volume and in money terms compared to the small farmers. This is very obvious that the large farmers have more surplus than the smaller ones. Even if small and marginal farmers sell their sales are in the nature of distress sales. The interaction of large farmers is obviously greater with the market economy, compared to small and marginal farmers.

Per Capita Expenditure and Size of Holdings

It is often believed that the per capita expenditure is much higher in respect of big farmers than the small and marginal. The economic condition and consumption level should be high in families which have larger size of operational holdings. To establish this relationship, correlation co-efficients and regression co-efficients have been calculated for all the five towns under study. The correlation co-efficients between the per capita expenditure and the size of holdings for Badnagar and Dewas are negative but not significant, the co-efficients are (—0.19) and (—0.29) respectively. The co-efficients for Dewas is also significant at 5 per cent. The co-efficients for other three towns of Depalpur (0.09), Shajapur (0.37) and Alot (0.18) are positive. Only co-efficient for Shajapur is significant at 1 per cent. The regression equations are shown in the Table 6.4 with Y=per capita expenditure and X=size of holding.

TABLE 6.4

Per capita expenditure and size of holdings

1.	Badnagar	Y=728.20	—5,79 X (0.64)	R^2=0.0347
2.	Depalpur	Y=419.49	+2.03 X (0.65)	R^2=0.0078
3,	Dewas	Y=703.30	—6.38 X** (2.23)	R^2=0.0856
4.	Shajapur	Y=392.10	+4.95 X* (2.80)	R^2=0.1380
5.	Alot	Y=556.16	+11.54* X	K^2=0.0329

* Significant at 1 per cent
** Significant at 5 per cent

The regression co-efficients for Badnagar and Dewas are negative, of which for Dewas it is significant at 5%. The other towns show a positive co-efficient but it is significant for Shajapur at one per cent, for two other towns of Alot and Depalpur, the co-efficients are not significant.

The said hypothesis cannot be taken as correct in all the cases but at least for those towns which show a positive regression co-efficient, it can be calculated that in the surrounding regions of Shajapur, Depalpur and Alot, the farmers with large size of holdings have higher per capita expenditure level than small and marginal farmers. With inorcase in the size of operational holding, the expenditure on food, clothing and other household consumer goods, also increases. With the increase in per capita expenditure, interaction with the market towns also increases.

Borrowings and Size of Holdings

This hypothesis has been tested in many areas and it was found that with increase in the ownership of operational holding, the capacity to borrow or the actual borrowings from banks and cooperatives increases. This is true because of larger securities required by the banks. When the two variables are correlated we find that in the case of Shajapur and Alot, the co-efficients come out to be negative and significant in case of Alot. The other three towns show positive correlation confirming the above hypothesis. The co-efficient of correlation is significant in case of Depalpur only.

When regression equations were calculated, a result similar to correlation analysis was found in all the five regions. The co-efficients and other related statistics, are shown in the table below. The bank/cooperative borrowings (Y) is explained with the help of ownership of operational holdings (x).

TABLE 6.5

Borrowings and size of operational holdings

1. Badnagar	Y=0.29	+0.005 X (0.74)	R^2=0.289
2. Depalpur	Y=0.38	+0. 01** X (2.59)	R^2=0.1113
3. Dewas	Y=0.28	+0.002 X (0.68)	R^2=0.0036
4. Shajapur	Y=1.19	—0.007 X (1.10)	R^2=0.0240
5. Alot	Y=0.96	—0. 03* X	R^2=0.3181

* Significant at 1 per cent

** Significant at 5 per cent

This statement, that with the larger size of holding, borrowings would be larger, stand correct only in case of Depalpur, Badnagar and Dewas where the co-efficients are positive but hypothesis cannot be accepted in the case of Depalpur and Badnagar because the regression co-efficients are insignificant. This can only be accepted in the case of Dewas. The two regions of Shajapur and Alot have even negative co-efficients. This may be attributed to the lower level of bank borrowings throughout the region. Also this may be due to the fact that bank finance is now being made available to small and marginal farmers.

Interaction Field of Towns

The question asked was : "From where do you obtain the central function, consumer items and agricultural inputs and repair of agricultural implements?" The simple question provides the location of the consumers and their preferences for making purchases and availing consumer goods. The consumer behaviour provides the extent of interaction field. For the delineation of such fields for the towns of Malwa, a number of factors are selected by considering the nature of the market and the region, which include, (i) retail shopping, (ii) repair of agricultural implements, (iii) postal service, (iv) Banking services (v) educational service, (vi) Medical service and, (vii) recreational service. The individual functions have been plotted on the map, with a straight line joining the location of the consumer and the market centre. Seven tributory areas have been identified for respective functions, by taking the maximum extent of consumer travel over the space.

Retail Trade

Map No. 10 shows the consumer travel preference for obtaining retail consumer goods like sugar, chillies, condiments, clothing, shoes, etc. Shajapur, Badnagar and Alot are small towns and if we look at the map, the boundaries of interaction almost confine to the tehsil boundaries. The consumers' travel of catchment area of Shajapur town is limited in the west because the competing town Tarana is very close to the market, while the markets in north (Agar) and south (Sonkachh) are far off, thus the retail trade is extended to a larger distance. The market centre draws consumers from other tehsils also. Shajapur being located near the western boundary of the tehsil services the Tarana tehsil as well. Badnagar and Alot being smaller centres, the consumers drawn to these centres, travel a few kilometers. Retail trade of these centres also cuts across the political boundaries. Ujjain and Khachrod the two towns being far away in the north and east, Badnagar town extends the retail trade to a greater distance. Also is a bordering town to Rajasthan. Thus the area is restricted to a large extent within the boundaries of Madhya Pradesh. The town serves the tehsil territory only. Dewas town is a large urban centre and offers wide range of commodities and thus draws consumers from greater distances. Dewas town is located at the fringe of Indore city. Thus the interaction of the town is very limited rather confined to a few kilometers. In all other sides, this town being the largest to the competing towns, has the larger interaction.

Repair of Agricultural Implements

The farmers avail the service of repair of agricultural implements like tractors, threshers, pump sets, electric engines, and visit the nearby market centre. Agriculture in Malwa region being traditional, the farmers visit the nearby town for getting the agricultural implements repaired. Other traditional implements are repaired at the village level only and thus the zone of repair of agricultural implements is confined to very smaller area in the case of all the towns. The map reveals that only nearby villages get this service from the centre. The travel for repair is very smaller and this confirms that the movement is very limited and confined to the nearest possible market centre.

Education

Almost all the villages lack higher education facilities. Education after eighth standard is availed from the towns. The nearby villagers commute daily for college and higher secondary level education and the distant students reside in the hostels or in the town. Alot, Depalpur and Badnagar have education facility upto higher secondary level. Thus the school going children are drawn only from walkable distance. The tributary area is confined to 5 to 6 kms. only. It is only Shajapur and Dewas which provide both levels of education, htgher secondary and the college. Because of higher level of this service, these centres extend the service to the larger area in all directions.

Postal Service

The postal service net is extended to the villages also and there is no price differential. Thus the choice of centres is limited. The only principle which operates in the region is that of least efforts or the minimum travel. People move to the nearest post office and for such functions as are available at villages also, their travel is confined to less than 5 kms. only. In all the five towns it is seen that few people avail this facility and that too from the immediate surrounding.

Medical Service

Medical facilities are not ubiquitous in nature, specialised medical facilities are confined to the town level only. Thus the surrounding countryside depends on the towns for this facility. Alot, Depalpur and Badnagar towns have lower level medical facilities. These towns, therefore, have limited interaction in this respect. Only Dewas and Shajapur which are district headquarters and have bigger hospitals, provide some specialised medical facility. The extent from which they draw consumers of this service is comparatively large. These centres draw consumers from more than 20 kilometers.

Banking Service

With the development and modernisation of agriculture, the requirements of finance of farmers have increased. The capital investment in tractors and other farm equipments and installation require large sum which the farmers borrow from banks. The requirements of seeds, fertilizers are met from the cooperatives. The requirement of finance draw people to tehsils or district headquarters where branches of banks are located. Alot, Depalpur and Badnagar, being very small towns, have lower order banking service and thereby serve a very limited area. Dewas and Shajapur, being the district headquarters and also comparatively large centres, have higher order banking service. The tributary area extends to a larger distance.

Recreational Service

Recreational facilities are very limited in most of the towns. They do not have wide range of facilities, like drama, dance, music. Only important recreational facility available may be the cinema. Villagers coming to the town market for selling their agricultural produce, may also visit the cinema located in the town. They do not come specifically for availing of this function. The interaction of rural areas with urban centres with reference to recreational facility is very limited. Though the map reveals larger extent of the tributary area, it needs to be made clear that people from rural areas do not come for availing of recreation facility only. It may bc due to some other facility that they come and along with that if they find time, may go to the cinema house. It is only from the immediate surrounding area that mostly people come for recreational purpose. The recreational linkages of rural areas to urban areas are almost absent.

Several facts are revealed by the above discussion. (i) The tributary areas of services do not overlap. There is exceptional choice at fringe which move to two centres. (ii) People move to the nearest market centres for a large number of functions. (iii) Distance of the competing centre is important in the determination of the limits of the maximum area served by the centre. If a competing town is nearer, the extent is restricted to large extent. (iv) The level of service provided and the type of service extended, have direct relation to the interaction field. Lower order or inferior services have lesser extent of tributary areas in all directions. (v) Smaller centres have smaller tributary area than the larger ones.

Demarcation of Interaction Field

Every urban centre, according to the level of service which it provides to the surrounding area, has a field of interaction. This area fully depends on the centre for the central functions and services. In turn, the surrounding area supplies the local produce to the market centre. Thus both forward and backward linkages may be seen. As discussed above, these interaction fields, can be delimited empirically as well as mathematically. The empirical boundaries depend upon the information collected about the origin of the consumer coming to a particular town. Mathematical expressions are based on masses which attract the surrounding population and the distance which produces the friction of space.

In the present study, both empirical and theoretical boundaries of the interaction zones for five towns have been drawn and compared with each other. The attributes of seven service functions of education, postal, banking, medical, repair of implements, recreation and retail trade service, are selected for the demarcation of overall field of influence of these towns. The outermost boundaries of these tributary areas based on functions are taken to delimit the regional boundaries. The theoretical boundaries are drawn on the basis of break point concept of Raillys' law of retail gravitation and lastly they are compared to find whether there is any concurrence between the theoretical and empirical boundaries.

The interaction field of Dewas is elongated to north and south because the Indore city lies in the west, and Sonkuchh in the east which restrict the zone to a great extent and both the boundaries have less distance from the centre. There seems to be a clear identify between the two boundaries. The concurrence is seen with the help of correlation coefficient between the extent of two boundaries. The correlation coefficient is 0.89 which confirms that the extent is very similar when delineated both theoretically and empirically.

The field of interaction of Shajapur also has greater extension towards north and south because there is no competing town nearby in these directions. Tarana in the west and Shajapur in the east of Shajapur, restrict the boundaries to limited distance only. When the boundaries of theoretical empirical zones are compared, the correlation was found to be 0.62 which also shows a high level of concurrence between the two boundaries.

Alot and Depalpur, both being smaller towns, have limited

interaction fields, confined, by and large, to the tehsil boundaries. Because of larger centres in the surrounding areas, these centres do not show any concurrence between theoretical and empirical boundaries. A similar pattern may also be seen in the case of Badnagar which also has a smaller field and shows a lower level of concurrence.

This analysis shows that the hierarchy of interaction fields may be clearly seen with the availability of central functions and the level of commodity provided by the centre. The smaller towns have a very restricted interaction zone. When type of interaction is analysed, it is apparent that the linkages of rural and urban areas are mostly agricultural sector oriented. The farmers sell their agricultural produce in the market and purchase their daily household requirements from the nearest market. The interaction of the towns with villages is also restricted by intervening opportunities in the form of periodic markets. On the whole, it can be concluded that the linkages are poor and the interaction is very limited. Only in the case of bigger towns, the interaction is wider but that too only with reference to agricultural produce and retailing.

REFERENCES

1. Hagerstrand, T (1957)—Migration and Area : Survey of sample of Swedish migration fields and Hypothetical considerations on their genesis—Lund series in Geography Series B, Human Geography, 13, pp 27-158.
2. Isard, W. (1960)—Methods of Regional Analysis MIT Press.
3. Christaller, W. (1966)—The central Places of Southern Germany.
4. Loesch A (1954)—The Economics of Location (Translation by WH Woglom) New Haven.
5. Zipf, G.K. (1949)—Human Behaviour and the Principle of least effort Cambridge
6. Huff, D.L. (1960)—A topographic Model of Consumer space preferences, Regional Science Association, papers and proceedings 5, pp 159-73.
7. Murdie R.A.(1965)—Cultural difference in consumer travel Economic Geography, Vol 41, pp 211-33.
8. Baumol WJ and Ide, EA (1965)—Variety in retailing management Science Vol 3, pp 93-101

9. V.L. Prakasha Rao (1983)—Urbanisation in India—spatial aspects-pages 100-103.
10. Berry, BJL (1967)—Geography of Market Centres and Retail Distribution, Printice Hall.
11. Helvig, M(1964)—Chicagos External Truck Movement: Spatial Interaction between Chicago Area and Its Hinterland, Research paper Chicago Univ. No. 90.
12. Zipf. GK (1949) Op. cit.
13. Dahl, S, (1957)—The Contacts of Vasteras with the Rest of the Sweden, Lund Series in Geog. Series B, Human Geography, 13, p. 206-43.
14. Skinner, GW (1964), Marketing and social structure in Rural China, Journal of Asian Studies, Vol 34.
15. Johnson, EAJ. (1972) : The integration of agrarian, commercial and industrial activities in functional economic areas, in Market Towns and Spatial Development, NCAER, New Delhi.
16. Bracey, HE : (1953) Towns as rural service centres. Transactions of the Institute of British Geographers, 19, p. 95-105
17. Smails, A.E. (1947)—The Analysis and Determination of Urban Fields, Geography Vol. 32 pp 151-161
18. Green F.H.W. (1950)—Urban Hinterlands in England and Wales, Geographical Journal, 16, pp 65-88.
19. Carruthers, WI (1957) : A classification of service centres in England and Wales Geographical Journal Vol 22, pp 371-385.
20. Reif, B (1973) : Models in urban and regional planning-Leonard Hill books.
21. Haggett P. (1967) : Locational analysis in Human geography Edward Arnold.
22. Stewart, J.Q. (1929)—Methods for the study of Retail relationships University of Texas, Bulletin 2944.
23. Stewart, WJ : (1929)—The Development of Social Physics American Journal of Physics, Vol 18, pp 239-53.
24. Zipf, GK, (1949) op. cit.
25. Converse PD (1951)—Development of Marketing : Fifty years of Progress in HG Wells (ed.) Changing Perspectives in Marketing Urbana Univ. Illinsis.
26. Hieff, DL (1963)—A Probability Analysis of shopping Centres Trading Area, Lane Economics, Vol. 53 pp. 81-90.

CHAPTER 7

URBAN DEVELOPMENT POLICY

The chapter highlights the main findings of the previous chapters and rises certain policy issues to be tackled by urban development policy. The outlines of such a policy have also been presented in this chapter.

An analysis of the process and pattern of urbanisation in Madhya Pradesh in general and of Malwa region in particular, reveals that the State does not have any urbanisation policy worth the name. Urban growth has taken place mainly in response to market forces and follows the pattern of economic development which itself is lopsided and mostly unplanned. Functions and facilities continue to be located in an unplanned and haphazard manner, dictated mainly by political expdiency. Planning in the State is very weak and there is no plan formulation machinery at the micro level. There is no regionalisation of the state for the purpose of regional planning. Under these conditions, urbanisation is bound to be haphazard and unplanned. Only a few piecemeal and adhoc measures in the direction of town planning, slum improvement, urban water supply, have been areas taken. There is no plan for the integrated development of urban areas.

Urban development cannot be viewed in isolation from rural development. It is linked with economic development, particularly rural development. Rural economy in the state continues to be exploitative, lacking diversification. It continues to push out the rural educated and rural unemployed to urban centres in search of employment and better living. Most of the rural areas lack the basic amenities of life. There seems to be no marked change in the occupational pattern of working force in the state. In 1981, 76.26% of working force was engaged in agriculture as against 79.42% in 1971. There has been only a marginal shift of working force from agriculture to household industries and other occupations. This shift has been more biased in favour of "other workers" than household industries. Although so much is being talked about the development of HH industries in the state, only 3.8% of working force in the state was engaged in such industries in 1981 as against 3.64% in 1971. Out of 45 districts, only in 15 districts the percentage of workers in HH industries has registered an increase in 1981 over 1971. There is virtual stagnation in agricultural growth, reflected in decline in agricultural productivity of major crops. Irrigation is scanty, available to only 11% of the gross sown area. Land reforms have not been effectively implemented. Feudal and semifeudal production relations pervail and in certain parts where modern inputs have been provided, we find the emergence of capitalist farming. The type of agricultural development that is taking place in the state, does not give rise to many linkages between rural and urban areas.

Madhya Pradesh is one of the less developed and less urbanised States of India, but with vast potential for development, provided the forces of growth are released by the development process and correct strategy of development is followed. The state has witnessed rapid urbanisation in recent years, partly because of industrial and agricultural development and partly because of designation of new settlements as 'urban' in the state by the State Government. The number of towns in the state has increased from 232 in 1971 to 303 in 1981 and the decennial urban population growth was 56.07% during 1971-81 as against 36.6% in the country as a whole. The URGD was 36.9% in 1981 as against 20.95% in 1971. Urbanisation in the state was slow till 1951 and this was quite consistent with the overall pattern of slow economic development witnessed in the State. The real spurt in urban growth was witnessed since 1951 when urban population registered an increase of more than three times but rural population less than doubled and total population just doubled. Rapid urbanisation is mostly due to migration from rural to urban areas and increase in number of towns.

Madhya Pradesh is a State of small towns. More than 75% of all towns belong to this category, with population of less than 20,000 each. Most of the very small towns are outgrown villages, with most of the characteristies of rural life. In 1981, nearly 47% of urban population lived in Class I towns, numbering 14, 18% in medium towns, numbering 28, 35.1% in small towns, numbering 261. Though the number of small towns has increased from 109 in 1901 to 261 in 1981, their percentage share in urban population has gone down from 72.5% to 35.16% in the same period. The State does not have a single metropolitan city. The problems imposed by urbanisation in the state are of such dimensions that can be effectively tackled in the initial stage of urbanisation, provided the state formulates an appropriate policy for the integrated development of rural and urban areas. In the absence of such a policy, these problems are bound to assume serious dimensions.

The phenomenon of relatively slow growth of small towns in the urban hierarchy has been variously interpreted. Some feel that slow growth is only transitional and as "trickle-down" forces are strengthened, small and medium towns will find their place in the urban hierarchy. To some, the erroneous strategies which have been highly capital intensive and agglomerative, are responsible for emergence of lop-sided and concentrated problem of urbanisation. To us, it is the absence urbanisation policy and gradual dilution of the planning process that has resulted in distorted growth of not only urban but also of rural areas.

While discussing the pattern of urbanisation in the state we have highlighted spatial dimensions of the problem. There are wide regional variations in the level and growth of urbanisation in the State. The eastern region, the largest in size with 33% of the geographical area of the state, accounted for 27% of the total cropped area. This is due to a very large percentage of area under forests (nearly 42% of total area under forests in the state). The eastern and inland eastern regions are rich in mineral and forest resources which can provide a basis for a number of mineral based and forest based industries. Inland western region and western region, out of which the Malwa region is carved out, possess better agricultural resources in terms of soil quality, water resources, irrigation and infrastructural facilities. The productivity per hectare of crops is higher in western and northern regions compared to the eastern and inland eastern regions. The irrigation intensity is the highest in inland western region (108), followed by northern region (106) and the lowest in eastern region (104).

The eastern region has the lowest level of urbanisation, with only 14.2% of its population living in urban areas, but its share in total urban population of the state has gone up from 18.8% in 1971 to 20.4% in 1981, whereas that of western region which is the highly urbanised region of the state, has gone down from 30.5% to 20% in the same period.

The eastern region has recorded the highest annual rate of growth of urban population during 1971-81 (6.7%) accompanied by a very low rate of growth of rural population (1.47%) and of total population (1.64%). URGD is the highest 5.12(%) in this sub region, followed by inland eastern region. In these regions huge investments have been made in coal, cement, forest based and mineral based industries. This fact has given rise to rapid growth of urban population in the region. Relatively faster growth of urbanisation in eastern and inland eastern region and slower growth in western and northern regions, has led to convergence in the inter-regional disparities in the levels of urbanisation in the state.

The western region which is relatively more urbanised, has the largest number of towns, followed by inland western region. This region has the largest number of cities, five out of 14 in 1981 and also the largest number of small towns, 71 out of a total of 261. The smallest increase in the number of small towns has taken place in the eastern region. But the cities of of eastern region have manifested very high growth rates of population. This is mainly due to migration caused by industrialisation. Western region is better served by towns,

built their own houses, must vacate Government accommodation which they are getting at concessional rates. They are earning huge amounts by renting their own houses. All public sector undertakings and corporations should be asked to build their own accommodation instead of paying fabulous rents on private accommodation. At present in certain localities in big cities rents have gone up to fantastic heights because the Government agencies, autonomous corporations and commercial banks, are paying very high rents on buildings which they get on hire.

Decentralisation of industrial units and their location in small towns can help in reducing pressure of migrants on big cities. Today in Bhopal alone, out of a total population of 6.72 lakh, about 1.3? lakh live in slums. A recent survey shows that nearly 30,500 families have encroached upon Government land and have erected hutments in 156 slum areas in the state capital. This is just one typical example of increasing pressure of migrants on the city. Decentralisation of industries simply does not mean creating new industrial centres within the proximity of big cities. Such a decentralisation would rather increase pressure on existing big cities. A well thought-out and a scientific policy of location of industrial units in a decentralised manner, needs to be formulated and related to the process and pattern of urbanisation in the state.

Most of the small towns in the State are mandi towns, having activity pattern with rural bias. The growth of small towns largely depends upon the growth of agriculture in their hilnter-lands. At present as we have seen, the economic base of small towns is very weak. Their hinterlands do not extend beyond a very limited area and their linkages with rural economy are very weak. Production-oriented functions are very few. Tertiary activities provide the maximum employment and within the tertiary sector, the informal sector absorbs them to the maximum extent. Some of the small towns are growing industrial centres but such towns have not been provided adequate functions and facilities, with the result that their linkages are poor. Moreover, the type of industrial units which are coming up, have weak linkages with the local economy. These small towns have not emerged as growth centres. Industrial dispersal policy should encourage location of industry at suitable growth centres with due weightage to rural growth centres which occupy higher levels in the hierarchy of settlements. It is not necessary that every backward district in the state is to be developed through industries. Most of the backward districts can be developed through agricultural development. A uniform policy of location of industries, irrespective of degree of capital intensity, linkages and lines of manufacture, would hardly trigger off growth in the area. There is considerable scope to locate small cement, sugar, paper, food processing and other agro-based industries in the small towns of Malwa region. For rapid agricultural development, besides technological development, institutional changes of far-reaching importance and abolition of exploitative agencies, are very essential. The development of Narmada Valley Project, is expected to usher in agricultural and industrial development. The impact of the project on settlement pattern and urbanisation in the region, needs to studied and plan for the region needs to be prepared much in advance of the completion of the Project.

The main ingredients of urban development policy should be, (i) to locate new industries away from big cities, (ii) to integrate and strengthen the interdependence between towns and the surrounding rural areas and (iii) to diversify the occupational base of rural areas.

An integrated approach to the development of small and medium towns implies that all the objectives must be looked upon as a single package with a view to minimising potential contradictions and trade-offs within and among objectives and using the each objective to further others. The present programme is basically adhoc without adequate coordination. The whole concept of integrated development cannot be based simply on physical plans.

The integrated strategy for such towns should include, providing infrastructure, units for processing of local products, housing and welfare functions, repair shops and work-sheds for agricultural tools and implements and agro-based industries. The annual budgetary allocations of different sectors like medical and health, education, environmental sanitation, urban development and housing, should be channelised through development priorities within the integrated development programmes.

Urban planning requires effective urban administration. At present responsibility of urban development is being shared by multiplicity of agencies with overlapping and sometimes conflicting functions. At present we have in a city urban development authorities like, the municipal committee/corporation, the Town and Country Planning Department, the Slum improvement Board, the Environ ental Planning and Coordination organisation (EPCO), the Pollution Board, the Housing Board the Urban Development Authority, the Public Health Engineering Department, the Public Works Department, the Captal Project (in Bhopal city only) and the newly created Directorate of Urban Development to look after the implementation of conferring ownership rights on Government land to the slum-dwellers. The overlapping responsibilities are several. This leads to conflicts between the development decisions of sectoral authorities and urban regional development authorities. There is no regional planning authority to coordinate the activities of these urban development authorities. Even at the State level, there is no agency to coordinate, harmonise and integrate the plans of development of multiplicity of agencies operating in the field of urban development. Rural and urban development are being viewed separately. At present an urban development plan is primarily a land use plan. It contains proposals for zoning in various commercial, residential and industrial areas, allocation of land for public purposes, open spaces, hospitals, schools and infrastructure development. The M.P. Town Planning Act of 1973, includes regions surroundings the towns and cities for the purpose of development plans. But regional plans prepared under the Act are also land use plans. Thus the whole concept of regional and town planning needs to be thoroughly changed. All this is possible only when we create strong and effective planning machinery at the state and regional levels.

In the Sixth Five Year Plan (1980-85), a centrally sponsored scheme for the Integrated Development of Small and Medium Towns (IDSMT) was evolved by the Central Government.

The scheme recognising the importance of these town, envisages that "for proper development of these towns, it is necessary that an integrated development programme of each town is drawn, keeping in view its locational importance and linkages in the region." For this purpose, the Govt. of India selected for development 200 small and medium towns in the country with a population of 1 lakh and below on the basis of 1971 census and have allocated an outlay of Rs. 200 crores (at the rate of Rs. one crore per town) during the sixth plan period, to make these towns more viable and functionally efficient. The IDSMT programme includes 8 towns of Madhya Pradesh of which only one Dewas, is from Malwa region. We do not know the basis on which these towns have been selected. Of the 8 towns, four viz. Bilaspur, Rewa, Burhanpur and Katni, have crossed the 1 lakh population limit and have attained the status of Class I towns in 1981 census. Under the scheme, the central assistance would be available to the states on a matching basis, for the following components of the scheme : (i) Land acquisition and development, (ii) Traffic and transportation (iii) Development of mandis/market, provision of industrial estates, provision of other service and processing facilities for the benefit of agricultural and rural development in the hinterland. Components for which funds are to be found from state plans, but which must from part of the Integrated scheme are : (i) Slum improvement/upgradation, urban renewal and small scale employment generation activity, (ii) Low cost schemes of water supply drainage, sewerage and sanitation (iii) preventive medical facilities/health care, (iv) Parks and play-grounds (v) assistance for the purpose of making modifications, whatever necessary, in city master plans to permit mixed land use.

The central financial assistance will be given to the State Governments as loan, repayable in 25 years including a moratorium of five years.

The main focus of the Integrated urban development programme has been to meet the requirement of the resident population and also to attract migrants to the small and medium towns. The master plans which have been formulated do not conceive the integrated development of the towns and therefore do not conform to the goals of providing need-based programmes, most appropriate community's 'values' and 'circumstances'. The existence of multiplicity of urban development agencies stands in the way of the preparation and implementation of integrated development programmes for these towns.

A Workshop[1] organised by the Centre for Urban Studies of the Indian Institute of Public Administration, New Delhi, in 1981, to discuss the critical areas and issues for policy options relating to the integrated development scheme of the Government of India, has made the following recommendations relating to the scheme :—

(i) Suitable strategies having bearing on the migration pattern should be evolved to meet the main objective of the scheme of arresting the flow of migration to metropolitan areas. This might include strengthening and diversification of economic base of the towns which might give boost to urban economic growth and social development.

(ii) An inventory of migratory and floating population along with the availability of workers by type of work and industry should be made for optimum utilisation of local resources and skills and also to ensure that ecological balance is not disrupted by pollution or over-utilisation of these resources.

(iii) The long term plans should be prepared and environmental/factors including provision of shelter, social services and infrastructure should be given priority in the development of small and medium towns.

(iv) The coverage of towns only of one lakh population should be changed to include towns having larger population also ; otherwise very remote areas will satisfy this condition having not so much felt needs for development.

(v) Towns in backward areas should be selected so that the migrating population of these areas is attracted towards small and medium towns covered under IDSMT scheme.

(vi) Unorganised informal sector should be given due share in the investment pattern of these towns. Mere capital investment in infrastructure is not enough.

(vii) The ceiling for the total cost of the project as well as the central assistance is too meagre to develop small and medium towns, as effective growth centres with better environment.

(viii) There are a large number of small and medium towns having activity pattern with rural bias and for such townships, the integrated strategy should include (i) veterinary hospitals for towns of 50,000 and above population, (ii) housing for agricultural and landless labourers (iii), social services for the aged and children of working mothers, (iv) opening of more repair shops and work-sheds for agricultural tools and implements (v) units for processing of local products.

With a view to increasing the operational efficiency of the IDMST programme, the local authority has to become more professional and the state Town Planning Department as an important agency to coordinate and execute various programmes. The organisational set-up of the local implementing agency, particularly their administrative and financial wings should be adequately strengthened and their procedures streamlined for efficient implementation of the programme. In particular, the implementation agencies, should have adequate powers delegated to them for the sanction of estimates and for prompt implementation of the programme. An effective machinery for coordination, monitoring and evaluation of the programme should be set up by the State Government at the town level under the Collector and at the state level preferably under the Chief Secretary or Development Commissioner. The machinery at the state level should be responsible for the formulation of the plan frame, to give general policy direction, review the progress regularly and ensure timely flow of funds and other resources for the implementation of the scheme. The integrated development programme should be prepared by the Town and Country

Planning Department in consultation with the local bodies, assessing their needs and resources available for development.

In Madhya Pradesh, no steps seem to have been taken on the lines suggested above, for the formulation and implementation of Integrated Development of small and medium towns. In the Sixth Five Year Plan of the State, in the chapter on Urban Development, no mention is made of the scheme and towns in which it would be implemented, the plan formulation machinery and the organisational set-up for the implementation of scheme. It is only mentioned that town plans for 35 towns would be prepared and certain programmes of slum clearance, housing for economically weaker sections, environmental improvement of slums have been included in the Plan. Interestingly, in the plan document, there are separate chapters dealing with local bodies development, state capital project, water supply, Housing, Rental housing, Police Housing and Urban development. All this shows lack of integrated approach to different urban problems. Multiplicity of urban agencies continue to operate in different fields. The role of urban local bodies in urban development is only secondary. Most of their functions of urban development have been taken over by other agencies like Slum Improvement Board, Urban Development Authority, Public Health Engineering For instance, in the same city of Bhopal, provision of water supply in old city is the responsibility of Municipal Corporation, whereas in new city the responsibility is that of Public Health Engineering. For instance, in the same city of Bhopal, provision of water supply in old city is the responsibility of Municipal Corporation, whereas in new city the responsibility is that of Public Health Engineering Department and in BHEL township, of the Management of the factory.

If we recapitulate our main findings in this Study of rural-urban interaction, we find that consumer preferences, even at the lowest level of demand of various items of consumption and inputs, are strongly biased in favour of big cities, like Indore, Bhopal, Ujjain and Ratlam, due to frequent contacts of migrants of their native places and also due to increase in income of big cultivators. The bigger cities are extending their tentacles deep into the countryside with which accessibility is so well established that items of daily consumption are getting supplied directly from the cities to the consumers in smaller places through net-work of traders having contact with large traders in the cities. This explains why the settlement hierarchy is very weak and lopsided at the lowest levels. This also explains as to why small towns are not growing at a fast rate in respect of functions and facilities and also not playing their due role in regional development. Unless heavy inputs, particulariy social inputs, are provided to small and medium towns, they would remain stagnant and also may deteriorate. No piece-meal approach will pay much dividends.

Urbanisation in the State is bound to be accelerated with industrial and agricultural development. Different studies conducted elsewhere reveal a positive correlation between urbanisation and economic development. The poor economic base of small towns and of rural areas, have accentuated the process of migration to large cities due to 'push' factors. In view of fast expected rate of urbanisation in Madhya Pradesh, it is high time that the state formulates an integrated urban-rural development policy.

There is the need for integration between agricultural, industrial, infrastructural and urban development policies and measures. Locational aspect of planning needs to be given due emphasis. But all this is possible only when there is strong planning machinery at the state, regional and local levels and there is commitment to planning. At the national level, gradually planning is being diluted and the economy is fast drifting to the market system, with further liberalisation of regulations and control of private sector. In the absence of micro level planning, the targets of macro plan, are bound to be frustrated. Urbanisation policy should, therefore, be an integral part of overall planned development of the State.

INDEX

MAPS

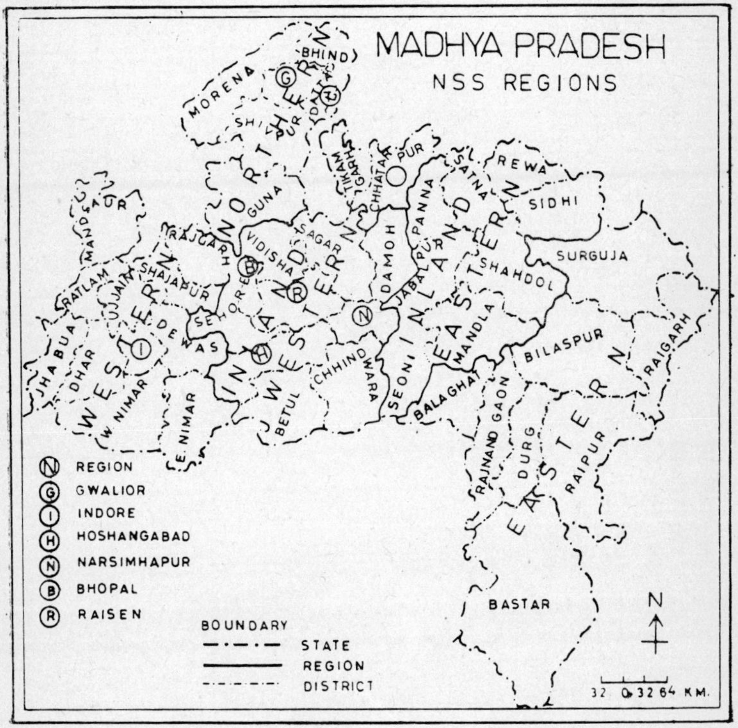
MADHYA PRADESH
NSS REGIONS
BHIND
MORENA
DATIA
GUNA
TIKAMGARH
CHHATARPUR
REWA
SATNA
SIDHI
PANNA
MANDSAUR
RAJGARH
VIDISHA
SAGAR
DAMOH
RATLAM
UJJAIN
SHAJAPUR
SEHORE
JABALPUR
SHAHDOL
SURGUJA
JHABUA
DEWAS
MANDLA
BILASPUR
RAIGARH
DHAR
W. NIMAR
E. NIMAR
BETUL
CHHINDWARA
SEONI
BALAGHAT
RAJNANDGAON
DURG
RAIPUR
BASTAR
NORTHERN
WESTERN
INLAND WESTERN
INLAND EASTERN
EASTERN
REGION
GWALIOR
INDORE
HOSHANGABAD
NARSIMHAPUR
BHOPAL
RAISEN
BOUNDARY
STATE
REGION
DISTRICT
N
32 0 32 64 KM.

MAP-1

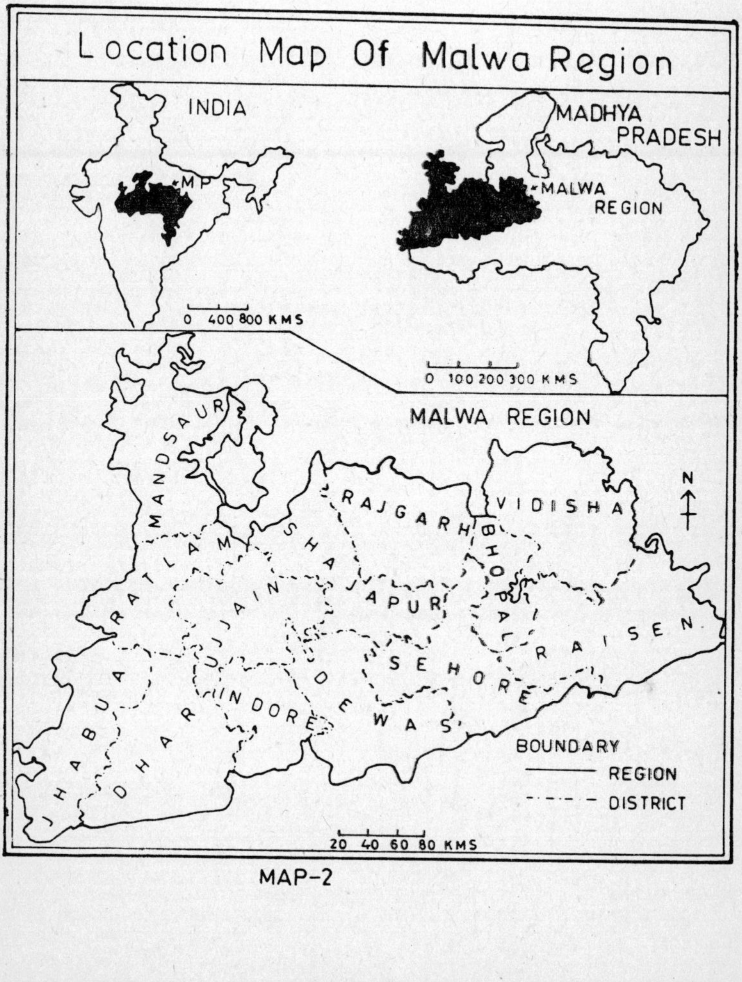
Location Map Of Malwa Region
INDIA
MP
0 400 800 KMS
MADHYA PRADESH
MALWA REGION
0 100 200 300 KMS
MALWA REGION
MANDSAUR
RATLAM
UJJAIN
SHAJAPUR
RAJGARH
VIDISHA
BHOPAL
RAISEN
SEHORE
DEWAS
INDORE
DHAR
JHABUA
N
BOUNDARY
REGION
DISTRICT
20 40 60 80 KMS

MAP-2

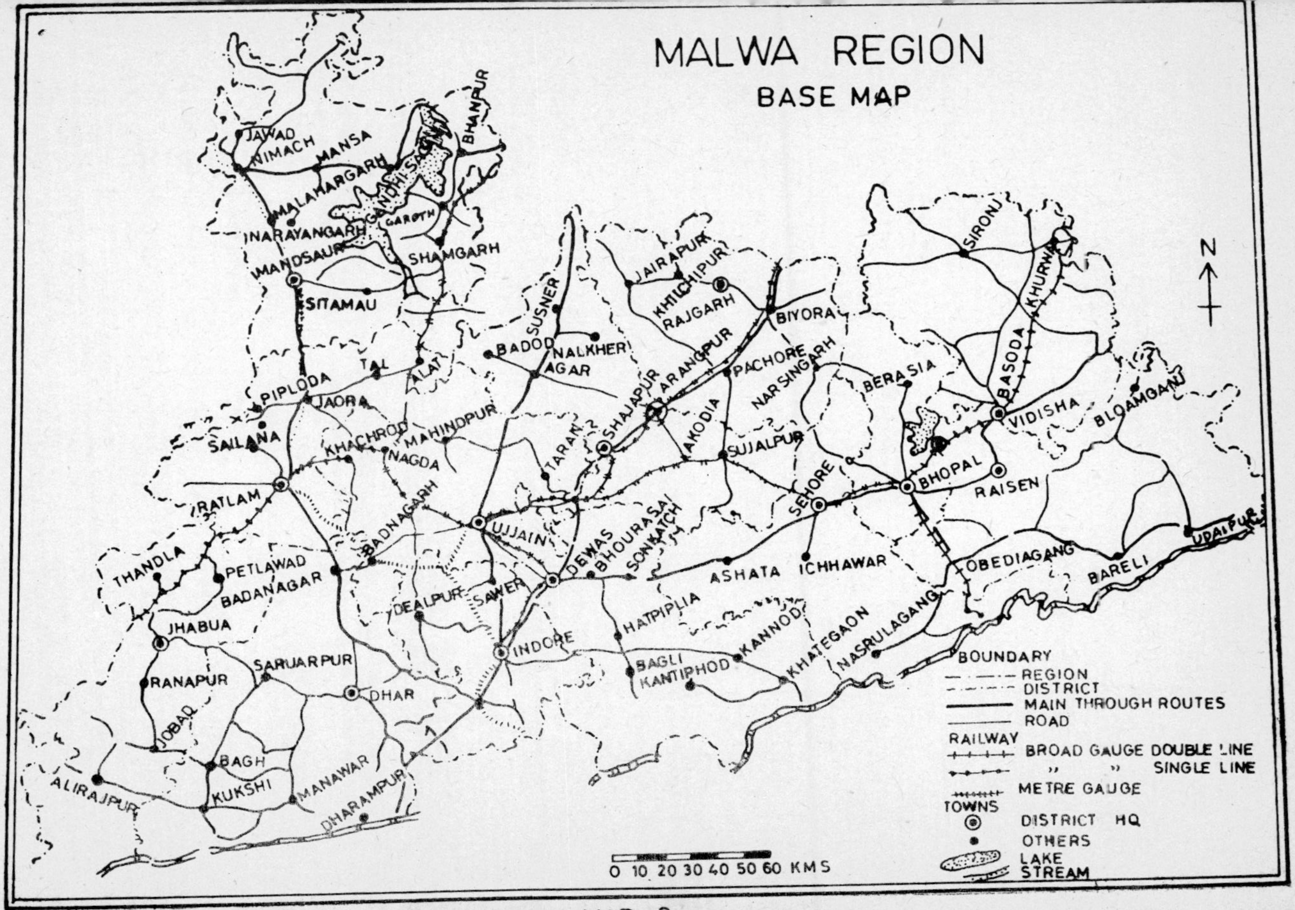
MALWA REGION
BASE MAP
N
JAWAD
NIMACH
MANSA
MALAHARGARH
GANDHISAGAR
BHANPUR
NARAYANGARH
GAROTH
MANDSAUR
SHAMGARH
SITAMAU
SUSNER
BADOD
NALKHERI
AGAR
TAL
ALAT
PIPLODA
JAORA
SAILANA
KHACHROD
MAHINDPUR
NAGDA
RATLAM
BADNAGARH
UJJAIN
TARANA
SHAJAPUR
JAIRAPUR
KHILCHIPUR
RAJGARH
BIYORA
PACHORE
NARSINGARH
AKODIA
SUJALPUR
BERASIA
SEHORE
BHOPAL
RAISEN
VIDISHA
BASODA
KHURWAI
SIRONJ
BLOAMGANJ
UDAIPUR
BARELI
OBEDIAGANG
ICHHAWAR
ASHATA
DEWAS
BHOURASA
SONKATCH
THANDLA
PETLAWAD
BADANAGAR
DEALPUR
SAWER
INDORE
HATPIPLIA
KANNOD
KHATEGAON
NASRULAGANG
BAGLI
KANTIPHOD
JHABUA
RANAPUR
SARUARPUR
DHAR
JOBAD
BAGH
KUKSHI
MANAWAR
DHARAMPUR
ALIRAJPUR
BOUNDARY
REGION
DISTRICT
MAIN THROUGH ROUTES
ROAD
RAILWAY
BROAD GAUGE DOUBLE LINE
" " SINGLE LINE
METRE GAUGE
TOWNS
DISTRICT HQ
OTHERS
LAKE
STREAM
0 10 20 30 40 50 60 KMS

MAP - 3

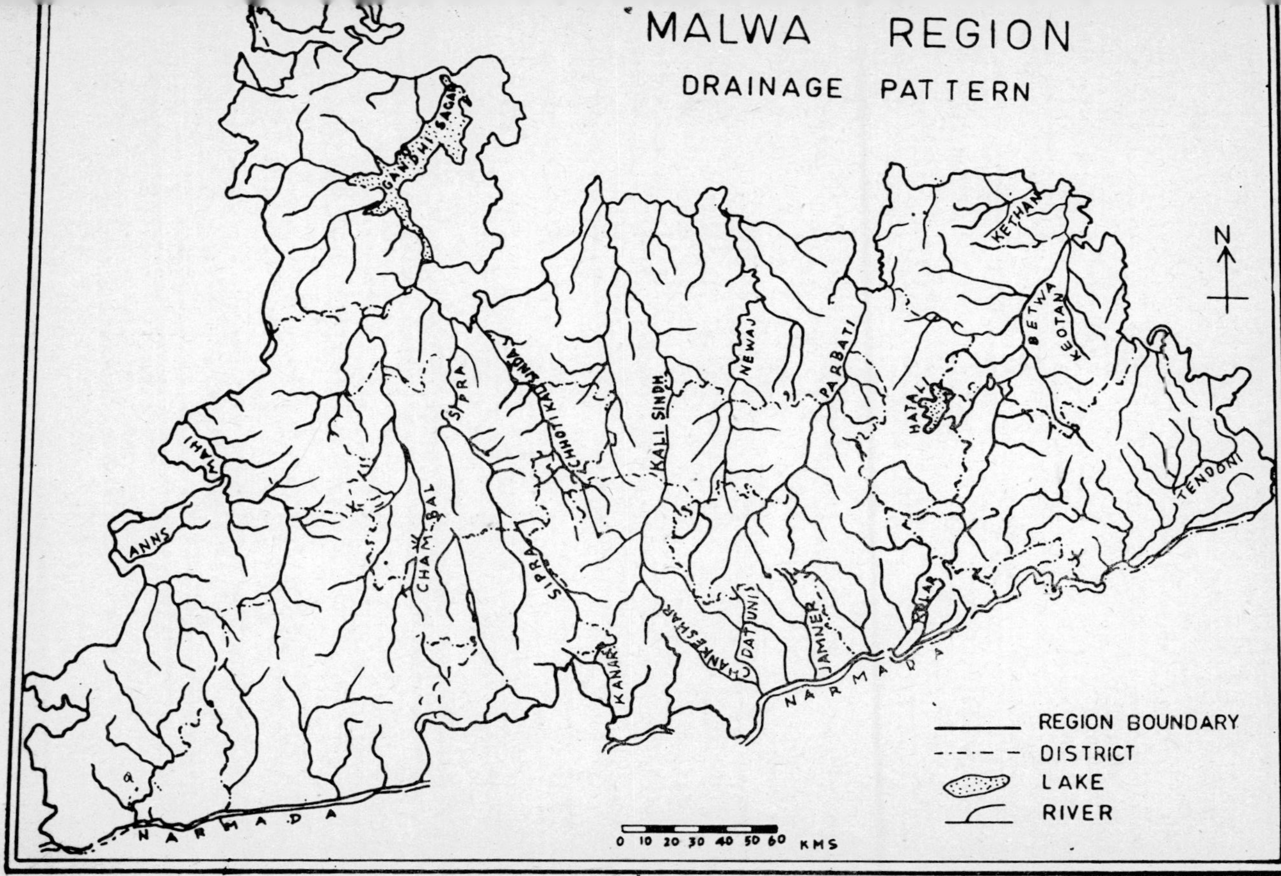
MALWA REGION
DRAINAGE PATTERN
N
GANDHI SAGAR
KETHAN
BETWA
KEOTAN
TENDONI
HATALI
PARBATI
NEWAJ
KALI SINDH
CHHOTI KALI SINDH
SIPRA
CHAMBAL
MAHI
ANNS
KANAR
CHANKESHAR
DATUNI
JAMNER
KOLAR
NARMADA
REGION BOUNDARY
DISTRICT
LAKE
RIVER
0 10 20 30 40 50 60 KMS

MAP - 4

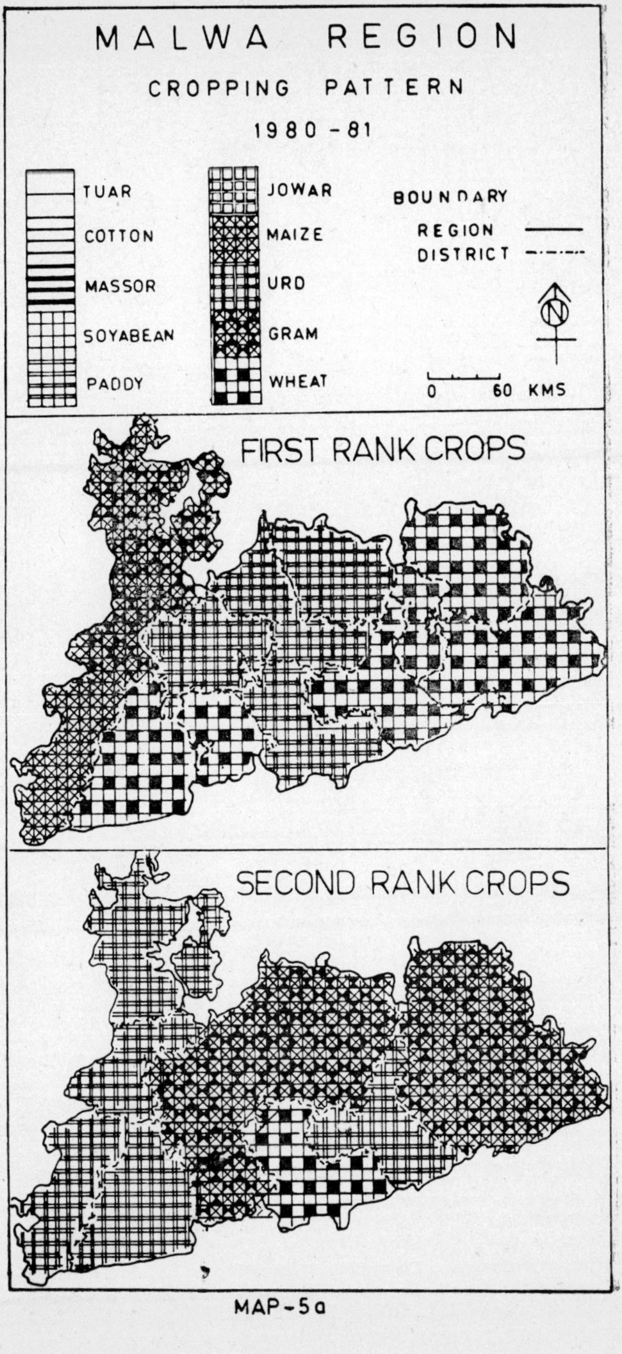
MALWA REGION
CROPPING PATTERN
1980 - 81
TUAR
COTTON
MASSOR
SOYABEAN
PADDY
JOWAR
MAIZE
URD
GRAM
WHEAT
BOUNDARY
REGION
DISTRICT
N
0 60 KMS
FIRST RANK CROPS
SECOND RANK CROPS

MAP-5a

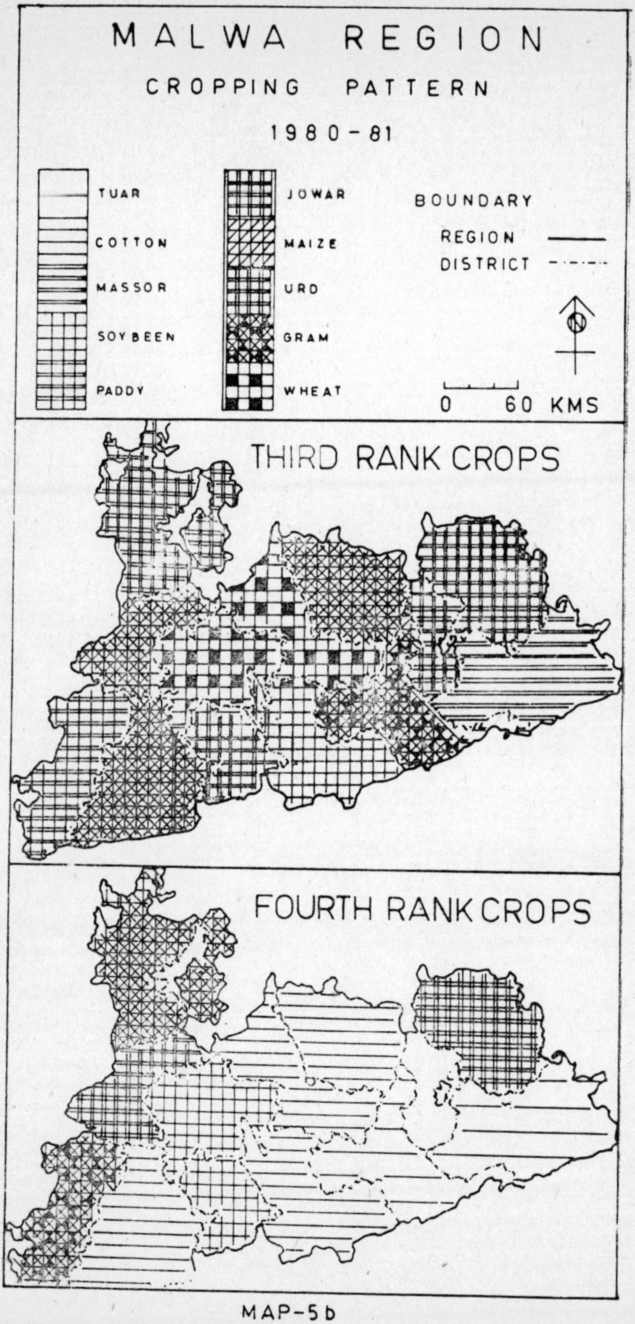
MALWA REGION
CROPPING PATTERN
1980-81
TUAR
COTTON
MASSOR
SOYBEEN
PADDY
JOWAR
MAIZE
URD
GRAM
WHEAT
BOUNDARY
REGION
DISTRICT
N
0 60 KMS
THIRD RANK CROPS
FOURTH RANK CROPS

MAP-5b

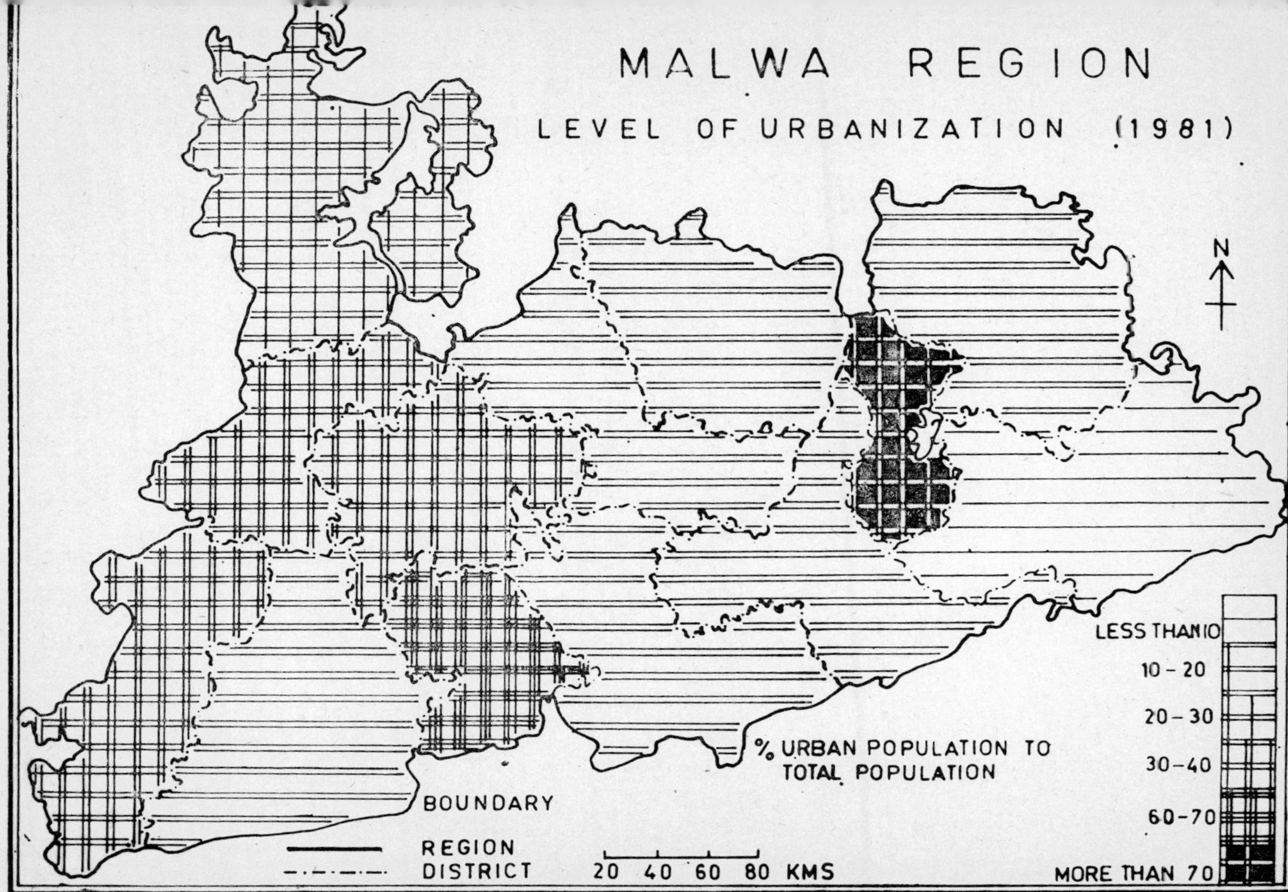
MALWA REGION
LEVEL OF URBANIZATION (1981)
N
LESS THAN 10
10 - 20
20 - 30
30 - 40
60 - 70
MORE THAN 70
% URBAN POPULATION TO TOTAL POPULATION
BOUNDARY
REGION
DISTRICT
20 40 60 80 KMS

MAP-6

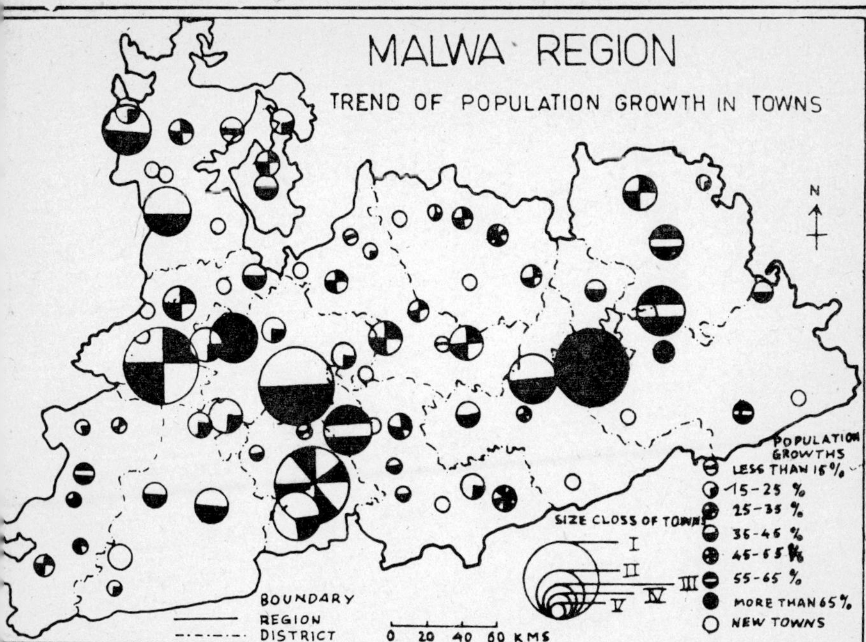
MALWA REGION
TREND OF POPULATION GROWTH IN TOWNS
N
POPULATION GROWTHS
LESS THAN 15%
15-25 %
25-35 %
35-45 %
45-55 %
55-65 %
MORE THAN 65%
NEW TOWNS
SIZE CLOSS OF TOWNS
I
II
III
IV
V
BOUNDARY
REGION
DISTRICT
0 20 40 60 KMS

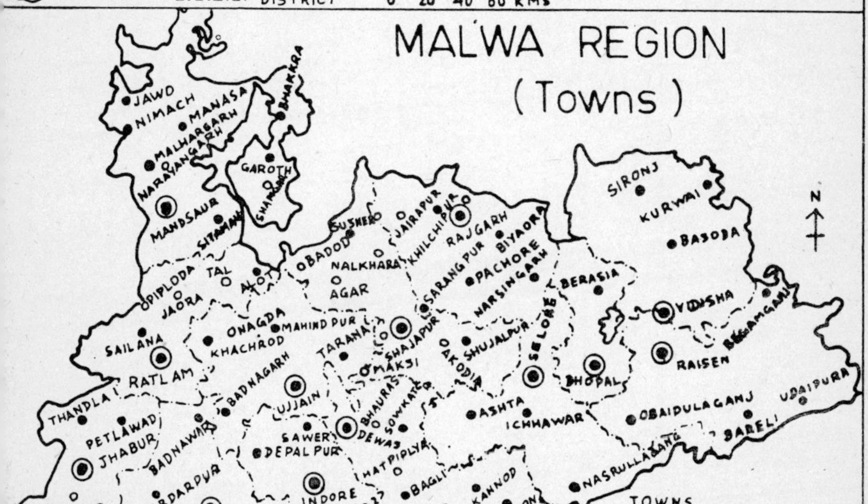
MALWA REGION
(Towns)
N
JAWD
NIMACH
MANASA
MALHARGARH
NARAYANGARH
BHAKKRA
GAROTH
MANDSAUR
SITAMAU
PIPLODA
JAORA
TAL
ALOT
SUSNER
OBADOD
NALKHARA
AGAR
JAIRAPUR
KHILCHIPUR
RAJGARH
BIYAORA
SARANGPUR
PACHORE
NARSINGARH
SIRONJ
KURWAI
BASODA
BERASIA
VIDISHA
RAISEN
SAILANA
RATLAM
ONAGDA
KHACHROD
MAHIND PUR
TARANA
SHAJAPUR
MAKSI
SHUJALPUR
AKODIA
SELORE
BHOPAL
BADNAGARH
UJJAIN
BHAURASA
SOWKATCO
ASHTA
ICHHAWAR
OBAIDULAGANJ
UDAIPURA
BAREILI
THANDLA
PETLAWAD
JHABUR
BADNAWAR
SAWER
DEWAS
DEPAL PUR
HATPIPLYA
BAGLI
KAHNOD
NASRULLAGANJ
RANAPUR
SARDARPUR
INDORE
JOSAT
BAGH
DHAR
MMOW
KANTIPHOD
KHATEGAON
ALIRAJPUR
KUKSHI
TOWNS
TOWNS
TAHSIL HQ
DISTRICT HQ
BOUNDARY
REGION
DISTRICT
0 20 40 60 KMS

MAP-8

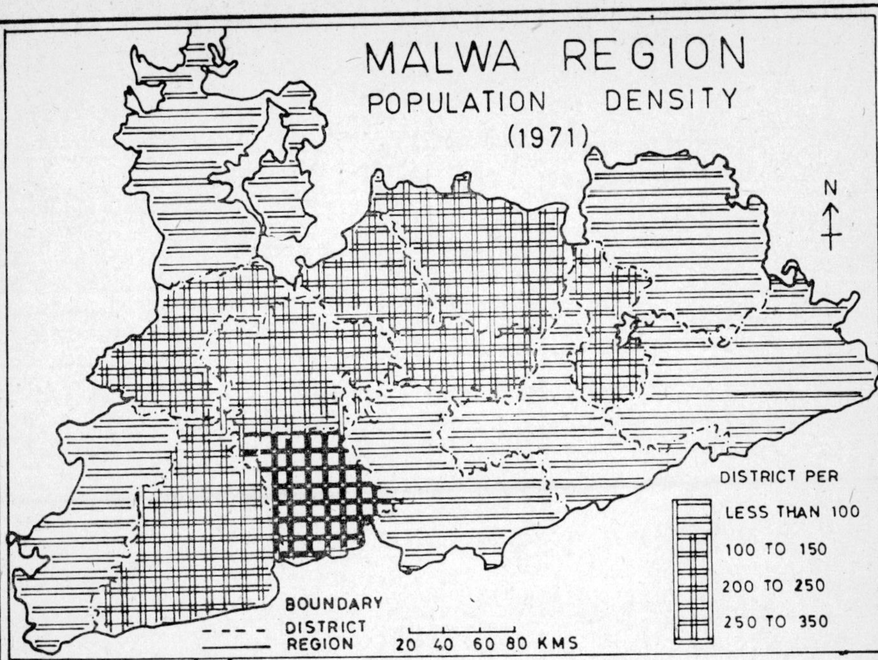
MALWA REGION
POPULATION DENSITY
(1971)
N
DISTRICT PER
LESS THAN 100
100 TO 150
200 TO 250
250 TO 350
BOUNDARY
DISTRICT
REGION
20 40 60 80 KMS

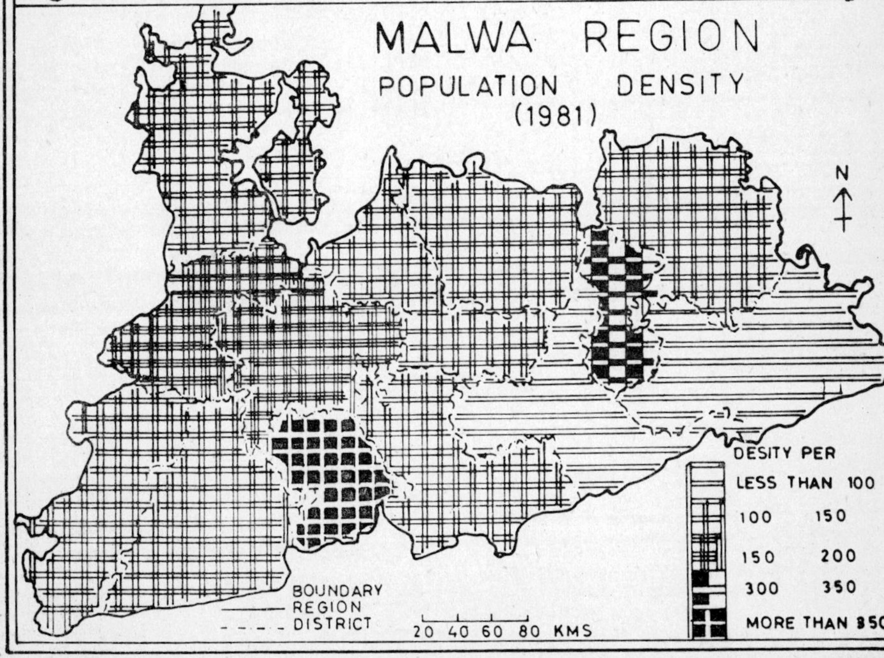
MALWA REGION
POPULATION DENSITY
(1981)
N
DESITY PER
LESS THAN 100
100 150
150 200
300 350
MORE THAN 350
BOUNDARY
REGION
DISTRICT
20 40 60 80 KMS

MAP-9

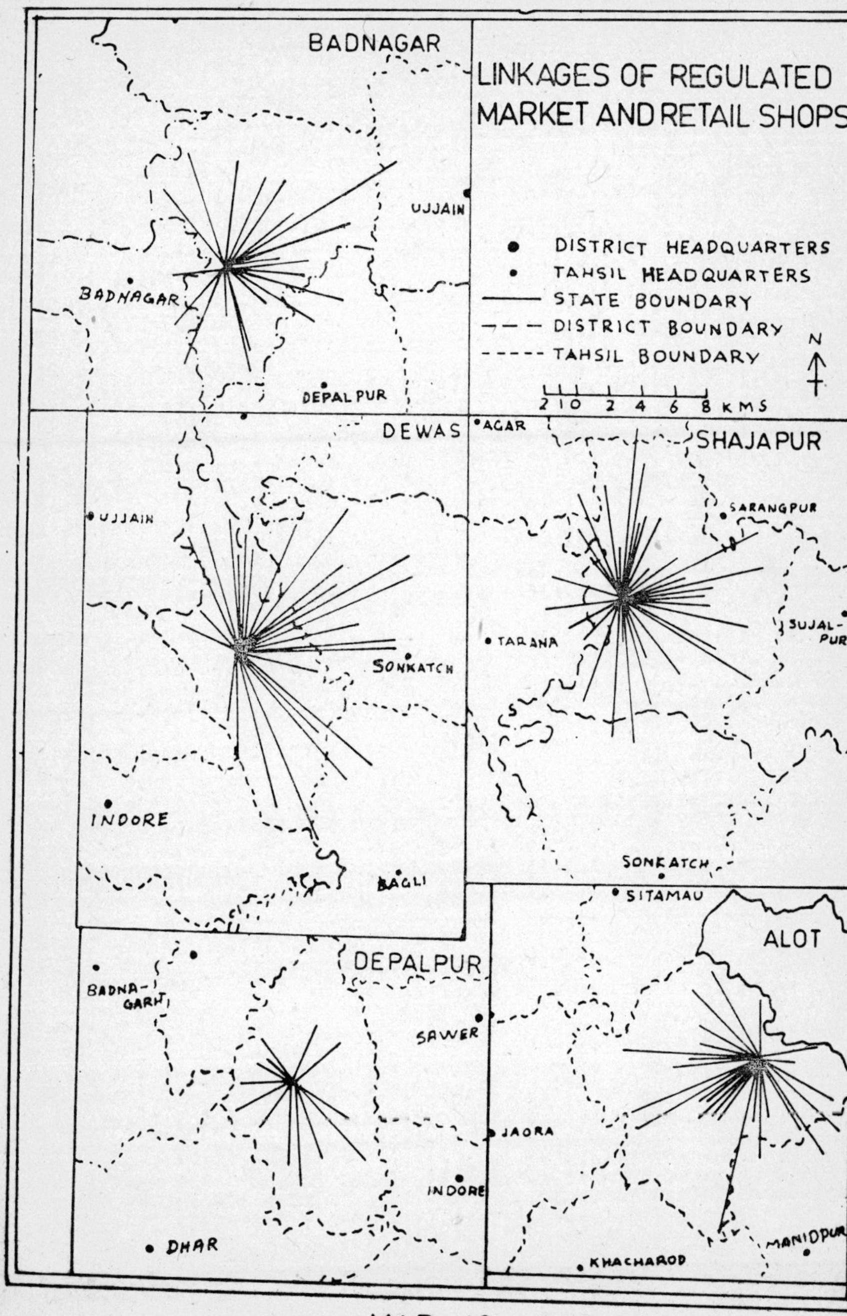

LINKAGES OF REGULATED MARKET AND RETAIL SHOPS
DISTRICT HEADQUARTERS
TAHSIL HEADQUARTERS
STATE BOUNDARY
DISTRICT BOUNDARY
TAHSIL BOUNDARY
N
2 1 0 2 4 6 8 KMS
BADNAGAR
UJJAIN
BADNAGAR
DEPALPUR
DEWAS
AGAR
UJJAIN
SONKATCH
INDORE
BAGLI
SHAJAPUR
SARANGPUR
TARANA
SUJALPUR
SONKATCH
SITAMAU
ALOT
DEPALPUR
BADNAGARH
SAWER
JAORA
INDORE
DHAR
KHACHAROD
MANIDPUR

MAP-10